COGNITIVE PROCESSES IN CHILDREN'S LEARNING

COGNITIVE PROCESSES IN CHILDREN'S LEARNING

Practical Applications in Educational Practice and Classroom Management

By

PREM S. FRY, Ph.D.

and

JUDY LEE LUPART, Ph.D.

The University of Calgary
Calgary, Alberta, Canada

CHARLES C THOMAS • PUBLISHER
Springfield • Illinois • U.S.A.

Published and Distributed Throughout the World by

CHARLES C THOMAS • PUBLISHER

2600 South First Street

Springfield, Illinois 62794-9265

© *1987 by* CHARLES C THOMAS • PUBLISHER

ISBN 0-398-05270-0

Library of Congress Catalog Card Number: 86-14367

With THOMAS BOOKS *careful attention is given to all details of manufacturing and
design. It is the Publisher's desire to present books that are satisfactory as to their physical
qualities and artistic possibilities and appropriate for their particular use.* THOMAS
BOOKS *will be true to those laws of quality that assure a good name and good will.*

Printed in the United States of America
Q-R-3

Library of Congress Cataloging in Publication Data

Fry, Prem S.
    Cognitive processes in children's learning.
    Bibliography: p.
    Includes index.
    1. Cognition in children. 2. Learning, Psychology of.
I. Lupart, Judy Lee. II. Title.
BF723.C5F78   1987   155.4'24   86-14367
ISBN 0-398-05270-0

ABOUT THE AUTHORS

PREM S. FRY is an educational psychologist trained at the Pennsylvania State University and the University of Michigan. She is professor of educational psychology and chairman of the general studies program at the University of Calgary, Calgary, Alberta, Canada. A former Fulbright Fellow, Woodrow Wilson Fellow, and Killam Scholar she has published widely in child development, educational psychology, and educational journals. She serves on the editorial boards of several psychology journals. Recognized with a Distinguished Teaching Award in 1983, she is a Fellow of both the American and Canadian Psychological Associations and editor of the book *Changing Conceptions of Intelligence and Intellectual Functioning.*

JUDY L. LUPART has a background of teaching and administrative experience in the area of special education. Her research has focused upon the learning, reading, memory, and attention abilities of mildly handicapped children. At present, she is on Faculty of the University of Calgary with the department of educational psychology. She is the current chairperson of the special education/rehabilitation program and her primary teaching focus is in Special Education.

This book is warmly dedicated to
our children
Shaun Fry,
Vanessa and **Michael Lupart**

PREFACE

SINCE WE HAD a specific purpose and readership in mind when we prepared this book we ought to share that information with the reader. The book is designed for the classroom teacher and is intended to be an introduction to the psychological study of basic cognitive processes in children. Because of space limitations we focused on processes of perception, attention, memory, problem-solving and metacognition — areas of primary interest to the classroom teacher. Since the book is written primarily for classroom teachers and teacher-trainees who are not necessarily majors in psychology we have tried to avoid technical vocabulary of psychology. Some technical terms are introduced but their use is deliberate and based on the conviction that teachers' precise understanding of cognitive processes requires these technical terms.

The text has a dual orientation presenting both theoretical concepts concerning cognitive processes and educational applications of these in the classroom. Research efforts of cognitively-oriented educators are briefly reviewed but always with the objective of translating such knowledge into improved practice for the classroom teacher. The underlying assumption is that teachers' basic understanding of children's perception, memory, attention, problem-solving and metacognitions should help to make interactions with the children in the classroom more sensible and effective.

Having taught child psychology in the Faculty of Education for several years, we know that the mention of research and experimental psychology studies can produce sheer panic in some teacher trainees. Our intention in this book has been to discuss the practical implications and applications of children's cogitive development in as intelligible and nontechnical a fashion as possible and avoiding the technical jargon of experimental psychology. Each chapter has two parts. In the first part we review important theoretical concepts of the cognitive process under consideration. In the second part we discuss the practical applications of the theoretical concepts to educational practice and classroom management.

For the advanced reader, reference citations indicate sources of further information. We have made no attempt to review all of the studies of cognitive processes in large part because there are far too many studies to be covered in a book this size. In addition, most of the details of such studies would be of interest to experts in cognitive processing. Instead our intention was to show what general facts have been discovered and what these facts mean to the teacher and educational practitioner. Toward this end, we begin each section with a statement of the problem under consideration and end each chapter with a summary of the major points of information of relevance to the classroom teacher.

P. S. Fry acknowledges with gratitude the assistance of the Social Sciences and Humanities Research Council of Canada and the Killam Resident Fellowship Committee in granting her a leave fellowship. We wish to acknowledge with thanks the invaluable help provided by Lynne Hill and Gladie Lys in typing the manuscript and Margaret J. Samuelson who helped with organizing the library materials.

Payne Thomas and Michael Payne Thomas at Charles C Thomas, Publisher have been vigilant, informative, and supportive throughout the production process and have made our association with the publishers a real pleasure.

CONTENTS

COGNITIVE PROCESSES IN CHILDREN'S LEARNING

CHAPTER ONE

INTRODUCTION

THIS BOOK on perception, memory, attention, problem-solving and metacognitive processes in children's learning was conceived as a series of topics concerned vitally with what we currently know about children's knowledge and the controversy surrounding the cognitive basis of this knowledge. Most existing cognitively-oriented texts are primarily introductions to Piaget's conceptualization of cognitive development, and there is little attempt to compare or contrast the Piagetian approach with other cognitive views about what children know, why they retain some aspects of their knowledge and are unable to retain other aspects, when they attend and what they attend to, and finally how aware they are of their own and others' knowledge states.

The text has a dual orientation comparing and contrasting, wherever relevant, two contemporary theories and approaches to children's cognitive development: Piagetian and information processing. Each chapter attempts to identify for the benefit of the classroom teacher (1) the major components of the child's knowledge base, (2) the manner in which information and knowledge is acquired, remembered and used, and (3) the important cognitive strategies and mechanisms responsible for the development of the knowledge base. We shall refer to this body of information as the process approach to cognitive development and we shall examine the major cognitive processes (perception, memory, attention, problem-solving and metacognition), each of which contributes to the activity we call thinking or information processing. Since information processing and Piagetian theory are currently the most viable theories and approaches representing the diverse efforts of child psychologists, we believe it is important that classroom teachers become quite familiar with the basic concepts of information processing and Piagetian theory as inherent in children's perception, memory, attention and problem-solving functions, and children's metacognitive knowledge about these processes.

3

The Scope of the Text

The text covers the major dimensions of cognitive development in children and the related basic processes: perception, memory, attention, problem-solving and metacognitive knowledge. Individual chapters are devoted to an overview of major dimensions of cognitive research and questions of how the teacher's knowledge and understanding of children's functioning in the perceptual, memory, attention, problem-solving and metacognitive awareness domains have special applications in classroom activity, education and special handicaps of children. Wherever relevant, the skills and abilities of younger children are contrasted with those of older children in order to help teachers adopt a developmental perspective. There is an attempt to show how cognitive processes occur at all ages, but they develop to a greater extent as children get older. For example, the number of dimensions to which the child can attend, or the number of items the child can remember or bring within the scope of metacognitive awareness, are likely to change with age. The cognitive strategies the child uses for organizing knowledge and information, and their specific level of functioning, are also likely to change with age. However, the processes of perceiving the environment and storing, retrieving and processing information cut across age levels and are therefore of primary interest to all classroom teachers at the kindergarten, elementary, junior and senior school levels.

Chapter 2 focuses on perceptual development during childhood. It presents an overview of the theories of perceptual development (both the information-processing and Piagetian approaches) and discusses the significance of the perceptual development to cognitive development of the child.

Chapter 3 addresses the question of how knowledge of the child's attention process might be applied to the practical problems confronting almost every type of handicapping condition among children. The frequency with which attentional problems are mentioned by the classroom teacher, coupled with the self-evident relationship between attention and learning, attest to the central role that attention plays in the information processing, memory, problem-solving and metacognitive awareness of children. This chapter proposes a two-dimensional view of attention, one of which is based on a traditional distinction between voluntary and involuntary attention, while the second dimension reflects the temporal properties of attention, either short-term or sustained. Aspects of interest to the classroom teacher include a discussion of interactive strategies for improving span, focus and selectivity, and promoting alertness, stimulus selection and vigilance in the young learner.

Chapter 4 addresses issues in memory development. Because of current interest in the information-processing and Piagetian model of memory functioning, the multistore model, the levels-of-processing model, and the Piagetian model are all considered.

Toward the goal of encouraging classroom teachers to give their students a problem-solving orientation to learning, Chapter 5 addresses the question of how children understand and attempt to solve problems and how children can be taught cognitive strategies to improve their performance in problem-solving ways. In this chapter, both information-processing and Piagetian approaches to problem solving are considered, although briefly, and a few illustrations of the synthesis and analysis approach on sets of specific problem-solving tasks are presented.

Chapter 6 considers metacognitive awareness, a relatively new area of cognitive development which has received increasing attention and one which plays an important role in children's communication of information and a number of other domains such as attention, memory, comprehension and problem-solving. Whereas the earlier chapters (Chaps. 2, 3, 4, & 5) consider what children are able to do in terms of perceptual, memory, attentional and problem-solving skills, Chapter 6 addresses the question of when and how children become aware of their own cognitive states. Levels of metacognitive awareness about memory, attention and problem solving that the child is capable of achieving are also considered.

Each chapter, including Chapter 7 "Concluding Remarks," addresses the question of how knowledge of various dimensions of cognitive development might be applied to the practical problems facing the classroom teacher, and specific recommendations and suggestions for the teacher are included. In Chapter 7 we identify a number of unifying themes that cut across discrete cognitive processes, structures and constructs, and attempt to relate these to the cognitive development of the individual learner in the classroom and the role of the teacher. We draw attention to specific Piagetian views and information-processing views on perceptual development, memory and problem solving. We elaborate on the future role of the classroom teacher as a custodian of individual differences in children, as a promoter of metacognitive awareness in the child, as a designer of cognitive strategies, and the teacher as a "cognitive engineer" in the classroom. We hope that teachers will view these suggestions and recommendations for implementing cognitive concepts and strategies in the classroom as developing ones rather than a final statement of facts.

CHAPTER TWO

PERCEPTION

IT IS AXIOMATIC that an understanding of children's perceptual development is of crucial importance to the teacher, especially to teachers of young children. Such an understanding influences the provision of educational materials of auditory, visual and sensory appeal, the general structure of the learning environment, and the expectations of the teacher concerning the individual child's capacities for attention to the stimulus field, distraction, and stimulus differentiation. Perhaps the main educational impact of the study of children's perceptual development has been in making teachers aware of the exteroceptive aspects of the study of the environment that are perceived and responded to by the child. This is the information-processing view. In contrast to this view is the Piagetian view, which holds that perception is an internal construction of reality. This internal construction depends upon the child's cognitive development and the way in which children structure their experiences.

There is evidence for the operation of both these processes in perceptual development: exteroceptive and interoceptive. In fact, contemporary opinion views these two processes as complementary rather than antagonistic. Knowledge of theories of perceptual development (interpreting both the internal and external world of the child) are of intrinsic importance to the teacher's function. These theories are discussed in ways that would facilitate the teacher's understanding.

The Exteroceptive Perspective

The view supports the notion that children have basic abilities and strategies that increase their contact with the auditory and visual environment. However, children's perception is activated by stimuli impinging from outside. The child is not simply an information responder

7

but an information seeker (cf. Banks & Salapatek, 1981; Linn, Reznik, Kagan, & Hans, 1982). The information-processing view is directed toward discovering what characteristics of the external reality are perceived by the child and what specific characteristics can be discovered and become known to the child. The exteroceptive theorists focus on the attributes or characteristics of the physical world that give rise to perception and the processes by which children come to perceive the world as they do. Within this framework the essential questions of interest to the teacher are whether children learn to recognize things by their unique features, or by learning what specific properties objects have, or whether they recognize something if it shares attributes common to some idealized exemplar or prototype of a class of objects. Different theories of perceptual development attempt to view these questions from a different perspective. Some of the more clearly formulated positions follow.

Differentiation Theory

From this theoretical perspective perceptual development is believed to involve the discrimination of those features of stimuli which allow us to distinguish among objects and things in the external reality. This notion is predicated on the assumption that the physical world is made up of rich and varied features which are initially undifferentiated to the young learner but which gradually become more differentiated with increasing exposure and practice. Objects acquire more distinctive features. With increasing training learners begin to detect features that distinguish sensory phenomena and allow for more complete representation of the stimulus objects (Gibson, 1969; Gibson, Gibson, Pick, & Osser, 1962).

There is good evidence that children's perception of meaningful differences changes with age, and more and more transformations are noticed by children. Younger children tend not to perceive rotations or reversals (e.g., ⅃ ⅃ − ⅭⅭ ; dd−bb; ⅄⅄ − ⅩⅩ); older children do (Gibson, Gibson, Pick & Osser, 1962). All age groups use distinctive features to recognize objects, and the ability to recognize more complete representations increases with age (Murray & Szymczyk, 1978) (see Fig. 2-1).

The improvement with age in children's ability to process information about object features and to use distinctive feature information implies that with experience children learn to distinguish dimensions of

FIGURE 2-1
An Example of Picture Stimuli

Source: Murray, F. S. & Szymczyk, J. M. (1978). Effects of distinctive features on recognition of incomplete pictures. *Developmental Psychology, 14,* 356-362.

feature variability and to appreciate featural differences. Recently, a redefinition and reinterpretation of the differentiation theory has been suggested by Garner (1979) in terms of what characterizes distinctive features of the external objects and stimuli. According to Garner, a stimulus has both dimensional and featural characteristics. Dimensional characteristics of objects are those that exist to some degree in all stimuli of a given class, whereas featural characteristics are those that exist within a set of stimuli. The children's ability to differentiate between dimensions and features is axiomatic to the teacher's understanding of the perceptual discrimination experienced by the child. Most teachers observe that young children have difficulty in recognizing and differentiating between stimuli that both vary dimensionally and featurally (i.e. where all stimuli have the same amount of a given attribute and vary along two or more dimensions). For example, the letters **p, q, b,** and **d** have **loops in common** but vary as to the **left and right direction of the loop** and the **upward and downward vertical line** to which the loop is attached. Young children exposed to recognition tasks involving dimensional and featural distinctions should have greater difficulty in the task than older children, especially under conditions where the exposure to the stimuli array is very brief as opposed to prolonged.

In recognition tasks involving patterns or stimuli that vary only in respect to features ⊏⌴⌴⌵ , similar confusion should be experienced by the young child who cannot scan all relevant features of the stimulus within the brief time (6 or 7 msec or less) allowed in the exposure. There is good evidence that perception of meaningful differences, both dimensionally and featurally, is more accurate with age (Elkind & Weiss, 1967) and when fewer features and dimensions need to be recognized by the young learner (Garner & Haun, 1978). Implications and applications of these findings for teachers are discussed at greater length in the next section.

As teachers will discern in later chapters on memory, attention and problem solving, there are age-related changes in scanning and focusing strategies used in attention, in subprocesses of memory, and in the amount of time the learner needs for coding and decoding into the information-processing system (Hoving, Spencer, Robb, & Schulte, 1978). Hence, perceptual development and ability to perceive featural and dimensional differences may reflect cognitive developmental changes that broaden the child's intellectual base. As the child moves from one stage of development (sensorimotor) to another (preoperational and concrete operational), there is a corresponding improvement in the child's ability to focus and a resulting improvement in perceptual differentiation skills (cf. Piaget & Inhelder, 1969). The changes may also reflect improvement in the use of the information-processing system itself (Hoving, Spencer, Robb, & Schulte, 1978). Cognitive developmental changes as they relate to perceptual development (cf. Laurendeau & Pinard, 1970) are discussed later in the chapter.

Prototype Theory

According to this view perceptual development in children takes place as a result of their comparing and contrasting objects on the basis of similarity with a prototypical exemplar of a class of objects. If a given object shares a number of characteristics of the prototype, then the child recognizes or identifies it as a member of that class of objects (Pick, 1965).

There is good evidence to show that children, like adults, make use of prototypes in their perception of things and, on the basis of prototypes, are able to present a complete representation of objects shown to them in broken-line or unfocused pictures (see Gollin, 1961; Murray & Szym-czyk, 1978). Discerning teachers observe quickly that even very young children have little difficulty (on the basis of prototypes) in recognizing somewhat distorted contours of different four-legged animals, four-wheeled vehicles, and winged airplanes, even when these are presented to them as a vast array of objects or things.

With increasing age and experience, children's knowledge of proto-type improves. Even exemplars that the child has not experienced before can be readily identified as class members on the basis of prototype comparisons (Posner & Keele, 1968). With age children become more adept at this type of recognition and specification of class members. With age there is an increasing elaboration of semantic capabilities in children (Saltz, Dixon, Klein, & Becker, 1977) leading to their being able to recognize more elaborate prototypes. As a result, as children grow older they need less information for identifying objects accurately.

Currently, there is a great deal of research in perceptual development inspired and stimulated by information-processing accounts of rules and principles that govern children's perceptual organization. Information-processing theorists propose that all children have basic abilities, plans and strategies that allow them to relate with and respond to the external world in terms of visual, auditory and other sensory stimulation (Haith, 1980). This position is in sharp contrast to the Genevan view that young children and infants respond to stimuli in their environment in a predominantly reflexive manner.

Currently, there is clear theoretical formulation (cf. Banks & Salapatek, 1981) of the position that children who receive strategy training in how to use prototypes or make other discriminations can be helped in perceptual learning. However, much of the current research has not been developed within a strictly "differentiation" or "prototypical" theory model. It is uniformly accepted by most information-processing theorists (e.g. Oden, 1979; Stevenson, 1972) that both prototype learning and distinctive features discrimination learning occur simultaneously in children and contribute equally to their perceptual development. Hitherto researchers have merely been able to describe the perceptual capacities of children, i.e. what they can perceive or recognize and under what conditions. It is expected that more and more future studies of perceptual development in children will attempt to discover general rules and patterns that guide their perceptual organization.

Interoceptive Perspective

This view supports the notion that initially children and infants respond to their environment in a primarily reflexive fashion and that their sensory receptors are excited by interoceptive stimuli. Gradually, children begin to structure their experiences initially in terms of schemes (figurative component of perception) and subsequently in terms of refinement of the schemes (operative component). According to the interoceptive perspective, perceptual development is seen as the child's increasing ability to recognize objects in the environment through a series of internalized action patterns. Perception involves both assimilation and accommodation — the application of some organized schemes to an object, person or event. According to Piaget (1963) and Inhelder (Piaget & Inhelder, 1969), improvement in mental schemes and the structure of the intellect therefore govern what is perceived. Piaget emphasizes that schemes and internal mental structures that govern perception are not static but are continually developing in quality. Concern with the development of perception therefore requires an understanding of the internal mental structures and internal activities throughout the developmental sequences and stages.

The basic premise of the perceptual-cognitive developmental approach as formulated by Piaget is that motivation for perceptual growth is intrinsic. Piaget's theory sees the child as striving to survive and function successfully by taking in information in interaction with the environment. The growing child's perception of the environment is not passively registered but is actively constructed throughout the developmental stages through the basic processes of assimilation and accommodation.

Perception of Objects, Time and Space

Piaget has suggested that since perception is rooted in knowledge about things (i.e. schemes), perception changes with age as a function of schemes and stage-related changes in children's operative knowledge. As postulated by Piaget and Inhelder (1969), perceptual development is not merely the refining of the schemes as reflected in the increasing sharpening of the child's ability to recognize the external world; it involves also an improvement in the child's operative structure. Piaget has argued that intellectual structures organize perception, and perceptual development occurs in the same step-like, stage-related manner that governs cognitive development. Piaget has suggested that the young child acquires knowledge of objects based on the acquisition of four primary concepts: objects, space, time and causation. Piaget reasoned that important developments in perception in early developmental periods include the infant's understanding that objects have identities of their own that are independent of seeing, hearing, touching, smelling and tasting. At the sensorimotor stage of development, children acquire a progressive sense of **object permanence,** although such representation of an object is still tied for many months to visual displacement of the object. Sometimes, the child takes note of the invisible displacement of the objects and shows himself able to deduce them as well as to perceive them through thought (Piaget, 1955).

Piaget also provides a detailed analysis of children's development in the **spatial field.** Young children begin to move objects about and to experiment with the relations between objects, rather than being totally concerned with the object itself or the relation of the object to the subject himself. Late in the sensorimotor stage, children are able to represent spatial interrelationships and represent displacements of the body, itself.

The notion of object permanence and spatial relations implies also a dimension of **time;** so, together with object permanence and spatial perception, the young child develops an early awareness of time. Perception of time, like that of space, is constructed little by little and involves the elaboration of a system of relations. A mature understanding of logical time (i.e. knowledge about the position that events occupy in our existence) results from the coordination of two dimensions: succession (when events begin and end) and duration (how long something lasts). For the sensorimotor infant, temporal information is used only in a practical sense. However, according to Piaget (1955), from the fourth substage of the sensorimotor period infants demonstrate an appreciation of logical time: they begin to act purposefully, ordering action schemes and exercising one action scheme so that another might be used (e.g. putting an object down, opening the door, picking up the object in order to get through the door). With age, children begin to differentiate before and after in time from before and after in space. As development progresses from the preoperational to the concrete developmental stage, the child's concepts of time, distance, speed and succession become differentiated.

Although preoperational children demonstrate practical uses of logical time, their understanding of it is still quite unclear for several months and years. Their knowledge of succession and duration (i.e. what stimulus comes on first, goes off last, or is the longest) reflects the young child's inability to understand duration independently of succession. The accentuation of perceptual cues for assessing succession interferes significantly with judgments of duration across the age levels.

Perception of Causality

It is not until the end of the first year that the child demonstrates behavior that can be attributed to an appreciation of causality (Piaget, 1955).

By the end of the sensorimotor period, infants have obtained a practical sense of causality. Till now the child's own activity was conceived as the center of production, but more and more it is recognized as subject to pressures emanating from an external universe. Children are capable of attributing causality to events beyond their immediate observation and recognize links between events that are independent of their own activity.

More precisely, by the end of the second year, children cease to place their own activity at the center of causality and instead conceive of causality as maintaining relations of mutual dependence with objects. However, for several years of the preschooler's life, children's understanding of cause and effect remains quite subjective and in this sense is different from that of adults. Cause and effect are not entirely separate and may be perceived as interchangeable. Young children justify events in the phenomenal world as caused by actions of higher beings (artificialism), or animism and dynamism (inanimate objects having life or human strength and qualities). As children grow older, they are able to differentiate between the physical properties of objects, and their perceptions and attribution of causality are increasingly based on physical attributes of objects and the relationships that obtain between properties of objects (Laurendeau & Pinard, 1962).

Perceptual Development and Cognitive Development

Although there is a great deal of controversy surrounding the Piagetian position that intellectual structure organizes the perception and that perceptual development follows the same step-like sequence associated with cognitive development, these issues are of particular concern to teachers, who must grapple with the essential question of whether or not children's perception develops in some kind of systematic and predictable fashion. Also of great interest to the teacher is the question of whether intellectual structures organize perception and whether perception is characterized by constructive developmental processes, or, as theorized by differentiation theorists and prototype theorists, by the discrimination and discovery of properties and features of objects in the physical-phenomenal world.

Cornell (1978) has argued against the idea that intellectual structure organizes the perception of reality. He notes there is too much unevenness in development, and therefore stage-related changes in children's operative knowledge and mental structures cannot be assumed uniformly to organize their perception of objects, time, space and causality. Furthermore, there is good research evidence (see Acredolo, 1978; Lamb, 1973; Liben, Moore & Golbeck, 1982) to indicate that children's perceptions of objects, time, space and causality are influenced by many other subjective factors such as familiarity versus unfamiliarity with the object (Lingle & Lingle, 1981). Other factors noted to be influencing perception include the familiarity or unfamiliarity of the environment in which the child experiences objects and events (Liben et al., 1982). The more unfamiliar the surroundings, the more allocentric will be the child's responding. Similarly, it has been demonstrated that children's perception of causality is influenced by task characteristics and task demands, such as the nature of instructions (see Huttenlocker & Presson, 1979) given to the child, the nature of motor response required for performing the task (see Gelman, 1978) and the background of experience the child has with the particular task. Lacking background and experience with new objects or the novel surroundings, children may be compelled to rely upon animistic explanations of causality in the phenomenal world.

Whereas some developmental effects are found in perceptual research, there is substantial evidence to the contrary. Burns and Brainerd (1979) have argued that if children's perception of time, space and of causality is affected by cognitive structure as conceived by Piaget, then we should not expect training or minor transformations in the stimulus conditions to produce substantial changes in children's perceptual responding. However, the training effects have been shown to be substantial in several experiments conducted by information-processing theorists. Teachers must therefore work from the ambiguous premise that the influence of intellectual structure on children's perception is not as distinct and pervasive as Piaget has claimed. Training effects appear also to be influential.

In defense of the Piagetian position, it should be noted that some strong cognitive-developmental effects and trends have been found in children's perceptual and conceptual understanding of time and causality. In older children compared to younger children, there appear to be more sophisticated levels of conceptual understanding and underlying competence in the Piagetian sense. The fact that older children reason about developmentally more advanced concepts of causality better than younger children implies that cognitive structures are influential to some degree in organizing perception.

Given the current state of knowledge about the relationship between cognitive developmental factors and children's perception, the notion of perception and cognitive development going hand in hand cannot be accepted unequivocally.

The Role of Activity in Perceptual Development

Another aspect of perceptual development which is of interest to the teacher is the extent to which perceptual ability is based upon action and object manipulation and whether there is evidence to suggest that increasing activity (whether self-directed or parent- and teacher-directed) facilitates the elaboration of perceptual skills.

The role of activity in perceptual development has been a subject of research exploration for a long time beginning with Hebb (1949) and Piaget (1963). Early animal studies by Held and Hein (1963) proposed the practical importance of activity in the development of visual perception. Other research studying the perceptual development of infants and children (e.g. Schofield & Uzgiris, 1969; Zaprophets, 1965) has confirmed that there is an increase in active systematic scanning of both tactile and visually presented stimuli. Also, motor activity directed at objects serves to create motor images that facilitate object recognition (Zaprophets, 1965).

Harris (1971) proposed the notion that perceptual ability of infants and children is facilitated as a consequence of actions carried out in a variety of sensory domains. In accordance with this line of reasoning, Harris examined the relative influence of haptic and visual exploration of the development of infants' and children's object knowledge. He concluded that object knowledge in infants and children is facilitated by a combination of visual exploration (see the object) and haptic exploration (object manipulation). Older children however, rely more and more on visual exploration in object recognition and object permanence. Other research (e.g. Gottfried, Rose & Bridger, 1978) following a similar line of reasoning has supported the idea that much of what infants and children perceive is based in activity that involves visual exposure, visual manipulation (seeing an object from various positions), and visual/ haptic manipulation (seeing and touching objects). However, these researchers concluded that superior object recognition resulted from the visual conditions alone (as contrasted with visual/haptic conditions), suggesting that haptic manipulation may, in some cases, interfere with the child's object recognition and permanence. Somewhat later research (Ruff, 1982; MacKay-Soroka, Trehub, Bull & Corter, 1982), however, noted that haptic manipulation may be very important to the acquisition of certain kinds of knowledge about objects such as three-dimensional properties of the object (Ruff, 1982). For purposes of strategy training, the preceding research suggests that if young children are being trained to remember properties of objects, it would be important in testing to reinstate the exact conditions under which they first became familiar with the object (haptic/visual or visual). For example, if the child was first initiated to an object with opportunity to both see and manipulate, replication of these exact conditions would improve the child's recognition of object properties. Similarly, if the child was only allowed to look at the object the first time around, then in strategy training the inclusion of haptic manipulation of the object may interfere with the child's acquisition of object knowledge.

By far the strongest advocate of the notion that the child's perception is based in action is Piaget (1963). Piaget believes that perception is a consequence of actions carried out on things. Infants' and children's visual, auditory and tactile experience with objects leads to the development of action schemes, and perception is therefore the assimilation of objects into visual and haptic-action schemes. Piaget believed, for example, that the child's knowledge of size and shape constancy emerges reliably with opportunity to experience, assimilate and coordinate information about a variety of objects. Not unlike information-processing theorists, Piaget (1963) believes that by the third substage of the sensorimotor development, children are able to respond to various sensory modalities, primarily visual, auditory and touch. They are able to recognize integrative properties of sight and sound and respond to stimuli in their environment to the extent that they develop expectancies about specific objects (e.g. the ball rolls, the rattle shakes) and persons (e.g. father smiles, mother coos) in their environment. Piagetians believe that although perception initially emerges from reflexive action schemes, these reflexes quickly become modified and strengthened as a result of the child's active exploration and assimilation of objects in the environment. Perception is therefore viewed as a consequence of a series of actions, and perceptual development is the construction of cognitive schemas leading to the acquisition of knowledge about objects. Thus, Piaget, more than other theorists, advances the notion that the child's perceptual development serves as the operative component of the intellect. Through interactions with the environment, infants and children adapt to and organize schemes about objects, time, space and causality. Although perception is regarded to be subordinate to other intellectual processes, it contributes significantly to knowledge and the intellect.

EDUCATIONAL AND CLASSROOM IMPLICATIONS AND APPLICATIONS

In view of a number of points of correspondence between Piagetian and information-processing views of perception and perceptual development, the educational implications and applications of these views will be covered generally to incorporate both viewpoints. Wherever necessary, specific restrictions and qualifications will be discussed separately for preschoolers and older children; and elaborations of strategies that pertain only to information-processing approaches will be noted.

Strengthening the Role of Activity

Based on the current acceptance of the view that perception is based on action, and that such construction leads to perceptual development, the obvious implication for teachers is to advocate action involving various sensory modalities. As noted earlier, certainly there is good evidence that activity facilitates the elaboration of perceptual skills.

Discerning teachers will emphasize the need for infants, preschoolers and children to vigorously and actively explore the environment visually and haptically. Recognizing that experience is important to perceptual development in both Piagetian and information-processing theory, teachers must use their own judgments as to what kind of activity is necessary and appropriate with different age groups. Picture-sorting tasks, structured exercises in habituation-dishabituation activities, and visual and haptic manipulation of various shapes and sizes may be useful activities with older children, who can be expected to sit in a chair and concentrate for a period of time on a task. Infants and young children may assimilate just as much by a more unstructured environment that allows them to wander about a room and engage in visual scanning which also involves considerable activity for the young child.

As with object knowledge, teachers should note that activity factors have been found to be influential in children's spatial reasoning. Children display much better spatial knowledge when there is encouragement to be involved in activities of spatial reconstructions. For example, teachers who involve their young children in furniture arrangement in the actual classroom, hanging pictures and plants, or preparing toy furniture for a model doll house provide their young learners with opportunity for valuable spatial learning and knowledge.

Teachers should note that children have better spatial perception when that knowledge is tapped in ecologically meaningful situations taken from real-life settings as opposed to reconstructions involving unfamiliar surroundings and arrangements (Liben, Moore & Golbeck, 1982).

Discerning teachers should note that reconstructive activity involving three-dimensional displays and objects of different sizes and shapes shows promise for improving children's ability to perceive scenes and arrangements from a variety of perspectives (Laurendeau & Pinard, 1970) and thereby refining their overall perceptual skills.

Although it should be noted that practice in reconstruction activities alone does not mediate children's perceptual performance, there is much support for this type of strategy training in the experimental literature. Teachers of both young and older children may find it reassuring to know that different kinds of visual and haptic explorations appear to improve children's perceptual development. Teachers should note that preschoolers develop much better spatial perception if allowed to explore novel environments on their own compared to when they are led through physical spaces by an adult (Feldman & Acredolo, 1979). By contrast, older children who are presumed to be less egocentric are able to coordinate several dimensions simultaneously (e.g. coordinating right and left, front and back) and are able therefore to make substantial gains in spatial relationships and perceptions through teacher-directed reconstruction activities and exercises.

The decision as to how much activity is needed for perceptual development and what procedures are typically appropriate for youngsters and older children requires a personal judgment call by teachers and parents, who are in the best position to assess, on an individual basis, the physical energy level of the child, the scope of the motor capabilities the child shows, and the number of persons in the environment with whom the child interacts. As would be obvious to the teacher, the greater the motor capabilities of the child, the greater will be the number of reconstruction types of activities and arrangements in which the child may engage. The fewer the number of adults in the child's environment, the more general will be the visual exploration possible for the child. If the child has interactions with a number of adults, the greater is the scope for more focused visual activities.

The Use of Discrimination Training in Perceiving Distinctive Features and Dimensions

Children's ability to respond effectively to featural differences in objects in the environment can be improved by providing discrimination training via card-sorting exercises, for example. Children can be trained to recognize objects and their distinctive features by being taught about the distinctive features through a series of comparisons with a standard.

Given a recognition task in which two objects have only a few distinctive features (e.g. the loops and lines in the letters **b** and **d**), the child's attention is directed to the relevant distinctive features. The object is exposed for a few minutes and the child has an opportunity for visual scanning and haptic manipulation of the letters. The child's attention is directed to the similar features (the loops) and the distinctive features (the direction of the loops). On the basis of experimental research evidence (cf. Pick, 1965; Garner & Haun, 1978), it can be predicted that trained children perform better in recognizing distinctive features than untrained children.

Early discrimination training tasks should include:

- objects with fewer features,
- explicit instructions for visual scanning of distinctive features, and
- extended exposure time (much more than the usual 7 msecs).

Gradually and with more practice, the number of distinctive features can be increased and there can be more rapid presentation of the object, with instructions for more focused attention on distinctive features as opposed to general visual scanning.

In designing discrimination training for teaching children distinctive features and dimensions, teachers must bear in mind the fundamental rules that detection of featural differences by children is primarily dependent upon (a) complexity of features and (b) the amount of processing time needed to code and decode information about the features of the object. Given increasing age and cognitive development, the distinctive features to be distinguished by the child can be made more elaborate. Discrimination patterns with more features can be added, and recognition tasks presented to the older child can be made to vary along a number of dimensions. For example given a discrimination task in which the letters **p, q, b,** and **d** have to be sorted out and associated with pictures of pony (**p**), quacking duck (**q**), baby (**b**), and dog (**d**), the teacher must ensure that the child has pretraining for recognizing dimensions such as (a) a **loop** to the **right** or **left** and (b) a loop on the **upward** or **downward** portion of the **vertical** line.

Discerning teachers would be justified in assuming that the child's increasing ability to respond to featural differences after pretraining is reflective of an improvement in the use of the processing time and may result also from discrimination learning as originally proposed in differentiation theory.

Helping Children in Perceptual Improvement Through Prototypes

As proposed earlier in this chapter, perceptual retention (recognition of distinctive features of objects) can be facilitated by encouraging children to compare new experiences of objects to a prototypical exemplar of a class of objects or things. A corollary to the idea that perception improves through the organization and development of knowledge about classifying sensory experiences (cf. Caldwell & Hall, 1970) should suggest to the attentive and discerning teacher the idea of training children to use prototypes in order to improve perception. Young children in their daily living, experience a vast smorgasbord of differently sized, shaped, colored and styled objects but generally have limited perceptual ability to recognize or identify objects accurately. Studies examining the use of prototypes by children suggest that children can become more adept at this type of recognition if they are trained to use different strategies, such as abstracting prototypes, in learning about objects.

Preschoolers can be trained to abstract prototypes by encouraging them to engage in **matching tasks** and gradually providing overlays to see if the child understands whether the overlay and the figure match exactly. If they do not match exactly, the child must be required to consider whether the transformed object is longer, shorter, wider or narrower than the standard. One way to create a prototype is to help the child perceive an average of values in a set of forms. Assuming that in training the child saw a set of trees or a set of plants with branches or stems ranging from short to long, a prototype based on an average of these values would lead the child to recognize as most familiar new trees or plants that had branches or stems of average length to those experienced before.

Likewise, children can be trained by the teacher to recognize the distinctive features of houses by means of exposure to pictures of houses of varying shapes and sizes — tall and short, wide and narrow. By requiring the child to compare each new transformation to a standard exemplar, it would be possible for the child to perceive in what respects a new transformation is similar to or different from a previous experience with an exemplar. More and more complex discriminations (such as houses with chimneys, houses with turrets, houses with arches) can be learned by children with the gradual introduction of new dimensions in the perceptual training programs.

A teacher training children in modal prototypes of colors (for example, green or orange) may expose children to dark green and very light green or dark orange and very light orange. The teacher might help the child create prototypes from the most commonly experienced shades of green and orange (modal prototypes). If children in training had exposure to green and orange (either dark or very light green, or dark orange or very light orange), it can be anticipated that the child trained for model prototypes will find new color shades of green and orange most familiar and recognize them spontaneously.

Teachers may find it useful to consider that after children have habituated to a set of dark and very light green and orange colors, they are likely to show much greater interest (dishabituation) to several different and new shades of green and orange not previously experienced. Further habituation-dishabituation exercises along similar lines can be designed by teachers for use with children of varying ages.

In other words, teachers can first train children in modal prototypes by requiring them to perceive within contrived limits. Subsequently, children may be trained to become more sensitive to the uniqueness of colors, sizes or shapes that they experience by arranging matching tasks comparing new colors, shapes and sizes to the previously experienced exemplars.

It may be reassuring for teachers to note that young children trained for prototypes not only become more adept at recognizing and identifying a class of objects, they also develop a better understanding of the class of objects. With some qualifications it can be anticipated that older children previously trained in prototypes may be able to perceive more fully and richly the uniqueness of new classes of objects, shapes, and colors they encounter in daily living.

Using Picture Stimuli Games

As part of their perceptual learning, teachers can encourage children to work with picture games requiring them to identify objects in broken-line patterns or unfocused blurred patterns. Other exercises requiring children to sort dot patterns into groups (with specific instructions for what patterns to use for sorting) have generally been helpful in stimulating children's perceptual learning.

Following habituation to a shape (for example, a triangle), teachers can encourage children to work with a series of test patterns in which certain components of the shape (e.g. corners or sides) are missing (see patterns B and C in Figure 2-2).

FIGURE 2-2
Set of Incomplete Triangles

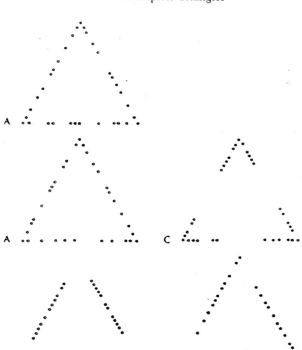

Source: Schwartz, M. & Day, R. H. (1979). Visual shape perception in early infancy. *Monographs of the Society for Research in Child Development, 44*(7, Serial No. 182), 1-63.

Training children for habituation to a shape such as a triangle involves repeated exposure to a triangular shape. When test patterns with missing components (see Fig. 2-2) are first shown to the child, there will be a certain amount of dishabituation, suggesting that the child perceives the new pattern being different from the earlier triangular shapes. However, with a certain amount of encouragement to reorganize and reprocess, children will quickly perceive the missing components; they will be able to sort out the missing links and complete the triangular shape. Therefore, teachers using picture-stimuli exercises as portrayed by Figure 2-3 are improving children's perception learning by means of the part-versus whole-method processing.

Certain cautions and precautions are advisable when picture stimuli are used with children of varying ages. At first, the picture stimuli used should involve very simple shapes and forms. However, with increasing age and assumed elaboration of semantic knowledge (i.e. what things are), children will be able to respond with interest to more complex forms and shapes, such as four-wheeled vehicles and airplanes with wings and tails. These can be introduced in the picture stimuli for older children.

Perceptual skills can be improved in older children by exposing the child to matching tasks that require reflective and highly focused visual responding rather than general visual scanning (see a sample item of a matching familiar figures test in Figure 2-3).

It is suggested that perceptual skills of the child are refined by the use of strategies (such as the matching figures test) that encourage performance in specific tasks requiring part (rather than whole) processing (Zelniker, Renan, Sorer, & Shavit, 1977). In order to match the standard exemplar with the items in the matching task, it is expected that the child must engage in very refined object-recognition activity. The increasing use of strategies that encourage more focused attention (part-method processing) will help the child to internalize perceptual feature differences and lead to more accurate recognition of shapes, contours and sizes.

With repeated practice and exposure to different forms, shapes and contours, children's perceptual abilities can be refined at a young age. By providing some feedback and instructional training, teachers can teach preschoolers and young children to sort more and more complex patterns with a higher degree of accuracy. Despite disagreement about how the process works, there is general optimism among information-processing theorists about the value of perceptual-training techniques with children. The reason for this optimism is found when one considers the range of experimental studies that show refinement in perceptual skills through discrimination training and prototype training. Experimental tasks (see Murray & Szymczyk, 1978; Garner, 1979) involving

Perception 25

FIGURE 2-3

Sample Items from the *Matching Familiar Figures Test* (in which children must match the standard on top with one of the items below).

Source: Kagan, J. (1966). Reflection-Impulsivity: The generality and dynamics of conceptual tempo. *Journal of Abnormal Psychology, 71,* 17-24.

differentiation and prototype learning demonstrate that trained children learn to recognize dimensional and featural differences more accurately.

Summary

This chapter has advanced the notion that neonates and infants are born with a set of rules that govern their reactions to the phenomenal world. All information-processing theorists agree that these so-called innate principles or rules govern perceptual organization (Haith, 1980). It is reassuring for parents and teachers to note that children at birth have basic abilities, plans, strategies or rules that increase their contact with the visual environment. Information-processing accounts of perceptual development stress that perceptual development occurs as one learns to discriminate between distinctive dimensions and features of objects and to respond to meaningful dimensions of one's environment.

Piagetian accounts of perceptual development argue that perception is rooted in the acquisition of four primary concepts: object, space, time and causality, and the child's perception changes as a function of the stage-related changes in intellectual structure. According to Piaget, it is the intellectual structures that organize perception and put a construction on reality.

Discerning readers will note that there is considerable overlap between the two positions in their explanation of how perceptual development occurs. One believes that perception is merely an initial activity performed by the child as information enters and flows through the processing systems. The other believes that perception emanates and eventuates from the intellectual structure and is subordinate to it. In this respect the Piagetian approach adds some notions beyond those advanced by information-processing theorists. However, there are a number of points of correspondence between the two positions. In fact, contemporary opinion views these two approaches to be complementary rather than antagonistic. Both positions advocate that perceptual development occurs through the child's interaction with the environment, through action and experience, and through strategy learning, discrimination learning, and abstraction of prototypical information from sensory experience.

Both approaches are of the view that interaction with the environment is very important to the development of the child's perceptual skills, and both stress the axiomatic contribution of teachers, parents and adults to the child's sensory exploration and perceptual integration.

REFERENCES

Acredolo, L. P., (1978). The development of spatial orientation in infancy. *Developmental Psychology, 14*, 224-234.

Banks, M. S., & Salapatek, P. (1981). Infant pattern vision: A new approach based on the contrast sensitivity function. *Journal of Experimental Child Psychology, 31*, 1-45.

Burns, S. M., & Brainerd, C. J. (1979). Effects of constructive and dramatic play on perspective taking in very young children. *Developmental Psychology, 15,* 512-521.

Caldwell, E. C., & Hall, V. C. (1970). Concept learning in discrimination tasks. *Developmental Psychology, 2,* 41-48.

Cornell, E. H. (1978). Learning to find things: A reinterpretation of object permanence studies. In L. S. Siegel & C. J. Brainerd (Eds.), *Alternatives to Piaget: Critical essays on the theory* (pp. 1-27). New York: Academic Press.

Elkind, D., & Weiss, J. (1967). Studies in perceptual development: III Perceptual exploration. *Child Development, 38,* 553-562.

Feldman, A., Acredolo, L. (1979). The effect of active versus passive exploration on memory for spatial location in children. *Child Development, 50,* 698-704.

Garner, W. R. (1979). Letter discrimination and identification. In A. D. Pick (Ed.), *Perception and its development: A tribute to Eleanor J. Gibson* (pp. 111-144). Hillsdale, NJ: Erlbaum.

Garner, W. R., & Haun, F. (1978). Letter identification as a function of perceptual limitation and type attribute. *Journal of Experimental Psychology: Human Perception and Performance, 4,* 199-209.

Gelman, R. (1978). Cognitive development. In M. R. Rosenzweig & L. W. Porter (Eds.), *Annual review on psychology* (Vol. 29). Palo Alto, CA: Annual Reviews.

Gibson, E. J. (1969). *Principles of perceptual learning and development.* New York: Appleton-Century-Crofts.

Gibson, E. J., Gibson, J. J., Pick, A. D., & Osser, H. A. (1962). A developmental study of the discrimination of letter-like forms. *Journal of Comparative and Physiological Psychology, 35,* 897-906.

Gollin, E. S. (1961). Further studies of visual recognition of incomplete objects. *Perceptual Motor Skills, 13,* 307-314.

Gottfried, A. W., Rose, S. A., & Bridger, W. H. (1978). Effects of visual, haptic, and manipulatory experiences on infants' visual recognition memory of objects. *Developmental Psychology, 14,* 305-312.

Haith, M. M. (1980). *Rules that babies look by: The organization of newborn visual activity.* Hillsdale, NJ: Erlbaum.

Harris, P. L. (1971). Examination and search in infants. *British Journal of Psychology, 62,* 469-473.

Hebb, D. O. (1949). *The organization of behavior.* New York: Wiley.

Held, R., & Hein, A. (1963). Movement-produced stimulation in the development of visually guided behavior. *Journal of Comparative and Physiological Psychology, 56,* 872-876.

Hoving, K. L., Spencer, T., Robb, K. Y., & Schulte, D. (1978). Developmental changes in visual information processing. In P. A. Ornstein (Ed.), *Memory development in children* (pp. 21-67). Hillsdale, NJ: Erlbaum.

Huttenlocker, J., & Presson, C. C. (1979). The coding and transformation of spatial information. *Cognitive Psychology, 11,* 375-394.

Kagan, J. (1966). Reflection-impulsivity: The generality and dynamics of conceptual tempo. *Journal of Abnormal Psychology, 71,* 17-24.

Lamb, M. E. (1973). The effects of maternal deprivation on the development of the concept of object and person. *Journal of Behavioral Science, 1,* 355-364.

Laurendeau, M., & Pinard, A. (1962). *Causal thinking in the child.* New York: International Universities Press.

Laurendeau, M., & Pinard, A. (1970). *The development of the concept of space in the child.* New York: International Universities Press.

Liben, L. S., Moore, M. L., & Golbeck, S. L. (1982). Preschoolers' knowledge of their classroom environment: Evidence from small-scale and life-size spatial tasks. *Child Development, 53* 1275-1284.

Lingle, K. M., & Lingle, J. H. (1981). Effects of selected object characteristics on object-permanence test performance. *Child Development, 52,* 367-369.

Linn, S., Reznik, S. J., Kagan, J., & Hans, S. (1982). Salience of visual patterns in the human infant. *Developmental Psychology, 18,* 651-657.

Mackay-Soroka, S., Trehub, S. E., Bull, D. D., & Corter, C. M. (1982). Effects of encoding and retrieval conditions on infants' recognition memory. *Child Development, 53,* 815-818.

Murray, F. S., & Szymczyk, J. M. (1978). Effects of distinctive features on recognition of incomplete pictures. *Developmental Psychology, 14,* 356-362.

Oden, G. C. (1979). A fuzzy logical model of letter identification. *Journal of Experimental Psychology: Human Perception and Performance, 5,* 336-352.

Piaget, J. (1955). *The construction of reality in the child.* London: Routledge & Kegan Paul.

Piaget, J. (1963). *The origin of intelligence in children.* New York: Norton.

Piaget, J., & Inhelder, B. (1969). *The psychology of the child.* New York: Basic Books.

Pick, A. D. (1965). Improvement of visual and tactual form discrimination. *Journal of Experimental Psychology, 69,* 331-339.

Posner, M. I., & Keele, S. (1968). On the genesis of abstract ideas. *Journal of Experimental Psychology, 77,* 353-363.

Ruff, H. A. (1982). Role of manipulation in infants' responses to invariant properties of objects. *Developmental Psychology, 18,* 682-691.

Saltz, E., Dixon, D., Klein, S., & Becker, G. (1977). Studies of natural language concepts. III. Concept overdiscrimination in comprehension between two and four years of age. *Child Development, 48,* 1682-1685.

Schofield, F. C. & Uzgiris, I. C. (1969). *Infant-mother relationship and object concept.* Paper presented at the meeting of the Society for Research in Child Development, Santa Monica, CA.

Schwartz, M., & Day, R. H. (1979). Visual shape perception in early infancy. *Monographs of the Society for Research in Child Development, 44* (Serial No. 182).

Stevenson, H. W. (1972). *Children's learning.* New York: Appleton-Century-Crofts.

Zaprophets, A. V. (1965). The development of perception in the preschool child. In P. H. Mussen (Ed.), European research in cognitive development. *Monographs of the Society for Research in Child Development, 30* (Serial No. 100).

Zelniker, T., Renan, A., Sorer, I., & Shavit, Y. (1977). Effect of perceptual processing strategies on problem solving of reflective and impulsive children. *Child Development, 48,* 1436-1442.

CHAPTER THREE

ATTENTION

DESPITE THE intuitive sense that we all have in conceptualizing attention, there is a very real problem with specifying just what attention is. For the teacher, attention may be demonstrated by various behavioral responses of students; the physiologist might examine certain autonomic patterns to determine associated attentional processes; and the clinical psychologist might refer to test results for indications of attention problems. When we examine the literature in this area, it is readily apparent that the study of attention is similarly problematic for academics and theoreticians.

Most scholarly and especially historical reviews of the work pertaining to attention refer to the classic descriptions of William James, presented nearly a century ago. The following quotation encompasses the flavor of his insights (James, 1890):

> Everyone knows what attention is. It is the taking of possession by the mind, in clear and vivid form, of one of what seem several simultaneously possible objects or trains of thought. Focalization, concentration of consciousness are of its essence. It implies withdrawal from some things in order to deal effectively with others (pp. 403-404).

Through the use of introspective research techniques, James and other early century psychologists identified attention as a central learning construct. Unfortunately, these early efforts were first criticized and later wholly abandoned as the behaviorists began to dictate the direction of psychological inquiry. For over 50 years, the study of attention was virtually nonexistent. Krupski (1980) has identified a number of factors leading to a renewed interest in the study of attention which began in the 1950s. These factors include:

> The introduction of operational definitions of attention-related processes, the highly productive attention-related research during World War II, technological advances, as well as the emergence of cognitive psychology (p. 103).

29

Efforts post-dating the 1950s have been directed toward the formulation of definitions and theories or models of attention. Psychologists will often refer to the components of attention as a useful and practical means of definition. Moray (1969), for example, suggested that there are seven different kinds of attentional processes which include vigilance, selective attention, mental concentration, search, activation, set and analysis-by-synthesis. Posner and Boies (1971) refer to the alertness, selectivity and processing capacity of attention, whereas Pribram and McGuinness (1975) organize their definition on the basis of the arousal, activation, and effort components of attention.

Although definitional attempts such as these are in many ways useful to our understanding of the important aspects of the concept, the lack of agreement with respect to those components that are critical to learning tends to thwart attempts at functional application of these definitions. The crux of the problem is identified by Mostofsky (1970), who suggests that "attention, implying as it does multivariate considerations of process (attentional), subject (attentive) and stimulus (attention-getting) will require multidimensional analytics" (p. 22).

It can be reasonably asserted that there is no definition of attention that has been articulated to date which satisfies all of the above problems. Similarly this assertion, it will become apparent, can be made with respect to existing models or theories of attention. However, it will also be seen that recent efforts have taken us much closer to the goal of a model of attention which can be used in applied settings such as the school classroom. This would help to explain typical development of attention processes and capabilities, and how these associate with learning and acquisition of knowledge.

Models of Attention

The traditional association of attention to the human learning system is primarily attributed to the reception and identification of information (Fishbein, 1976). These two aspects have also been closely associated with the concept of perception. For example, Gibson and Levin (1975) define perception as "the process of extracting information from stimulation emanating from the objects, places and events in the world around us" (p. 13).

In an attempt to clarify the relationship between perception and attention, Fishbein (1976) combines the views of Norman (1969), who emphasizes the selective aspects of attention, and Gibson (1969), who emphasizes exploration aspects to define attention as "any process that determines which of the actual or potential environmental information that gets selected for further processing" (p. 208). If we refer back to Gibson's (Gibson & Levin, 1975) definition of perception, it can be seen that attention is a very important aspect of perceptual learning. Whereas perception involves extracting or "pulling out" information from the stimulus environment, attention determines which of the stimuli will be selected for further processing. Hence, attentional processes include those processes which underlie how we orient our sensory receptors to the environment, how we identify information, how we explore the environment, and how we select information for additional processing. With this interrelationship in mind, we will consider three models of attention, two of which have dominated the research literature over the last thirty years.

Filter Model

The first attempt to specifically describe the role of attention within an information-processing framework was put forth by Broadbent (1958). The "filter" model assumes that only one stimulus can be perceived at a time and that in the case of two competing bits of sensory information, while the one item is immediately perceived, the other is held momentarily as an unanalyzed echo or image. Only after the perceptual analysis of the first item is completed can such echoes and images undergo perceptual analysis. The model, then, suggests a blocking off of less important or irrelevant perceptual information by means of selecting filtering in order that physical properties of high information value concerning the event or activity are those which get attended to.

The phenomenon is well illustrated in the classic dichotic listening and shadowing experiment. The subject wears headphones and two different messages are presented, one to each ear. Instructions are given to listen to a particular message and repeat this as it occurs, or in other words the person is to "shadow" the attended message. The average adult will find it relatively easy to carry out this task by simply selecting out the message to be shadowed and by tuning out the unshadowed message.

Cherry (1953), who pioneered the research in this area, found that although the unshadowed message was not discerned to any degree, certain aspects such as human voices versus buzzing noises or male versus female voices could be identified. To return to Broadbent's (1958) theory, this phenomenon is accounted for by the assertion that any incoming message can be selected and attended to on a physical basis (i.e. pitch differences in male and female voices).

Subsequent to the introduction of the filter model, various theorists and researchers have presented experimental results to refute the original model (Triesman, 1964) and elaborations and modifications of the model have been advanced (Deutsch & Deutsch, 1963). A major point of contention relates to the question of whether inputs are analyzed one by one, with analysis of the second occurring only after the first has been dealt with (i.e. Broadbent's view) or whether several inputs are analyzed simultaneously before selecting among them (i.e. Deutsch & Deutsch (1963) and Triesman's (1964) view). Other major adjustments concern whether the information gets selected early or later on in perceptual analysis and whether the selection is based upon physical or meaningful information about the events (Norman, 1976).

Even though the filter model has dominated the research literature (as it will be seen in subsequent sections of this chapter) for the past thirty-year period, there has been recent criticism regarding both the empirical and theoretical utility of the model (Douglas & Peters, 1979; Krupski, 1986). Indeed, there is no doubt that the dissatisfaction of the filter model and its depiction as a single-channel mechanism prompted the development of the popular alternative capacity model of attention.

Capacity Model

Like filter models, capacity models of attention were formulated within an information-processing framework. The major difference is that capacity models were more concerned with the deployment aspects of attentional abilities as opposed to the blocking or filtering aspects.

The major assumptions of this model are that there is a general limit to a person's ability to processs information, even though this limited capacity can be very flexibly deployed to single or multiple activities (Moray, 1969). In essence, the model suggests that structures of the brain that have received information input, can be activated by an additional input of attention from the limited attentional capacity. Different mental activities will necessarily impose different demands on the limited capacity (Kahneman, 1973). Those activities which are primarily sensory-based (i.e. select the darkest color) would demand less of this capacity than, say, responding to a question about the pros and cons of multiple-choice tests. Generally speaking, tasks such as the latter require greater effort to remain on task, thus making attending more difficult.

The model, in general, offers more possibilities for explaining information processing as well as processing difficulties than the filter model. For example, performance can be deficient as a result of limited capacity of the processor, inappropriate channelling of available attention to irrelevant inputs, or to a lack of attention to relevant inputs.

The capacity model has been widely adopted for research and applied uses, essentially because of the wide capability to account for a greater number as well as type of attention research studies. The model also provides some direction for comparison studies of differences in attentional processing of children and adults. For example, differences in attentional abilities have been explained by the reason that a person's capacity for attention is developmentally constrained and that increases in capacity are a direct function of age.

Even though the model is held to be a major improvement over filter models, there is current criticism of this model, as well (Gibson & Rader, 1979; Neisser, 1976). For example, Neisser (1976) objects to the prevailing notion of the individual's passive acquisition of information inherent in capacity and filter models alike and suggests that the interactive aspects of person and task are of central importance to any examination of attention. Such aspects are the central consideration in the most recent model of attention, the interactive model.

The Interactive Model

Despite the recency of this lesser-known interactive model of attention (Krupski, 1980, 1981, 1986), the roots of the model trace back to a paper written by Vygotsky in the late 1920s which has only recently been translated and published in Wertsch (1981). Vygotsky (1981) asserts that there are two forms of attentional development: the first relating to the inherited neurological mechanisms and "the organic processes of growth, maturation, and development of the neurological apparatuses and functions of the child" (p. 193). The second form, called voluntary attention, is described as a qualitatively distinct process of attention emerging from the sociocultural interaction of the child with the adults surrounding him. According to Vygotsky (1981):

> Voluntary attention emerges owing to the fact that the people who surround the child begin to use various stimuli and means to direct the child's attention and subordinate it to their control. By these means adults give the child the means with which he/she subsequently can master his/her own attention (p. 194).

Adults interact with the child is such a way as to mediate voluntary attention, and it is through such continued social interaction that the child gradually learns to self-regulate and control his/her own attention processes.

In summary, Vygotsky's (1981) view of attention emphasizes the importance of voluntary attention as a direct link to cognitive development and its cultural transmission through the child's social interaction with adults. The child can only gradually learn to master or control his/her voluntary attention by means of mediated practice in social interaction with adults who have themselves mastered voluntary attention. Although Krupski's (1980) interactive model adopts the notion of voluntary attention, the adult mediation aspect of Vygotsky's (1981) model is not included.

Krupski's (1980) interactive model of attention is structured along two dimensions, which are considered to be central to all attentional processing. The first dimension borrows from traditional work pertaining to involuntary/voluntary attention. This dimension reflects the level of volitional deployment of attentional processes. At the involuntary end are those attentional processes that are largely elicited by the "attention-grabbing" characteristics of the stimulus. This would include attention attractors such as bright colors, loud noises and violent scenes. In contrast, the voluntary attentional processes are those that are internally or intentionally exerted by the individual. This would include, for example, attentional processes that are implemented during one's studying for an examination or in one's critical reading of an article. In a sense, Krupski's (1980) description of this dimension has some similarity to the capacity model, in that the dimension reflects the degree and effort one must make in order to satisfy the attentional demands of the moment.

The second dimension reflects the temporal aspects of attentional deployment as being either short-term or sustained. The latter would include attentional demands lasting several minutes to hours, whereas short-term attention refers to brief episodes lasting for a few seconds (Krupski, 1980).

The model can be used then to classify mental tasks and activities along these two dimensions. For example, watching a situation comedy program on television might be categorized as an activity involving involuntary sustained attention processes, whereas pointing to the largest ball in a picture of two different-sized balls would be categorized as involving voluntary short-term attention.

It should be pointed out that Krupski's (1980) primary reason for developing this two-dimensional view of attention was to provide a system of organization of the voluminous literature associating attention problems and a variety of handicapping conditions. As such, the interactive view of attention is not a general model of attention in the same way that filter and capacity models are. Interestingly, much of the recent work pertaining to the development of children's attentional processes has been focused upon children with learning and/or attention-deficit problems (Hale & Lewis, 1979; Douglas & Peters, 1979; Hallahan & Reeve, 1980; Loper & Murphy, 1985).

Krupski (1980) used the two-dimensional framework for her analysis of experimental studies of attention in atypical children, and she was able to demonstrate consistent differences between mild to moderately handicapped children and their same age nonhandicapped peers in learning contexts requiring voluntary sustained attention. In contrast, such differences were not apparent in short-term involuntary attentional situations.

Krupski (1980) argues that these differences must be explored further, especially since the predominant learning context within the typical school classroom is one which demands voluntary sustained attention. She concludes that the interactionist view of attention, as opposed to a deficit or development lag view, offers the greatest utility not only in identifying more specific diagnostic categorization of attention problems in children but also for providing useful information pertaining to remedial intervention. In other words, Krupski (1980) is saying that by examining the specific task variables that lead to attentive and inattentive behavior in children with learning handicaps, teachers and remedial specialists can identify and capitalize upon those which maximize the learning capabilities of the child.

In summary, Krupski's (1980, 1981, 1986) view of attention has considerable appeal, in that existing research can be reorganized in a way that is more relevant to developmental studies and can provide a means for comparison of typical and atypical development. Moreover, this information can be readily utilized in remedial or educational settings. Such trends are already being described in the literature, (Krupski, 1980, 1981; Torgesen, 1981; Loper & Murphy, 1985). Other advocates for an alternative to filter and capacity models of attention have stressed the importance of investigating the cognitive dimensions of attention and especially metaattention (Neisser, 1976; Lupart & Mulcahy, 1984; Douglas & Peters, 1979; Miller, 1985)

The work of Miller (Miller, 1985) and her associates has been particularly instrumental in hypothesizing the important developmental interrelationships between knowledge and control of attention, in particular, and knowledge and control of the general cognitive system. In addition, she refers to the importance of social attribution theory (i.e. the child's perception of the causal effects of various external factors such as task difficulty and internal factors such as effort and motivation) and the important relationship to attention and metacognition.

Although Miller's work has focused upon the analysis of attention/ metaattention relationships, it has been developed out of the generic study of metacognition. Therefore, those aspects relevant to the cognitive/metacognitive dimensions of attention will be examined in the ensuing chapter on metacognition.

Before moving on to the next section concerning how attention is studied, one final point is in order. It was mentioned earlier that Krupski's (1980) view of attention did not include the aspect of adult mediation as did Vygotsky's (1981). As it will become evident in the chapter on metacognition, recent discussions on learning and metacognition have restated the importance of such mediation for the development of attention-related self-regulation (Brown, Bransford, Ferrara & Campione, 1983; Loper & Murphy, 1985), and it is predicted that this factor will become a primary consideration in future models of attention development.

How is Attention Studied?

Researchers tend to select a theory or model of attention to guide their experimental work and to use the results to support or refute the relevance of a model or theory. It is important to note that the model itself, along with the particular experimental paradigm that is adopted, may direct the researcher to view attention in a certain and perhaps biased way (Douglas & Peters, 1979). The most predominant research in the study of attention comes from distractibility studies, central/ incidental learning studies, selective attention studies, and physiological and reaction time studies. Each of these types of studies has similarly been utilized to examine the developmental aspects of attention and, therefore, each will be briefly described.

Distractibility Studies

Distractibility studies are based upon the assumption that attention given to distal distractors detracts from a person's ability to perform on a task. Most studies involve comparisons of distractible and nondistractible subjects and/or performance on a designated task under distracting and nondistracting conditions. The underlying assumption for such research is that distractible individuals are unable to screen-out the competing non-relevant stimuli, and therefore attention that should be allocated to the central task is diverted to the extent that performance reduction occurs.

Distractibility studies typically include some form of task-irrelevant stimuli (i.e. extraneous lights or noises) and the tasks can vary considerably (i.e., naming words, reaction time tasks, written tasks, story reading).

A study by Lasky and Tobin (1973) is a good example of this type of investigation. Learning disabled and nonlearning disabled were positioned midpoint between four speakers. The three experimental tasks consisted of (1) verbal response to auditory instructions, (2) written response to auditory instructions, and (3) written response to written stimuli. Relevant materials were presented through the front speaker, while auditory distractors were played out of the rear and side speakers. The two kinds of distractions included white noise and competing linguistic messages. Results showed no distraction effect of white noise for both groups, whereas the linguistic distraction resulted in greater distractibility for the learning disabled subjects. Lasky and Tobin (1973) concluded that the apparent difficulty for learning disabled students was due to the lack of distinct differences between the relevant and nonrelevant stimuli.

Many studies have been reported in the literature to suggest a greater susceptibility for learning disabled children to the effects of extraneous stimuli. Indeed, distractibility has been the most widely accepted clinical characteristic for learning disabilities since the inception of this field. However, a number of noted experts have recently challenged the validity of this assumption and the research upon which it is based. Hallahan and Reeve (1980) point out that distractibility study results have been notably inconsistent for both normal and learning disability groups. Douglas and Peters (1979) criticize the research for the failure to adequately define single groups, the failure to consider statistical artifacts such as the unusual variability of hyperactive as opposed to learning disabled groups, and the failure to consider initial differences between groups before exposing them to the distractor variables. Future studies of this type will have to be designed in such a way so as to avoid these problems.

Central/Incidental Learning Studies

Another predominant research approach developed by Hagen and his associates (Maccoby & Hagen, 1965; Hagen, 1967; Hagen & Hale,

1973; Hagen & Kail, 1975) involves the measurement of central versus incidental learning or recall. Although many variants of the experimental paradigm have been cited in the literature, the basic task requires an individual to remember the serial position of stimulus cards of line drawings of such items as animals, household objects or colored geometric shapes. The cards each contain a relevant or central stimulus (e.g. animal) and an irrelevant or incidental stimulus (e.g. household item). The child is instructed to memorize the order of the cards by concentrating on the central stimulus and given a number of practice trials.

Performance is assessed by first asking the child to recall the serial position of the central stimulus (the number correct is the central recall score) and then asking the child to name the paired incidental stimulus that appeared with each of the central stimuli (the number of correct pairings is the incidental learning score). The extensive examination of children and adults of all ages using this paradigm has revealed clear developmental trends in children's attending behavior.

In general, the very young child (four years and younger) does not appear to distinguish the central versus incidental aspects of the task and most likely attends to the stimulus most salient. For example, if the task includes color and form elements, the younger child will most often attend to the color dimension, regardless of the relevance or irrelevance to the task. With increasing age, children demonstrate the tendency to attempt to take in all aspects of the stimulus situation, and this is clearly evidenced by a gradual increase in incidental learning scores up to about age 10 or 11. After this age, the typical sharp decline in incidental scores suggests that the relevant stimulus is strategically selected, as it is recognized as being the only information required for successful performance. In other words, children of about 12 years and older begin to approach this task with an "economy of effort" strategy similar to that used by adults in the same or similar task situation.

Other developmental studies (Hale & Taweel, 1974; Brown, Campione & Gilliard, 1974) have expanded this hypothesis somewhat further to suggest that the more attentional-proficient older child adjusts attentional requirements to fit the task demands. In other words, if the task is such that breadth of attention (as opposed to selective attention) is relevant to performing well, then the older student will be more likely than younger children to implement this strategy. This emphasis upon strategic selection and application of task relevant attentional processes is most notable in the current literature in this area.

Selective Attention

A significant offshoot of the central versus incidental learning research has been the study of selective attention. Selective attention studies have been used extensively to examine how the ability to select and process relevant information changes and develops with increasing age. In addition, studies of this type have been used in the examination of children having significant attentional problems. Both the "filter models" and "capacity models" have figured prominently in the development of this type of research investigation.

A classic example, based on the filter model of attention, is Cherry's (1953) cocktail-party phenomenon. This refers to the notion of a person having the ability, on the one hand, to block out all competing conversations to attend to the conversation in which he is involved or, if he so desires, to shift his attention to an alternate conversation within earshot. The latter might indeed be triggered by such salient cues as loud laughter or hearing one's name being spoken.

Studies of attention based upon the capacity model have generally been concerned with the examination of a person's ability to be completely engaged in a particular or primary task and yet be influenced by features or aspects of secondary tasks. Generally it has been found that individuals can attend to more than one task at a time. Moreover, with adults, given the practice and flexibility to self-pace their performance, they can simultaneously execute two tasks almost equally well as performing on one of the tasks.

Findings from adult studies such as the above research relating to central/incidental attention further led investigators of selective attention to examine how the selective attention capabilities of younger children differed from older children and adults (Wright & Vlietstra, 1975; Pick, Christy & Frankel, 1972). For example, Pick, Christy and Frankel (1972) examined second graders and sixth graders using a task involving a same or different decision. Total stimuli included 72 pairs of colored wooden animal shapes varying in shape, color, and size. The relevant dimensions were utilized: one in which the students were cued concerning the relevant dimension prior to presentation of the pair of animal shapes and the other in which this information was given only after the animal pair had been briefly exposed to the child. Each child was examined under both conditions a week apart. Performance was assessed by the time required to make a decision (i.e. same or different) and pressing the appropriate response button. These times were indexed as a measure of selective attention, in that the greater a child's capacity for selective attention, the more quickly one should be able to execute a correct decision.

The results revealed the predictable finding that the older students produced shorter reation times. Of greater importance was the interactive effect of age and conditions. Grade six students showed significantly faster reaction times in the condition where they were pre-informed of the dimension relevant to the task, suggesting they were better able to take advantage of the prior information than the grade two students. Pick, Christy and Frankel (1972) concluded that the capacity for selective attention increases with age in normally developing youngsters, and suggested that the ability to visually focus exclusively upon relevant information is a primary aspect of this development.

The study of performance differences in selective attention has been generalized widely to children with attention and/or learning problems* and to tasks relevant to school performance, such as reading (Laberge & Samuels, 1974; Gibson & Levin, 1975).

A set of studies by Willows (Willows & McKinnon, 1973; Willows, 1974) has combined both aspects to demonstrate the relative importance of being able to ignore irrelevant information. Good and poor grade six boys were asked to read aloud passages in which lines of red type were inserted between the focal text which was printed in black type. Subjects were asked to ignore the red typed lines. The findings revealed that poor readers required more time to read the passage, and made more errors both in the mechanics of the oral reading task as well as in a subsequent comprehension check, than did their proficient reading peers.

Overall, the findings of selection attention studies and central/incidental learning studies appear consistent with the conclusions drawn by Gibson and Levin (1975) who assert that: "Optimally adaptive perception must consist of some balance between heightened attention to information required by task demands and some incidental exploration of other potential input" (p. 28).

Physiological, Reaction Time, and Vigilance Studies

Physiological studies have been carried out in an attempt to directly link internal environments (mental processing, heart rate, galvanic skin response) and external stimuli (flashing lights, loud sounds, bright colors). The mechanism that has been closely associated with attention and

---

*See Hallahan and Reeve (1980) for a comprehensive review.

held to be responsible for the regulation of internal and external information is referred to as the orienting reflex.

The orienting reaction (OR) was first described by Pavlov (1927) as a "What is it?" response to novel stimuli. This concept has since been examined and elaborated by the Soviet psychologist Sokolov (1963a; 1963b; 1960). Essentially, the hypothesis is that as a stimulus is repeatedly presented, the person records a variety of the dimensions of the stimulus (e.g. quality, intensity, frequency, duration) in the form of a neuronal model within the cerebral cortex. The accumulation of stimuli information is made possible through the elicitation of the OR. Its function is preparatory, in that it prepares the organism for optimal reception of information about the stimuli. The OR ensures increased receptor sensitivity by allowing the focusing of attention and preparing the organism for responding. Once a neuronal model is established, all succeeding stimuli are compared to it. If a newly presented stimulus contains information discrepant to the existing neuronal model, the OR occurs to effect further analysis and its magnitude is proportional to the degree of stimulus discrepancy. As a result of elicitation of the OR and further analysis, the new stimulus information is added to the neuronal model.

Physiological indices such as heart rate deceleration, pupil dilation, and inhibition of motor activity have provided reliable indications of this OR response to novel stimuli. Recent work in this area has been particularly promising in associating predictable physiological responses with mental activity (i.e. heart rate deceleration for attention to the external environment and heart rate acceleration associated with internal decision making or problem solving) (Kahneman, 1973). There is, at present, a considerable body of theoretical and empirical investigation to support the notion of a consistent relationship between autonomic response patterns and attention and information processing (Lacey, 1967; Coles, 1974; Coles & Duncan-Johnson, 1975; Bernstein, 1969; Tursky, Schwartz & Crider, 1970). The several reported investigations involving attention and effort (using autonomic indices) and information-processing tasks, collectively suggest that sensory analysis requires minimal effort and attention, whereas the deeper levels of cognitive analysis progressively demand greater attention for successful processing.

Developmental studies have been reported to support this cognitive/ physiological relationship. Stroufe (1971), using heart rate indices with 6-, 8-, and 10-year-old boys, found greater and more reliable heart rate decelerations in the older children. Consistent with the theory, age differences reflected a developmental improvement in attentional set.

Similarly, Jennings (1971), using Piagetian tasks, found the expected heart rate changes to correspond to the degree of cognitive effort required.

Reaction time and/or vigilance performance studies have been widely reported in the literature as traditional measures of attention, and these measures have been used in combination with the above-described autonomic response pattern studies.

In a typical reaction time study, subjects are presented with stimuli (i.e. light flash, different letters, different pictures) over a series of trials (i.e. "n" number of times in which the material is presented). The subject's response (i.e. time to press a button) is recorded as reaction time and constitutes both the completion of a trial and the activation of the next trial. An example of this task would be the displaying of the question, "Does this word start with **b**?" on a slide screen for four seconds, an interval of 10 seconds and then the presentation of the stimulus word "brain" on the screen for one second. Reaction time is measured from this point to the subject's indicating his response through button press, resulting in the completion of that particular trial.

Sample differences in reaction times, as well as differences in subject response times, after presentation of varying materials or stimuli have been used in making interpretations about attention processing and attentional development. The increasingly complex and sophisticated studies using reaction time and automatic responding indices would appear to be a particularly promising avenue of investigation. Unfortunately, studies of this nature cannot guide the work of the classroom teacher.

Vigilance studies will often include a reaction time component to assess the subject's ability to monitor stimuli over a lengthy time period. Although a variety of experimental formats have been utilized,* the typical vigilance study requires the subject to attend to successive presentations of stimuli (i.e. tones, lights, words in a series) and to respond in a particular way (i.e. oral response, button press) when a specified change in stimuli occurs (i.e. different intensity of light, a specific sequence of signal words). The person's ability to correctly detect the key signals over a prolonged time period is interpreted as a reflection of one's ability to voluntarily sustain attention (Krupski, 1980). The importance of this ability to monitor and maintain attention over prolonged periods of time, and the obvious implication this has when school-related tasks are considered, is most apparent.

---

*See Broadbent (1971) and Mackworth (1970) for complete reviews.

In summary, a wide variety of research approaches have been utilized to study attention in young children. This diversity has been ad-
vantageous to the degree that many dimensions of attentional processing
in normal and exceptional children have been identified and examined.
However, this has also resulted in considerable confounding of some of
the factors most central to practical applications. Nevertheless, there are
certain developmental trends that have been well documented in the literature, which are of considerable interest to educators.

The Development of Attention

Studies of young children have shown that learning is dominated by
external cues in the environment. However, with increasing age and experience, the young child's attentional abilities are ever changing and
improving. Gibson (1969), who is a leading authority in this area, has
described mature attention as the optimization of attention and
describes the course of development as follows: "First, the tendency for
attention to become more exploratory and less captive; second, the tendency for exploratory search to become more systematic and less random; third, the tendency for attention to become more selective; and
fourth, the inverse tendency for attention to become more exclusive" (p.
456).

Evidence for a developmental trend in environmental scanning and
exploration efficiency was apparent in a study conducted by Zinchenko,
Chzhi-tsin, and Tarakanov (1962). The tasks induced subjects of three
to six years of age to visually attend to irregular shapes and then identify
the shapes when they were again projected on a screen. From the results
of this study, Zinchenko et al. (1962) concluded that with increasing age,
children demonstrate greater efficiency in familiarization tasks to attend
to and isolate the relevant aspects of the shape, that familiarization and
recognition tasks become increasingly differentiated, and that scanning
behavior becomes more economical. Similar age/efficiency trends in
tactile exploration were reported by Abravanel (1968).

Vurpillot (1968) recorded the oculo-motor activity of children between three and nine years of age in order to examine the development
of scanning strategies and their relation to visual differentiation. The results of this study led Vurpillot to hypothesize a succession of four stages
in scanning strategy development. Stage one children appeared to have
no definite criterion of same or different, as scanning behavior was random and responses were unrelated to the information collected. In stage

two, same and difference definitions were assumed by the existence or absence of a common element. No spatial frame of reference was apparent and visual scanning involved only portions of the stimulus. At the third stage, the same and difference definitions were similar to adult formulations, and comparisons were employed within a limited spatial and temporal frame of reference which included only the elements that could be scanned and memorized in a few seconds. At stage four, a systematic strategy of scanning and a wide frame of reference was evident (Vurpillot, 1968, p. 649).

Selective auditory attention was examined in children, ranging from kindergarten to grade four, on a task requiring the selection of one auditory message when two were simultaneously present (Maccoby & Konrad, 1966). The results of this study indicated that with increasing age performance was improved. The authors suggested that "language familiarity allows older children to benefit by the redundancies in the material to be selected as well as the ability to exclude irrelevant information (nonsense words)" (Maccoby & Konrad, 1966, p. 121).

The above studies reveal a gradual progression of attending abilities as they pertain to selected visual and auditory tasks. Key words to describe these qualitative differences that are increasingly apparent as the child matures are efficiency, economy, and systematic strategy. It should further be noted that each of the key words suggests the tendency for greater internal or cognitive regulation of attentional processing. Indeed, a number of recent literature reviews (i.e. Gibson & Rader, 1979; Day, 1975; Wright & Vlietstra, 1975) have suggested a direct link between attention and cognitive development.

For example, Gibson and Radar (1979) focus directly upon the developmental aspects of attention in suggesting that:

> The child gains progressively in the specificity of correspondence between what information his perceptual processes are engaged with (what he is attending to) and its utility for performance in the service of his needs. He gains in flexibility because more alternatives become open to him. He gains in preparedness for events in readiness for performance. And he gains in how much he can do because of the increasing economy of his pickup of information (p. 17).

Wright and Vlietstra (1975) have provided a very careful analysis of exploratory versus search attentional behaviors as they relate to information processing. The authors describe the two aspects as entirely distinct processes that are developmentally and cognitively linked. A critical shift in attentional control emerges when the person is able to move from passive intake of information to active, planful and deliberate attending. In their description of this important developmental progression, Wright and Vlietstra (1975) note that:

> This developmental change appears to be marked by a transitional period in which the intentional and goal-directed aspects of deliberate search are fairly well developed, and the capacity of salient features to capture attention is no longer particularly helpful, even when such features are informative, but is still a major source of interference when they are distracting or irrelevant (p. 196).

Similar conclusions suggesting the importance of developmental considerations in assessing attentional proficiency have been reported by Day (1975), who found that with increasing age children:

1. demonstrate more systematic, task-appropriate strategies for acquiring visual information;
2. show an increasing ability to maintain optimal performance across variations in the content and arrangement of stimuli;
3. exhibit visual scanning which becomes more exhaustive and more efficient;
4. show an increasing focus on the portions of visual stimuli which are most informative for the specific task;
5. show an increase in the speed of completion of visual search and comparison tasks;
6. show an increase in the size of the useful "field of view" (pp. 186-187).

In summary, the conclusions of those who have extensively reviewed the literature pertaining to developmental aspects of attention very clearly point to the notion that attention is extricably tied to cognitive development. Changes in attention which traditional models have insufficiently characterized as quantitative appear to be recognizable qualitive differences which maximize and optimize the attention of the growing child or adult. In other words, attention begins to take on a strategic role in the child's learning processes and the child becomes increasingly adept at managing his/her own attentional processes. This focus is increasingly becoming the predominant view and is one which is very closely associated with the developing work in the broader domain of metacognition. Those aspects relevant to attention and the current emphasis toward self-regulation and motivation will be examined in the subsequent chapter on metacognition.

The following section will review the educational and classroom applications relevant to the attentional processes described in this chapter.

EDUCATIONAL AND CLASSROOM APPLICATIONS OF OUR UNDERSTANDING OF ATTENTIONAL PROCESSES

Given the observable fact that children attend to and explore their environment, it is valuable to the teacher and parent to ascertain what variables (both learner and environmental) determine these attentional behaviors and to what extent the attentional processes of children can be reconstructed by external forces to play a maximal role in children's immediate learning and their long-term cognitive development. Our purpose in this section is to reexamine psychological components of attention discussed in the earlier section, but this time more strictly in terms of how they apply to classroom instruction and learning, and how these analyses can be extended to promote more adaptive attention both in the classroom and the broader learning environment. The aim, therefore, is to link the findings of experimental research to the activities of the classroom as they relate to alertness, selectivity, and central processing—the three separable components of children's attention. The critical objective in this section is to build an interpretive bridge between theoretical concepts and basic research discussed earlier in the chapter and practical classroom application based upon a commonsense perspective.

The most practical needs of teachers and parents with respect to holding and maintaining children's adaptive attention and selective focusing on task performance are as follows:

- The development and maintenance of optimal sensitivity to their environment (alertness);
- Children's scanning of their environment in order to select the most salient dimensions and to focus on those features while excluding others (selectivity);
- Understanding the focal point of children's thinking, where the selected elements are brought together for identification, comparison and recording (central processing).

In spite of a great body of available research and theory in mental concentration, vigilance, search, activation, set, etc., much of the work has little applicability to an understanding of the development of attentional processes in young children. Therefore, the present examination of techniques and strategies for promoting adaptive attention in children is not intended to be comprehensive nor generalizable to a diversity of children. Only a few ground rules of relevance to children's attentional learning are presented here.

Alertness

A number of practically beneficial generalizations supported by the laboratory research on alertness, as a component of attention, reveal that alertness is best maintained when (1) the task is varied, (2) feedback is provided, and (3) the learning situation is kept interesting to the students. Teachers and learners recognize, all too well, that a task becomes boring if it is repeated often without a change. As recommended by Keele (1973) and Silberman (1970), even intriguing tasks can become boring unless a certain level of diversity and vitality is maintained. Two specific ways of maintaining alertness are to introduce variety and novelty and to provide feedback about performance on the task (Keele, 1973). Students and teachers remain alert when the classroom situation is characterized by new features and elements and unexpected offerings which have the effect of raising the arousal level of the student. In order to maintain interest in the classroom, teachers who confront students with unexpected questions and activities, change the artwork on the walls, and introduce variety into the schedule increase student alertness and, to a point, improve performance.

The optimal level of alertness, however, depends on the nature of the task (Fitts & Posner, 1967). Teachers need to recognize that short tasks built around concrete, personally relevant and meaningful problems keep the student alert and active. An adequate level of arousal is a sine qua non, but if the classroom always has a dramatically festive atmosphere with bright colors, loud sounds, and sharp contrasts that have their own variation, the perceptual salience may be enhanced for awhile stirring the average learner from a stupurous condition. However, beyond a certain point of unusual stimulation, such increases in alertness are likely to cause a deterioration in student performance, especially in difficult tasks requiring a narrowed focus on the specific task at hand. Difficult tasks requiring concentrated attention and alertness must, of necessity, have a delicately balanced level of stimulation and arousal. As pointed out by Roper and Nolan (1976), the teacher needs to be sensitive to the delicate balance between alertness produced through teaching conditions that are naturally stimulating and those external conditions that may heighten the arousal level considerably but will take attention away from matters of relevance. Samuels (1967) noted that novelty enhances alertness but it also distracts and may take over from alertness in matters of vital importance to attention.

Maintaining Alertness in the Classroom

The teacher's function of arranging learning situations that are interesting, and which stimulate moderate levels of alertness and attract student focus, requires careful consideration of the consequences of creating unexpected contexts that may generate high levels of arousal. Forcing all students to be alert at all times by introducing loud sound, sharp contrasts and visual displays is a high price for eliminating boredom. Planning effective use of classroom situations that are naturally and quietly interesting and appeal to students' motivations achieves a compromise between the extremes of boredom and repetition on the one hand and the strong effects of unusual stimulation of arousal level on the other hand.

The special needs of some students for constant alertness and stimulation and other students who find it unusually hard to stay alert can be met by rearranging the features of the task demands so that students are impelled to be alert. For the average student having normal problems of attention, the following recommendations may be of relevance to teachers in maintaining alertness in the classroom:

1. Arouse interest in a topic through discussion that requires the less alert student to think about a cut-and-dried problem in a new way that is personally stimulating.
2. Provide continual feedback on performance to students who have trouble staying alert. When students are kept informed about how well they are doing on the task, the job at hand seems more important and worth doing.
3. Provide moderate levels of music and other background noise which helps the average student stay alert, especially if tired or sleepy (Keele, 1973).
4. Arrange seating assignments so that students who have trouble staying alert are placed in the "action zone" of the classroom (Brophy & Good, 1974) where the teacher spends a greater proportion of time and where interactions among the higher-achieving students are most frequent.

   A frequent tactic used by teachers is to place the less alert students at the back of the class so that they do not distract the higher-achieving students, who tend generally to migrate to the front of the classroom.

   The teacher's essential function with respect to seating assignments is to spot students whose alertness lapses easily and to identify the action zone of the classroom. A practical function of the teacher is to strategically place the less alert student initially on the outskirts of the action zone; then encourage tasks with moderate levels of difficulty, provide continual feedback on performance, and finally to encourage the student to migrate permanently to the action zone. This strategy of placing the less alert students in the front of the classroom which is commonly the action zone is typically more successful than any other assigning strategy. According to Schwebel and Cherlin (1972), it shows the greatest decrease in percent of time inactive or on task-irrelevant behavior.

5. Rearrange the features of the task itself (Posner, 1973) so that the level of task difficulty is compatible with the child's training to handle the task. The optimal level of alertness depends on task difficulty (Fitts & Posner, 1967). Tasks that are too easy for the child are inherently monotonous. The child is sufficiently skilled in performing the task so that it can be done in a half-sleep state and does not require the child to be alert in the execution. By contrast, a task that has a high level of difficulty may have the effect of reducing the level of alertness in a child who perceives the task to be beyond the purview of the fundamental skills that he or she has mastered. The high level of difficulty of the expected and assigned task may initially have a strong effect on the arousal level, but the difficulty of the task itself and the student's sensitivity to this factor may cause a deterioration in the alertness. The narrowed focus of the child on the difficult nature of the task becomes too restrictive, with the result that important relevant details of the task are ignored. Under these conditions, level of alertness drops rapidly. The high level of arousal initially experienced by the child reflects a kind of failure of alertness and attention, requiring proper remedial action by the teacher.

6. Identify the child's precise problem and suggest a specific remedy. Teachers ask too much when they expect the average student to respond to rather difficult tasks with activity and alertness. For consistent long-term improvement in attention and alertness the teacher must identify specific features of the task, precise problems inherent in the task, and specific remedies with respect to training, fundamental skills, and selective attention to salient dimensions of the task. It is recognized in our discussion here that children's central processing has a sharply limited capacity. The frequent occurrence of attention problems among children are therefore

attributed less to known physiological deficits or mental handicaps in the central processing system, but more to the educators' and teachers' lack of ability to identify children's precise problems and to try specific remedies. In order that teachers and parents use specific techniques for assessing inattentiveness, and strategies that are effective for promoting alertness, what is required is a careful analysis of some of the factors that control children's attention span, selective attention, sustained attention and special problems of attention requiring special control processes and cognitive treatments.

A practical understanding of the following control processes and strategies may be of relevance to teachers in promoting children's adaptive attention in the classroom.

Selective Attention

In the chapter on memory (Chapter 4) we will note that although the nature of the sensory register functioning is similar across age levels, children do not process the contents of this memory store in such a way as to prevent decay of information from memory. One of the processes that is important to the operation of the sensory register is selective attention. Selective attention is a kind of screening device by which certain aspects of the situation or stimulus are scrutinized and other aspects are ignored. Selective attention includes three elements and with the young learners often reflects at least two stages of attention.

In the first stage, the learner learns what to attend to by picking out a designated object or event from a larger set.

In the second stage the learner learns which feature of the stimulus needs special attention and which other features of the same stimulus must be disregarded for the moment. Thus, in selective attention, the learner learns first what to look at and then what to choose. An examination of these two stages of selective attention reveals a progressive improvement of children's ability to move from random to selective attention as follows:

1. attending selectively to a specific set of **visual** information (letters, words and sentences),
2. listening selectively or attending **auditorily** to a variety of sensory stimulations (e.g. people talking, noise from the traffic in the hallway, traffic noises on the street), and
3. selectively inattending to less obvious sensations (e.g. heat, odors, headache, stomach rumbling).

At any given moment a great quantity of information is impinging on the children's sensory organs. Their ability for attending to stimuli, events, or contexts is influenced by the degree to which they can filter out unwanted sources of information and focus on a central message in a selective listening or visual task. Related to selective attention, therefore, is the problem of distractibility. For example, when a teacher asks a child to complete a sheet of addition problems and instead the child is observed to be studying multiplication numbers at the bottom of the sheet, or the child is confused by the fact that some additional items in the sheet are written in blue ink as opposed to black ink, then in these cases one could say that the child is selectively attending to stimuli or features that the teacher has designated as irrelevant to the task at hand. Teachers, therefore, should be aware of the problems of distractibility as related to selective attention and should guide the child's interest to focus on the task-relevant features in the array of information. Teachers of young children, in particular, have the responsibility to keep distracting stimuli to a minimum.

Selectively Attending to Specific Features of the Task

A frequent tactic in classroom instruction is to arouse selective attention to a task by the teacher announcing that the task is important and urging the children to pay special attention to it. However, these general instructions of the teacher for paying special attention do not pinpoint the specific features of the task to which the children should pay special notice in order to profit from the instruction, nor do they specify other incidental features of the task that are irrelevant and should be disregarded. Some of the most effective aspects of the direct instructional model reviewed by Carnine and Silbert (1979) and the discriminative learning model described by Siqueland and Rieber (1970) have important implications for teachers concerned with improving pupils' performance through selective attention. The major components that are commonly agreed upon in both the direct instructional model and discrimination learning include:

1. **Ordering of objectives** (e.g. "I first want you to look at all objects on page 1 that are **round** in shape").
2. **Assessing students' mental set** — the ideas, expectations and motivations the individual child brings to the learning situation. The emphasis is on identifying how much a child departs from the developmental level of other peers. The teacher should assess the

child's personal frame of reference. In other words, the teacher needs to remain sensitive to the aspects of the situation that the young student considers personally relevant. In the performance of a complex task, the teacher must draw the attention of the child to task-related characteristics of the stimulus which may not "naturally" stand out for the child. Unless the teacher draws the child's specific and selective attention to these details, the young child faced with an abundance of information may ignore the task-related features of the stimulus and rely more on the mental set — the personal ideas, expectations and meanings. The task of the teacher in this respect is to become acquainted with those expectations of the child that may be selectively sensitizing him or her to the personally less task-relevant aspects of the activity. For example, the student who is directed to identify specific numerical figures on a screen by pressing buttons may become so fascinated by the buttons themselves and their bright colors that he or she may end up identifying fewer numerical figures as a result of looking more frequently at the distracting events. This underscores the need to comprehend the child's specific motivations and ability to resist certain types of distractions in order to succeed in task performance. For example, in teaching addition, it is important that the teacher facilitate selective attention by keeping "distractibility" factors to a minimum (e.g. not mixing up one-digit and two-digit numbers for addition in the beginning of the exercises). Distractibility may be reduced by the teacher not using any sharp contrasts in color or sound.

3. **Directing attention to specific aspects of the task by means of query and interrogation.** Prevailing evidence indicates (Lovitt, 1975) that to maximize a child's success at a particular task, especially an academic task, teachers should have available an accurate assessment of the child's ability to perform the task. The teacher should be generally aware of the child's previous experience with tasks of a similar nature and the degree of autonomy with which the child was able to handle the task. Because of the child's limited information-processing capacity to filter input, sustained interrogation of the child and query by the teacher is necessary to ensure that certain stimulus features of the task have been detected and absorbed by the young learner. In any specific task performance, therefore, it is important for the teacher to ask specific questions or to give specific instructions that will draw the child's attention to stimulus features of the task. For example:

- "Did you notice that all numbers to be added first, are in the color blue?"
- "What is the color you must use to show corrections in the second line?"
- "When will you need to go to the line marked **Product**, at the beginning or the end of the adding?"

It is important for the teacher to bear in mind that such a procedure of sustained interrogation in a relatively new and unfamiliar task (for example, addition) leads the child to familiarity with the salient steps of the task. When faced with a similar situation, children begin, slowly but gradually, to rely on what they have learned in the past and, as a result, become more goal oriented in their search, i.e. in selecting the relevant, information features of the adding exercise according to prior experience. With experience and familiarity in a variety of addition exercises, the child is able, more automatically, to select the appropriate features and respond quickly and with specific reference to the various steps to be used in the exercise.

The exact amount of interrogation (concerning the selectivity of the child's sensory field) that the teacher needs to conduct will depend on the age of the child. With respect to ability for selective attention, younger children perform less well on discriminative-learning tasks because of developmental incapability to probe the environment for salient features of the stimulus. There is little the teacher can do to improve this lack of ability, except be objectively aware of developmental differences in selective attention. However, there are other aspects of the selective attention that the teacher can attempt to control even with young learners.

The teacher can facilitate attention to the task by picking out a designated feature of the task that will ensure accuracy in performance. For example, when a student is presented with a new and complex two-digit addition problem for the first time, the teacher can point out the significant features that require attention. If the task is to add two-digit numbers, it helps to know that the numbers form two columns. After the numbers in the right-hand column have been added, the total might come to another two-digit number which is the product of the right-hand column numbers when they are added up. If the student understands terms such as column, product, sum, etc., then giving instructions using these labels or signs directs attention to specific aspects of the task and specific steps to be taken in task performance. If the student does not understand labels or signs for terms such as product, addition, subtraction, then the first specific feature of the task would be to selectively attend to the meanings of the symbols used in task performance. In the addition exercises, it is selectively relevant for Johnny to be told that in adding two-place numbers, it is important that the numbers are properly aligned so that Johnny knows what numbers in a column are to be added. The important point here is that the teacher encourages selective attention by drawing Johnny's notice to the fact that (1) numbers to be added are appropriately placed in two columns (right-hand and left-hand columns), (2) numbers in the right-hand column must be added first, and (3) numbers in the left-hand column must be added later. The features of the task selected by the teacher help to channel Johnny's actions and behavior. Thus, it can be expected that in future task performance Johnny is likely to notice these perceptual salient and distinctive features of the task, to remember the symbols associated with the addition and subtraction task, and to act on the task in a way that his past experience tells him is important. In our illustration the selective instructions given by the teacher help Johnny's responses to become less exploratory and more systematic and selective (Gibson, 1969).

Enhancing the Salience of External Stimuli

Since attention is a kind of screening device by which certain aspects of a situation are scrutinized and other aspects are ignored, attention is influenced by both external and internal sources of information, and the teacher needs to be cognizant of both the external features of the stimulus or event that normally grabs the child's attention and also the internal sources of information — for example, the learner's mental set, motivations and expectations concerning the task or the event which will determine whether the learner will attend sufficiently to take in the event or to ignore it. The teacher needs to be sensitive to the delicate balance between a situation that is likely to be stimulating for the child and one in which relevant stimuli are overshadowed and drowned out by distractors, intrusion factors or competing stimulations. The external and internal influences on selectivity in children's attention need to be considered separately.

External Sources of Influence on Selectivity

Laboratory studies have reviewed some of the more commonly observed external influences on children's selectivity of attention. They conclude that bright colors, loud sounds, sharp contrasts and novel features attract the attention of learners, especially children.

What can the teacher do to make critical elements of the stimulus or relevant features of the task more noticeable to the child so as to facilitate selective attention?

(a) **Make the stimulus characteristics more prominent.** According to Pointkowski and Calfee (1974), this can be done by enhancing the natural perceptual salience of the task so that task-relevant dimensions stand out. In other words, emphasize critical features of a stimulus or facilitate selective attention to step-by-step procedures in a task. With young children, for example, the different steps in a task may become distinct when each step is given its own bright color. In the addition problems involving two-place numbers, initial instructions might be to add the right-hand column of numbers marked in blue first before proceeding with the adding of the left-hand column.

(b) **Eliminate irrelevant features.** An examination of the development of selective attention reveals that children, as compared to adults, have more difficulty in filtering out unwanted information and focusing on a central message in selective listening or visual task. Children are often distracted by competing tasks, and young children make more intrusion errors than older children. As might be anticipated, therefore, selective attention of children can be facilitated by teachers eliminating as many irrelevant features of the task as possible and by avoiding competing auditory distractions. Due to information-processing limitations, children are unable to attend simultaneously to two sources of stimulation: one instructing them on what to do and what is appropriate procedure, and another telling them what not to do and what mistakes to avoid in procedure. Thus, in our illustration of adding two-place numbers the teacher must focus only on what to do with numbers in the right-hand and left-hand column. Any simultaneous discussion of other irrelevant features such as what happens in three-place numbers and common mistakes that children make in adding two-place numbers should be avoided until after the children have mastered the basics of adding two-place numbers.

The hallmark of this approach involves discrimination teaching. This approach is teacher-directed and uses teacher-dominated activities, principally as follows:

a. **Stimulus similarity:** Teachers need to be aware that teaching to discriminate between two objects that are similar to one another is more difficult than teaching to discrimiate two objects that are distinctively different. For example, in drawing children's selective attention to geometrical figures, the teacher would be well advised to start the discrimination exercise by using two stimuli that are noticeably different (e.g. square and circle as opposed to a rectangle and square). In developing the child's selective attention to certain features of the stimulus under study, the teacher should initially use stimulus features that are very different. For example, on the task of identifying odd and even numbers, two noticeably different colors may initially be used to represent the numbers until such time as the child begins to understand the concept of odd and even numbers in terms of other distinguishing features.

b. **Separation between stimuli.** If the task requires the child to compare and contrast the stimulus features of two objects, the discrimination between two widely separated objects is going to be considerably harder for the younger children. Reducing the amount of space between the stimuli will make the stimuli easier to compare and contrast. In other words, selective attention is impaired when stimuli for comparison are located far apart. The child will find it harder to selectively examine pictures of two objects on far-apart pages of the text as opposed to two objects displayed side-by-side.

c. **Separation between stimulus and response locations.** The characteristics of the task that requires a separation between the place where the stimuli are presented and the place where responses are made makes the process of selective attention correspondingly more difficult for the child. When there is no separation between the stimulus and response locations — that is, when the learner responds directly to the stimulus (for example, when the child describes specific features of an object that is placed directly in front of him) — selective attention to the salient characteristics of the object is comparatively easy. However, when the locations of the stimulus and response are separated, selective focus on specific dimensions and task-relevant and task-irrelevant characteristics is less possible and discrimination responding is harder. For example, in a situation where the teacher gives instructions for a "ball-throwing" task in the classroom, salient features of the activity may be described on the blackboard. The response units are described to the child and learned by the child with the help of the blackboard. It follows that the ball's position on the blackboard may become the last cue the child sees when attending to the stimulus. If, subsequently, the child has to make the response in a different location (e.g. on the playground), the separation of the original stimulus and response from the modified stimulus and response changed, in terms of location, makes the discrimination much harder for the inexperienced learner. The theoretical explanation for this effect is that because the stimulus and the response units are separated in position, the latter becomes a salient cue requiring selective focusing and selective attention on the part of the learner. In classroom applications it should be quite obvious to the teacher that when locations of two response units or locations of the stimulus and response are separated, cues that are irrelevant to discrimination are confounded with the cues of the position (Shepp & Swartz, 1976). With young and inexperienced learners, therefore, teachers must ensure that locations of stimuli and responses are not changed too quickly. If the response units change with respect to location, the child must be given selective help for learning the position cue. The teacher must strike a balance between the change in location or position being too large or too small. If the transitions from one location to another are too large, the discrimination is impeded. If the transitions are too small, discrimination learning is unnecesarily slow and the child's selective attention is impaired. Generally speaking, however, teachers would be well advised to note that separating the locations of the stimuli from the locations of the responses interferes with learning because it makes the irrelevant transitional cues more salient. The reason for this effect is that the child is more likely to give selective attention to the positive-relevant dimensions when there are other more task-relevant dimensions of the task to consider.

d. **Providing instructional praise.** Another factor for the teacher to bear in mind when teaching the young child to respond selectively to task-relevant features of the event is that instructions alone are generally not as effective as instructional praise. Instructions are most effective when they are accompanied by small-step instructional demonstrations. Relatively small-step instructional demonstrations requiring a one-to-one relationship between the teacher and child are more effective than instructions for selective attention given to the entire class. The reason for this difference is that in the one-to-one interaction between learner and teacher, there is a greater chance of verbal analogues, such as verbally instructing the learner about small segments of the task, proceeding to larger segments only after the smaller ones are thoroughly understood. Thus, nonverbal and verbal shaping begins to occur, with the teacher providing to the child instructional praise for accurate responding and selective attention to task-relevant features. If the steps in shaping the selective attention are gradual enough, a young learner can solve a discrimination problem without ever making an error.

e. **Shaping selective attention through the use of prompts.** In the initial stages of shaping selective attention behaviors, the teacher uses prompts frequently in teaching a new task. Gradually, the prompts are made more superficial and are eliminated entirely when the children feel they have grasped the selectively salient dimensions of the task.

f. **Individualizing instructions** for children with attentional deficits. Most children may learn to attend selectively to task-relevant features of a stimulus or event by general instructions given to an entire class. However, some individual children who have attentional deficits or special attentional problems may get very confused by general instructions, especially if the range of ability in the class is large. Although it is unrealistic to expect the teacher to provide this one-to-one shaping experience for every child in the classroom, shaping of selective attention to specific features of the task would be most helpful in the case of learners identified as having difficulty in attending to relevant aspects of the situation. Often, these are children who in addition to having attentional deficits have problems of poor memory, low motivation, and limited self-reference. Such children often lack basic skills in selecting relevant information, possibly as a result of early failure in task performance. Unless instructed individually in how to attend and what to attend to, they do not benefit from the school experience despite other indications that they have a reasonably extended attention span to nonschool activities.

What kind of instruction might a teacher use to improve such students' attentional skills? A number of dimensions need to be considered.

Direct Instruction Approach

Direct instruction is a commonsense approach, focusing essentially on teaching the students with attentional problems to:

- take their time,
- teach them what to do in differentiating task-relevant features from task-irrelevant features,
- provide a strategy-training program to students who have difficulties in filtering out irrelevant dimensions of the task or in setting up

an independent set of rules that will lead them through the various steps of the task performance,

- give students the much needed instructional praise and feedback to practice the mechanics of applying the strategy till task performance becomes automatic (Wright, 1977). Norman (1976, p. 65) attributes automaticity to practice — the skill is practiced over an extended period of time, it is highly learned, then it becomes automated, requiring little conscious awareness and little allocation of mental effort.

Because children's attention can be affected pejoratively by nonoptimal organization, it is encumbent on teachers as presenters of materials to generate well-structured presentations. It has been proposed that more **concrete modes** of presenting information will dramatically improve children's attention. When one wants young children to consider certain items of information in a sequence as being more important and requiring the child's sustained attention, it behooves the teacher to present the information late in the communication or make the need to attend to the information maximally explicit, either through concretization or additional verbalizations about items to attend to and remember (Rohwer, 1973).

Although it is unrealistic to expect that the teacher can give direct attention and a one-to-one interactive relationship to each child, the application of this somewhat laborious procedure is most useful in learning situations in which an error would produce harmful consequences. For example, in the case of a child requiring practice in selective attention in order to cross a busy street or thoroughfare, one-to-one instructions in selective attention to specific features of the street-crossing task are most critical. Direct instruction in teaching the preverbal child to cross the street may be provided at two levels. At the first level the child selectively attends to the colors, shapes and contours of the traffic signs and lights (e.g. red light, walk and stop signals, pedestrian crosswalk) till he can make the necessary discrimination at an errorless level. At the second stage, direct instruction is supplemented with step-by-step practical demonstration of the act of crossing. This may be supplemented by a graphic explanation of the negative consequences of choosing to ignore the traffic signs and intersection lights. In having the child attend selectively to the positive and negative consequences of monitoring or not monitoring behaviors, the child learns to differentiate between the positive stimuli (green light, walk sign, traffic stops) and the negative stimuli (red light, don't walk sign) and their positive and negative consequences. Selective attention to both the positive and negative properties of the stimulus are important to a child's errorless-discrimination performance.

Assessing the Child's Level of Motivation

The teacher's assessment of the motivation level of the child to make the necessary discriminations and to attend to selective features of the situation is important to the application of techniques used with the young learner. It is important for the teacher to recognize that young children's behavior is obviously not motivated by the basic needs required for safety and survival. It is generally accepted that curiosity is a more impelling source of motivation for children's behavior in both academic and non-academic learning situations. In task performance, therefore, the teacher needs to have a fairly accurate assessment of the child's motivation or lack of motivation for selectively attending to the task at hand. This is especially warranted in situations where the harmful consequences of making an error in the task far surpasses the positive consequences of curiosity-motivated behavior. Once teachers get to know the student, they should be able to predict the circumstances in which the child will respond with alertness and attention. The child's motivation level can be too low to focus selectively on the task so that accurate performance is impaired, or it can be so high that it causes autonomic overactivity and interferes with accurate performance in the task at hand. It is suggested that the autonomic overactivity caused by too high levels of motivation may have a deleterious effect on adaptive attention and task performance. Between these extremes of motivation is an optimal range of motivation. Within that range, when new material is being learned, a moderate level of motivation enables the child to attend selectively to the task.

When the material has already been learned in some previous situations, a moderately high level of motivation will help the child to focus best on the task at hand. In this connection, the teacher's function is two-fold: first, to provide the child increased incentives and rewards only in tasks in which the child already has a well-learned response tendency to perform correctly; second, to avoid giving added inducements and incentives for those task performances in which the child's well-learned response tendency is incorrect. In short, based on the teacher's personal knowledge of the child, teachers need to note that if the child's well-learned response tendency is for correct performance, increasing the child's motivation by means of added rewards and inducements will help the child to focus more selectively and attentively and thereby improve performance further. But if the child's well-learned response tendency is toward incorrect performance, increasing the level of motivation too much will interfere with selective attention and thereby impair performance.

The theoretical explanation for this effect is that the child's attentional capacity is exceeded when the response tendency from past learning and experience is insufficient for accurate performance, so that additional motivation to perform gives the child too much to think about and distracts the child from selective focusing (Norman, 1976; Kahneman, 1973).

The optimal level of motivation for a child is individually determined, and the teacher's appropriate steering of the child depends upon the teacher's knowledge of the child's previous performance and response tendencies, the nature of the task requirements, and an optimal level of motivation that would promote in the child selective attention to the task at hand. If the teacher is aware that the child already has a well-learned response tendency for performing correctly in a task, increasing the child's motivation will strengthen both the response tendency and the selective attention and will thereby contribute to much higher levels of performance.

Special Problems of Attention Among Students with Attentional Deficits

Some students have attentional deficits that cause them to be grossly inattentive under normal learning conditions. Their inattention calls for a twofold special-action regimen. The first set of special action is aimed at changing dysfunctional and task-irrelevant behaviors of the student through behavior-modification strategies using reinforcement and instructional praise to shape task-relevant behaviors. In this approach the student is rewarded for keeping his selective attention on relevant features of the task. A detailed discussion of behavior-modification techniques for use with children having manifest attentional deficits is beyond the scope of this chapter, and the interested reader is referred to Becker (1972) for a discussion of how the teacher may handle classroom situations where little else helps children with special problems of attention. Such an approach works well and quickly to gain students' attention in special education classes where the ordinary classroom regimen is not effective and the classroom atmosphere becomes manifestly disrupted by the behavior of students, many of whom have a history of inattentiveness and disruptiveness. Through judicious use of reinforcement strategies, such students may be trained to become less disruptive and to focus more on the task. These students need direct guidance in how to solve problems, what specific features of the task to attend to, and how to handle assigned tasks. Behavior-modification techniques are used to provide the necessary direct guidance through a system of rules, reinforcements and ignoring of disruptive behavior. The teacher explicitly repeats the rules for appropriate attentive conduct several times a day (e.g. "Sit quietly while working; look at me while I'm explaining this procedure; follow each step exactly the way I show it to you"). The teacher monitors the student behavior closely and provides praise for appropriate task performance. In the early stages, the teacher may ignore task-irrelevant behaviors, but soon after the student has learned to maintain attention to the task, even for a brief period of time, the teacher provides ongoing feedback to the child as to successful performance in the task. The evidence suggests that judicious use of reinforcement for attentive focus on the task, praise for behaviors conducive to task performance, and one-to-one direct guidance and direct training of the student through the various steps of the task are effective techniques for promoting attention in special education classes.

These techniques and strategies are especially germane to students having problems of hyperactivity and impulsiveness. These are students who switch rapidly from one task to another; who are not able to focus on a task for longer than a moment or two. The actions and conduct of these students are disruptive, and they not only fail in their own work but disrupt the classroom regimen sufficiently as to make it difficult for other children to focus on the task at hand. Meichenbaum (1977), Cobb and Hops (1973), and Zelniker, Renan, Sorer and Shavit (1977) have identified a constellation of behavioral responses and perceptual processing strategies that are helpful to the impulsive child in focusing on the task: attending to the teacher, following teacher instructions and using explicit and implicit cognitive strategies such as overt and covert speech rehearsals, behavioral and cognitive rehearsals of the steps and instructions for completing the task. These are all actions that mark attention and provide practical methods for teaching impulsive students to pay closer attention to the task, to slow down by means of overt and covert self-instructions for slowing down, so that there is an opportunity to reflect on what they are attending to. Attentional training of hyperactive and impulsive children, and children who have other problems of autonomic reactivity is most effective when it is coupled with survival skills training in academic task performance. Attention even in normal children with no special problems of alertness, mental acuity, and mental capacities is a complex process, but analysis of the underlying components of attentional deficits in brain-damaged children, hyperactive and impulsive children, and other cognitively handicapped children requires the teacher to have specialized training in behavior-modification skills, cognitive skills training, and control of arousal and activation training to treat children with attentional problems that seriously limit their learning and task performance. Teachers working more closely with children having specific and more serious attentional deficits and disorders may wish to get training in specialized procedures relevant to special populations of hyperactive, impulsive, cognitively impaired, and brain-damaged children. A discussion of specialized procedures is beyond the purview of this chapter.

Summary

Our aim in this chapter was to link the experimental research on attentional processes reported earlier in the chapter to the activities of the classroom and the role of the teacher. Some of the practical implications discussed, especially with respect to the personal and situational factors that enhance or interfere with the components of alertness and selective attention, have little supporting basis in research. There is, in fact, little research demonstrating that the principles of selective attention as developed from discrimination learning and discriminative transfer have the suggested effects in real-life settings. The reason is that, until recently, most researchers who have studied basic attentional problems in information processing have not been concerned with the possible classroom implications or applications of their findings. Conversely, educational psychologists or educators interested in learning and teaching problems in the classroom, home, and other natural settings have not kept up with the experimental and laboratory studies. Therefore, the teacher should consider the practical implications that have been discussed in this chapter as reasonable procedures and suggestions to be tried out rather than as established guidelines that will necessarily work. The emphasis in this chapter has been on the practical applications of the three separable components of attention: alertness, selective attention, and discrimination in central processing.

The areas of alertness and sustained selective attention were selected for their practical applications because they are frequently cited as aspects of attention in which children (both nonhandicaped and handicapped) are often observed to demonstrate impaired performance in vigilance tasks thought to require high levels of alertness and selective attention.

A number of practically useful generalizations concerning components of attention have been supported by laboratory research. It appears reasonable to conclude that alertness is best maintained when the classroom task is varied, feedback (first positive, and then both positive and negative combined) is provided, and the salience of the learning situation is enhanced in terms of making it interesting and personally relevant to the students. Selectivity is also influenced by both external and internal factors. External sources of influence on selectivity include factors of natural prominence (bright colors, loud sounds, sharp contrasts, novelty that is unexpected in the naturalistic setting) that attract the child's attention and enhances alertness. Unfortunately, novelty factors that arouse interest and motivation may sometimes take attention away from the matters of task relevance. Thus, it is the classroom teacher's responsibility to maintain the right balance between novelty factors that maintain the students' alertness and the need to keep distracting stimulation in the background to a minimum. It becomes the teacher's function to enhance natural perceptual features of the classroom context and the classroom tasks so that relevant dimensions of the task are emphasized, irrelevant dimensions that may distract the child's attention are eliminated or kept to a minimum, and familiar tasks and events are presented with a touch of novelty that would maintain the child's interest.

Selectivity also depends immediately on what is personally motivating to the child. The motivation level of the child with respect to mental set for a given task performance may be too low to produce selective attention and good performance. It can be so high that it produces autonomic overactivity and interferes with selective attention, discriminative ability, and performance. Between these extremes is an optimal range within which it is the responsibility of the teacher to elicit a moderate level of motivation in tasks involving learning of new materials by the child. When the material has already been learned, a high-level motivation induction is best.

Successful performance of the task by the child requires that the teacher be fully cognizant of the task characteristics and the ideas, expectations, and previous experiences that the young learner brings to the situation. Task-specific characteristics for selective attention can be more parsimoniously considered by teachers in the broader context of mental and cognitive processing demands rather than within the poorly defined context of distractibility in attention. For this reason, it seems well advised for the teacher to use such concepts as distraction with caution, if at all. If it is used, it is critical that the teacher provide explicit description of distraction in terms of task-irrelevant dimensions. Thus, the main problem of the teacher is determining which aspects of the learning situation are relevant to task performance and which are irrelevant and should be ignored or eliminated. The child's limited central processing capacity prevents successful performance on more than one task requiring mental effort or discriminative capacity, but several discriminations can be accomplished when performance has been rehearsed frequently and has become automatic.

The evidence suggests that direct training on attention (using discrimination teaching, instructional interrogation and praise, small-step instructional demonstrations, strategy training in filtering out irrelevant dimensions) is effective with most children. Through direct training and shaping of selective attention, students can learn to pay attention to the task and can learn to slow down so that they have a chance to differentiate task-relevant and task-irrelevant features and to focus selectively on the former.

Research has also provided some backing for practical methods of measuring and enhancing attention in handicapped children who have been reported to exhibit impaired ability to sustain attention (Douglas & Peter, 1979). Children with a variety of learning handicaps are consistently observed to perform more poorly than nonhandicapped peers in tasks requiring alertness and selective discriminations. Strategy training for use with handicapped learners (or children with special problems of attention) has not been discussed at length in this chapter. It is argued that hitherto the classroom teacher's knowledge of the pronounced distractibility factors in learning handicapped youngsters is inadequate and contributes little to an understanding of their selective attention problems. Furthermore, the selective and sustained attention problems of learning handicapped youngsters are inextricably confounded with problems of memory and cognitive processing. Teachers need specialized training in understanding the attentional operations that may be contaminated by other incidental learning processes.

As a final point, it is instructive for teachers to remember that attention is a complex process. Although an analysis of the three separable underlying components of attention gives the teacher some broad and global insights into the treatment of attentional problems that limit learning in many students, much more refinement of the measurement tools and training strategies for dealing with attentional problems needs to be achieved before teachers can be noticeably effective in the classroom.

Assuming an interactionist position could also help the teacher in uncovering a number of specific task variables and child characteristics that are critical elements in the study of children's attentional problems. The high degree of voluntary and sustained attention required in certain tasks (tasks with active demands to respond quickly and efficiently) appear to influence the child's expression of attention. However, it is equally important for the teacher to assess the specific resources that a child brings to the task. In order to be moderately sure that the child is ready to meet the more rigorous demands for voluntary attention, it may be reasonable to group children in task performance on the basis of the specific attention problems they express (Berkson, 1973) rather than by age or stage development.

REFERENCES

Abravanel, E. (1968). The development of intersensory patterning with regard to selected spatial dimensions. *Monographs of the Society for Research in Child Development, 33,* No. 118.

Becker, W. C. (1972). Applications of behavior principles in typical classrooms. In C. E. Thoresen (Ed.), *Behavior modification in education.* The 71st Yearbook of the National Society for the Study of Education, Chicago: University of Chicago Press.

Berkson, G. (1973). Behavior. In J. Wortis (Ed.), *Mental retardation,* Vol. 5 (pp. 24-47). New York: Grune & Stratton.

Bernstein, A. J. (1969). To what does the orienting response respond? *Psychophysiology, 6*(3), 338-350.

Broadbent, D. E. (1958). *Perception and communication.* London: Pergamon Press.

Broadbent, D. E. (1971). *Decision and Stress.* New York: Academic Press.

Brophy, J. E., & Good, T. L. (1974). *Teacher-student relationships: Causes and consequences.* New York: Holt, Rinehart & Winston.

Brown, A. L., Bransford, J. D., Ferrara, R. A., & Campione, J. C. (1983). Learning, remembering, and understanding. In J. H. Flavell & E. M. Markman (Eds.), *Handbook of child psychology, Vol. 1: Cognitive development* (pp. 77-168). New York: Wiley.

Brown, A. L., Campione, J. C., & Gilliard, D. M. (1974). Recency judgements in children: A production deficiency in the use of redundant background cues. *Developmental Psychology, 10,* 303.

Carnine, D., & Silbert, J. (1979). *Direction instruction: Reading.* Columbus, OH: Merrill Publishing Co.

Cherry, E. C. (1953). Some experiments on the recognition of speech with one and two ears. *Journal of the Acoustical Society of America, 25,* 975-979.

Cobb, J. A., & Hops, H. (1973). Effects of academic survival skills training on low achieving first graders. *Journal of Educational Research, 67,* 108-113.

Coles, M. G. (1974). Physiological activity and detection: The effects of attentional requirements and the prediction of performance. *Biological Psychology, 2,* 113-125.

Coles, M. G., & Duncan-Johnson, C. C. (1975). Cardiac activity and information processing: The effects of stimulus significance and detection and response requirements. *Journal of Experimental Psychology: Human Perception and Performance, 55,* 75-84.

Day, M. C. (1975). Developmental trends in visual scanning. In H. W. Reese (Ed.), *Advances in child development and behavior,* Vol. 10 (pp. 153-193). New York: Academic Press.

Deutsch, J. A., & Deutsch, D. (1963). Attention: Some theoretical considerations. *Psychological Review, 70,* 80-90.

Douglas, V. I., & Peters, K. G. (1979). Toward a clearer definition of the attentional deficit of hyperactive children. In G. A. Hale & M. Lewis (Eds.), *Attention and cognitive development* (pp. 173-237). New York: Plenum Press.

Fishbein, H. D. (1976). *Evolution, development and children's learning.* California: Goodyear Publishing Company.

Fitts, P. M. & Posner, M. I. (1967). *Human performance.* Belmont, CA: Brooks/Cole.

Gibson, E. J. (1969). *Principles of perceptual learning and development.* New York: Appleton-Century-Crofts.

Gibson, E. J., & Levin, H. (1975). *The psychology of reading.* Cambridge, MA: M.I.T. Press.

Gibson, E., & Rader, N. (1979). The perceiver as performer. In G. A. Hale, & M. Lewis (Eds.), *Attention and cognitive development* (pp. 1-20). New York: Plenum Press.

Hagen, J. W. (1967). A developmental study of task-relevant and task-irrelevant information processing under distraction and non-distraction conditions. *Child Development, 38,* 685-694.

Hagen, J. W., & Hale, G. A. (1973). The development of attention in children. In A. D. Pick (Ed.), *Minnesota symposia on child psychology,* Vol. 7, (pp. 117-140). Minneapolis: University of Minnesota Press.

Hagen, J. W., & Kail, R. V., Jr. (1975). The role of attention in perceptual and cognitive development. In W. M. Cruickshank & D. P. Hallahan (Eds.). *Perceptual and learning disabilities in children (Vol. 2) Research and Theory* (pp. 165-192). Syracuse: Syracuse University Press.

Hale, G. A., & Lewis, M. (Eds.). (1979). *Attention and cognitive development.* New York: Plenum.

Hale, G. A., & Taweel, S. S. (1974). Age differences vs children's performance in measures of component selection and incidental learning. *Journal of Experimental Child Psychology, 18,* 107-116.

Hallahan, D. P., & Reeve, R. E. (1980). Selective attention and distractibility. In B. K. Keogh (Ed.), *Advances in special education* (Vol. 1), (pp. 141-181). Greenwich, CT: JAI Press.

James, W. (1890). *The principles of psychology,* (Vol. 1). New York: Henry Holt and Company. (Republished by Dover, 1950).

Jennings, J. R. (1971). Cardiac reactions and different developmental levels of cognitive functioning. *Psychophysiology, 8,* 433-450.

Kahneman, D. (1973). *Attention and effort.* Englewood Cliffs, NJ: Prentice-Hall.

Keele, S. W. (1973). *Attention and human performance.* Pacific Palisades, CA: Goodyear.

Krupski, A. (1980). Attention processes: Research, theory, and implications for special education. In B. K. Keogh (Ed.), *Advances in special education,* Vol. 1, (pp. 101-141). Greenwich, CT: JAI Press.

Krupski, A. (1981). An interactional approach to the study of attention problems in children with learning handicaps. *Exceptional Education Quarterly, 2,* 1-12.

Krupski, A. (1986). Attention problems in youngsters with learning handicaps. In J. K. Torgesen & B. Y. L. Wong (Eds.), *Psychological and educational perspectives on learning disability.* (pp. 161-192). New York: Academic Press.

LaBerge, D., & Samuels, S. J. (1974). Toward a theory of automatic information processing in reading. *Cognitive Psychology, 6,* 293-323.

Lacey, J. I. (1967). Somatic response patterning and stress: Some revisions of activation theory. In M. H. Appley & R. Trumbull (Eds.), *Psychological stress: Issues in research* (pp. 14-44). New York: Appleton-Century-Crofts.

Lasky, E. Z., & Tobin, H. (1973). Linguistic and nonlinguistic competing auditory message effects. *Journal of Learning Disabilities, 6,* 243-250.

Loper, A. B., & Murphy, D. M. (1985). Cognitive self-regulatory training for underachieving children. In D. L. Forrest-Pressley, G. E. MacKinnon, & T. G. Waller (Eds.), *Metacognition, cognition and human performance,* Vol. 2, (pp. 223-265). New York: Academic Press.

Lovitt, T. C. (1975). Applied behavior analysis and learning disabilities. *Journal of Learning Disabilities, 8,* 432-443.

Lupart, J. L., & Mulcahy, R. F. (1984). *Some thoughts on research in learning disabilities and attention.* In J. R. Kirby (Ed.), Cognitive strategies and educational performance (pp. 217-247). New York: Academic Press, Inc.

Maccoby, E., & Hagen, J. (1965). Effect of distraction upon central versus incidental recall: Developmental trends. *Journal of Experimental Child Psychology, 2,* 280-289.

Maccoby, E., & Konrad, K. W. (1966). Age trends in selective listening. *Journal of Experimental Child Psychology, 3,* 113-122.

Macworth, J. F. (1970). *Vigilance and attention.* Baltimore: Penguin.

Mackworth, N. H. (1977). The line of sight approach. In S. Wanat (Ed.), *Language and reading comprehension* (pp. 1-22). Arlington, VA: Center for Applied Linguistics.

Meichenbaum, D. (1977). *Cognitive-behavior modification: An integrative approach.* New York: Plenum Press.

Miller, P. H. (1985). Metacognition and attention. In D. L. Forrest-Pressley, G. E. MacKinnon, & T. G. Waller (Eds.), *Metacognition, cognition, and human performance, Vol. 2* (pp. 181-221). New York: Academic Press.

Moray, N. (1969). *Attention: Selective processes in vision and hearing.* London: Hutchison Educational.

Mostofsky, D. I. (1970). *Attention: Contemporary theory and analysis.* New York: Appleton-Century-Crofts.

Neisser, U. (1976). *Cognition and reality.* San Francisco: Freeman.

Norman, D. A. (1969). *Memory and attention.* New York: Wiley.

Norman, D. A. (1976). *Memory and attention: An introduction to human information processing.* New York: Wiley.

Pavlov, I. P. (1927). *Conditioned reflexes: An investigation of the physiological activity in the cerebral cortex.* London: Oxford University Press.

Pick, A. D., Christy, M. D., & Frankel, G. W. (1972). A developmental study of visual selective attention. *Journal of Experimental Child Psychology, 14,* 165-175.

Pointkowski, D., & Calfee, R. (1974). Attention in the classroom. In G. A. Hale & M. Lewis (Eds.), *Attention and cognitive development* (pp. 297-329). New York: Plenum Press.

Posner, M. I., & Boies, S. W. (1971). Components of attention. *Psychological Review, 78,* 391-408.

Posner, M. I. (1973). *Cognition: An introduction.* Glenview: IL: Scott, Foresman.

Pribram, K. H., & McGuinness, D. (1975). Arousal, activation, and effort in the control of attention. *Psychological Review, 82,* 116-149.

Rohwer, W. D. (1973). Elaboration and learning in childhood and adolescence. In H. W. Reese (Ed.), *Advances in child development and behavior,* Vol. 8, (pp. 37-51). New York: Academic Press.

Roper, S. S., & Nolan, R. R. (1976). *How to survive in the open-space school.* Occasional paper No. 10, Stanford Center for Research and Development in Teaching, School of Education, Stanford University.

Samuels, S. J. (1967). Attentional processes in reading: The effect of pictures on the acquisition of reading responses. *Journal of Educational Psychology, 58,* 337-342.

Schwebel, A. I., & Cherlin, D. L. (1972). Physical and social distancing in teacher-pupil relationships. *Journal of Educational Psychology, 63*(6), 543-550.

Shepp, B. E., & Swartz, K. B. (1976). Selective attention and the processing of integral and nonintegral dimensions: A developmental study. *Journal of Experimental Child Psychology, 22,* 73-85.

Silberman, C. E. (1970). *Crisis in the classroom.* New York: Random House.

Siqueland, E. R., & Rieber, M. (1970). Discriminative learning. In H. W. Reese & L. P. Lipsitt (Eds.), *Experimental child psychology* (pp. 151-194). New York: Academic Press.

Sokolov, E. N. (1960). Neuronal models and the orienting reflex. In M. A. Brazier (Ed.), *The Central Nervous System and Behavior.* New York: J. Macy.

Sokolov, E. N. (1963a). Higher nervous systems: The orienting reflex. *Annual Review of Physiology, 25,* 545-580.

Sokolov, E. N. (1963b). *Perception and the conditioned reflex.* New York: MacMillan.

Stroufe, L. A. (1971). Age changes in cardiac acceleration within a fixed foreperiod reaction-time task: An index of attention. *Developmental Psychology, 5*, 338-343.

Torgesen, J. K. (1981). The relationship between memory and attention in learning disabilities. *Exceptional Education Quarterly, 2*, 51-60.

Triesman, A. (1964). Monitoring and storage of irrelevant messages in selective attention. *Journal of Verbal Learning and Verbal Behavior, 3*, 449-459.

Tursky, B., Schwartz, G. E., & Crider, A. (1970). Differential patterns of heart rate and skin resistance during a digit transformation task. *Journal of Experimental Psychology, 83*, 451-457.

Vurpillot, E. (1968). The development of scanning strategies and their relation to visual differentiation. *Journal of Experimental Child Psychology, 6*, 632-650.

Vygotsky, L. S. (1981). The development of higher forms of attention in childhood. In J. V. Wertsch (Ed.), *The concept of activity in Soviet psychology* (pp. 187-240). Armonk, NY: M. E. Sharpe, Inc.

Wertsch, J. V. (1981). *The concept of activity in Soviet psychology.* Armonk, NY: M. E. Sharpe, Inc.

Willows, D. M. (1974). Reading between the lines: Selective attention in good and poor readers. *Child Development, 45*, 408-415.

Willows, D. M., & McKinnon, G. E. (1973). Selective reading: Attention to the "unattended" lines. *Canadian Journal of Psychology, 27*, 292-304.

Wright, J. C. (1977). *On familiarity and habituation: The situational microgenetics of information getting.* Paper presented at the Symposium on Attention and Cognition, Society for Research in Child Development, New Orleans.

Wright, J. C., & Vlietstra, A. G. (1975). The development of selective attention: From perceptual exploration to logical speech. In H. W. Reese (Ed.), *Advances in child development and behavior,* Vol. 10, (pp. 176-235). New York: Academic Press.

Zelniker, T., Renan, A., Sorer, I., & Shavit, Y. (1977). Effect of perceptual processing strategies on problem solving of reflective and impulsive children. *Child Development, 48*, 1436-1442.

Zinchenko, V. P., Chzhi-tsin, V., & Tarakanov, V. W. (1962). The formation and development of perceptual activity. *Soviet Psychology and Psychiatry, 2*, 3-12.

CHAPTER FOUR

MEMORY

THE ABILITY to store and retrieve information has long been recognized as a primary factor in learning. Indeed, intelligence tests have consistently included subtests purporting to tap those basic learning skills referred to as memory. One of the most common is the digit span task in which an individual is instructed to listen to a series of randomly ordered numbers, such as 9-4-2, and then is asked to repeat the numeral sequence. The number of digits presented within a series is increased until the person cannot accurately repeat the series, thereby establishing one's digit span capacity. It has been well established that "memory," as measured by a task such as digit span, is highly correlated with intelligence and that a person's digit span capacity **does** increase with increasing age.

Memory research for the major part of this century has attempted to delineate the key characteristics of memory through the study of "memory curves," depicting rates of retention, and the variables relevant to the learning and retention of new material such as nonsense syllables. Even though such studies have yielded considerable insight into the short-term, and to a lesser degree, long-term components of memory, and the complexities of the learning-interference-recall interrelationships, minimal effort was given to examining the memory performance differences of young children and adults. Consequently, these studies have had very limited utility for practical application in teaching young children and in classroom learning.

It has only been in the last few decades that memory researchers have directed their efforts to the important question of **why** adults are consistently better able to remember than children. The recent development of applied models of memory and the profusion of memory studies in the developmental psychology area have been the catalyst for our present and enriched understanding of what it means to remember. The change can be simply described as a shift from the measurable, observable products of memory to the cognitive processes and knowledge factors that create these products. Most important is that with this shifted interest to qualitative aspects of memory, and how these change and develop with increasing age, comes a prodigious understanding of young children's learning which **can** and **is** being readily translated into practical application for the classroom.

In the following section, an overview is provided of the significant models and theories instrumental in changing our view of children's memory development.

MODELS OF MEMORY

Multistore Model

The study of memory within an information-processing framework dates back to Broadbent's (1958) classic model of selective attention which incorporated a short-term memory store. The multistore model of memory has subsequently been modified and altered by a number of authors, including Waugh and Norman (1965), Atkinson and Shiffrin (1968) and Tulving (1968), but the essential features of these and present-day models (Lindsay & Norman, 1977; Klatsky, 1980) may be collectively described.

The multistore model of memory has a number of specific temporal-structural components including a sensory store, a short-term store and long-term store. Let us consider a specific example as we proceed to describe the components of this model. Try to imagine a grade three teacher reading a story aloud to the class when a loud sound is heard.

The processing begins when information from the external environment is entered into the infinite capacity store through the senses. In our example, the sound is held in auditory form but will remain for only a brief time (less than two seconds) unless the input is "attended" to or "recognized" in some manner. Thus, if the teacher chose to ignore the loud sound and continued on with the reading of the story, the auditorily registered input will decay. On the other hand, the teacher may have momentarily attended to the noise and recognized that it was the school buzzer. Once the information is recognized or associated with one's prior experience and selectively attended to, inputs can then be transferred to what is referred to as the short-term memory store (STM).

FIGURE 4-1

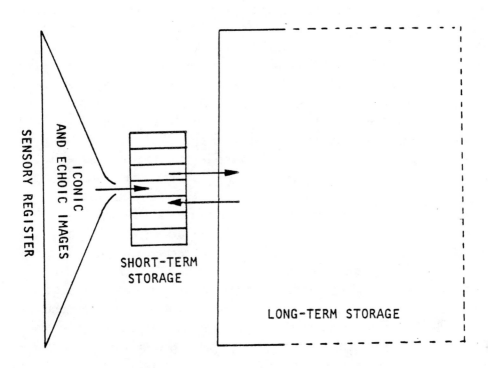

A three-storage system in the structure of memory.

Unlike the sensory store, the STM is considered to be a limited capacity store, meaning that this stage of memory can only deal with a limited amount of information at a given time. Miller's (1956) classic memory experiments which affirm capacity of the STM to be seven slots plus or minus two items have been widely accepted as the standard. It is also important to note that this capacity can be greatly enhanced by a process referred to as "chunking." Essentially, "chunking" is the process of connecting unrelated separate information inputs into more meaningful and economical organizational units. A good example of the chunking process would be in the case where the grade three teacher, prior to the reading of her story to the class, may have suggested that the students use the W5 (who, what, when, where, why) questions to help them remember the relevant story information. Thus, if a student is asked to recall a story immediately after the teacher's reading of it, it would be most useful to give the gist of the story (as it would be expressed if the W5 organization were used) as opposed to attempting to provide a verbatim word-for-word recall.

To return to the teacher's response to the buzzer in this example, we could assume that the STM capacity was totally allocated to the task of reading aloud the story. However, upon recognizing the school buzzer sound, the teacher may continue with the reading-aloud task but may also allocate some of the STM capacity for the "active" processing of the loud sound (Wickelgren, 1981). By keeping the buzzer concept active through rehearsal and attempting to relate the present to past experience, the teacher may initially interpret the buzzer to be the typical signal for a change of class period, and decide to finish reading to the end of the paragraph and then move on to the planned spelling unit. On the other hand, the teacher may recognize that the buzzer sound is different from the typical change of class tone and, upon further analysis, recognize this as the fire alarm buzzer. This being the case, the teacher would most likely have ceased the reading aloud activity and the STM memory capacity would likely be totally concerned with school procedures for responding to fire alarms.

Our experimental knowledge of the STM indicates that as a result of this rapid shift in STM capacity, it is very unlikely that the teacher would be able to correctly recall the last sentence that she had just read. In this case, the information just read was "forgotten" because of interference of immediate responses to the fire alarm. Experts such as Klatsky (1980) and Lindsay and Norman (1977) indicate that information in the STM can be forgotten by interference from other material or by passive decay in which the item or new information can be lost as a result of passage of time, estimated to be about 30 seconds.

The final storehouse within an information-processing model of memory is most often referred to as long-term memory (LTM). Although LTM is considered to be the most important and complex of the storehouses, it is recognizably the most difficult to study and accordingly the one we know least about. However, LTM has increasingly become the focus of present-day memory study, as research paradigms have shifted from an emphasis upon learning long word and/or nonword lists or paired associates to the use of meaningful materials such as recall of stories or recognition memory of classmates from high school yearbooks. Another factor that has recently brought the study of LTM into the forefront is a convergence of interest of several disciplines such as linguistics, cognitive psychology and education upon memory processes and learning, and cognitive development throughout the life span.

Researchers who have studied LTM describe it as the permanent storehouse of one's experience, acquired knowledge and working knowledge of language. In other words, all that one has come to know about the world is stored within LTM and as such can potentially be recalled minutes after learning the material or even several months or years afterward. However, most of us, as experienced and mature memory processors, are aware of our limitations when it comes to recalling information previously learned. We know, for example, that our memory is not perfect, and even if material was carefully learned at one point in our experience, the successful retrieval of the material will depend upon such factors as how long ago the material was learned, if there was adequate opportunity to utilize the information, if the material related to other areas of knowledge, if the material affected us emotionally, and so on.

If we return to our example of the grade three teacher recognizing the buzzer to signal a fire alarm, we can examine how the LTM might operate in this situation. The alarm would summon a number of associated memories such as:

This could be a dangerous situation.

I must remain calm, so as not to alarm the children.

What is the first thing to do?

I remember that we have to bring our registers outside. While I do that I can consider the other steps. That's right, the rules and procedures are posted on the North wall.

I will ask the students to line up single file, and proceed to the stairs, meanwhile I will obtain the procedures page.

The above example nicely illustrates what present-day theorists describe as the "associationistic" qualities that typify LTM (Baddeley, 1976; Wickelgren, 1981). That is to say that even though memories might be coded in many ways (i.e. the look on my mother's face when she received the surprise bouquet; the smell of the burnt pot roast; the feeling one has after a strenuous aerobic workout; the name of the city my sister lived in two years ago), these memories are stored and organized in such a way that, in any given situation, the person associates the present to what might be useful from the past. Just how this organization of LTM is achieved and whether this is an idiosyncratic process for each individual or whether common general organizational systems can be discerned are a few of the important areas that are currently being explored. However, it should be noted that recent developmental studies have revealed the close relationship between memory and learning, and how children increasingly apply reconstructive and organizational strategies to optimize their memorial capabilities. This important line of memory investigation will be discussed in greater detail in the following section.

In summary, the popularity and widespread use of the multistore memory model may be attributed to the specification of both storage structures and control operations, hence allowing for both capacity characteristics (i.e. sensory store, short-term store, long-term store), as well as the operations that account for the processing and transfer of information from store to store. For example, Waugh and Norman (1965) incorporated a rehearsal process into their modal model of memory to account for the transfer of information from primary to secondary memory, and later, Atkinson and Shiffrin (1968) expanded the rehearsal concept to that of "control processes" described as "transient phenomena under the control of the subject" (p. 106). However, even with the addition of specific processes to account for input transfer, the central focus of memory research using a multistore model concerned the various structures and capacities of the memory stores. Memory study up to the time of the early 1970s proceeded for the most part independent of inquiry into the interrelation with other higher mental processes and cognitive development, and hence the focus remained primarily upon reproduction memory (i.e. recognition, recall of nonsense syllables, digits).

An important shift to the current emphasis upon information meaningfulness and how information is processed and stored in LTM came from the work of Craik and Lockhart (1972). Their levels-of-processing memory model has had and continues to have a significant impact on our current thinking about memory and memory processes, and will be briefly described in the following section.

Levels of Processing

As an alternative to the multistore information-processing model, Craik and Lockhart (1972) proposed the "levels-of-processing" approach to memory, which emphasizes the perceptual analysis and encoding of stimuli. The proposed model encompasses a hierarchy of analysis, in which incoming information may be analyzed or processed at a shallow, "physical" level, a deeper "phonemic" level, or a deeper yet "semantic" level. Craik (1973) suggests that the memory trace is a product of these perceptual analyses and that "trace persistence is a positive function of depth of analysis" (p. 48). Therefore, information that is more deeply processed, analyzed or elaborated will be better remembered. The three classes of factors comprising the criteria of depth of analysis are described by Craik (1973): "(1) stimulus salience or intensity; (2) the amount of processing devoted (or the amount of attention paid) to the stimulus; and (3) the item's meaningfulness or compatibility with the analyzing structures" (p. 50).

Within the concept of the basic levels-of-processing memory system, Craik and Lockhart distinguish two types of rehearsal. Whereas maintenance rehearsal refers to continued processing at the same level of analysis (i.e. prolonging an item's accessibility without actually strengthening the durability of the memory trace), elaborative rehearsal involves the processing of stimuli to deeper levels (i.e. increasing the strength of the memory trace) (Mazuryk & Lockhart, 1974).

Although the general notion of depth of processing and its influence on retention have been retained, a number of modifications and extensions of particular aspects of the model have subsequently been advanced (Lockhart, Craik & Jacoby, 1975; Craik, 1973; Craik & Tulving, 1975; Craik & Jacoby, 1975). Most important is the notion that incoming information can be analyzed both laterally and vertically within the three "qualitatively coherent" domains, rather than necessarily undergoing the full gamut of analysis at each level. Thus, further processing can proceed either between domains or within a domain; and all further processing results in increased depth of processing, producing a stronger memory trace. The processing that takes place depends on the perceptual/cognitive ability of the processor to extract meaning from the presented stimuli as well as the interaction with factors such as the material, practice, context and set. Encoding that is well-practiced will require minimal processing or conscious awareness; that is, only those operations necessary or critical to effect deeper levels of processing are carried out. On the other hand, encoding of novel and/or difficult-to-process stimuli, or more important stimuli requires more analysis and attention, hence resulting in a richer memory trace.

Another important distinction incorporated into the levels-of-processing model is that of episodic versus semantic memory. Episodic memory is described as a structureless system which records the temporal sequence of encoded events or inputs. Semantic memory functions at encoding to interpret the stimulus in terms of "the system's structured record of past learning, that is, knowledge of the world" (Craik & Tulving, 1975, p. 291). The interpretation of the stimuli is achieved by means of complex analyzing and encoding operations which constitute

the memory trace. The inherent interrelationship of episodic and semantic memory may be understood, in that, to the extent that stimuli
have undergone deeper analysis or a greater number of elaborations by
the perceptual system, so too will the event be more richly or uniquely
specified in the episodic memory trace.

The distinction between episodic and semantic aspects of the memory system is of particular relevance when the notion of retrieval is considered. Whereas it has been suggested that there are a number of ways
in which optimal encoding may be achieved, various factors likewise determine the maximal retrieval of information. Lockhart, Craik and Jacoby (1975) suggest that both scanning and reconstruction processes are
operant in recognition and recall. The scanning process is simply a
backward search in episodic memory, which becomes increasingly less
efficient as more items are interpoled between initial processing and retrieval. On the other hand, interpretive or recall task requirements
which are specified some time after processing occurs, with minimal or
limited cue value, would likely require reconstruction of the retrieval
processes to relocate the desired encoding event. Reconstruction involves the cognitive structures of the processor which are "guided and
constrained both by the structure of semantic memory and by feedback
from episodic trace itself" (Craik & Jacoby, 1975, p. 176). Whereas
short-term retrieval is adequately achieved with the scanning of episodic
memory, whenever a longer delay between presentation and test is apparent, then "the richer encoding, and more powerful retrieval processes
(reconstruction), associated with semantic information give rise to superior memory performance" (Craik & Jacoby, 1975, p. 177).

By way of summary, then, the levels-of-processing model, as it is
presently understood, is most readily distinguished from the traditional
information-processing models, in that the segmentation and quantification of memory is bypassed in favor of an emphasis upon the analysis
of qualitative differences of memory operations.

It is important to note that it has only been within the last decade or
so that theorists and researchers have attempted to apply general models
(specifically formulated on the basis of research utilizing mature adult
subjects) to the study of children's memory. Initial studies of children's
memory were similarly fashioned after the adult studies described
above, in that memory tasks consisted of precise observations of retention capacities for nonsense syllables, digit, serial recall position data,
spacing effects, and so on. Accordingly, the consistent results of the
young child's inability to remember as well as the adult have been attrib-

uted to the smaller storage capacity (structural) which limited the amount of material that could be remembered. However, researchers such as Chi (1976) have been very critical of this approach, and, following an extensive review and evaluation of the literature, she asserted that there was no conclusive evidence to support the assertion that it is the STM capacity that increases with age. Alternatively, she presented substantial evidence to suggest that it is more likely that the processing strategies used by adults are unavailable or deficient in children. Chi (1976) concluded her analysis by proposing that such deficits could be explained in terms of "the lack of proper control processes or processing strategies as well as an impoverished LTM knowledge base rather than a limitation in STM capacity" (p. 599).

Interestingly, Chi's (1976) views reflected the predominant thinking of cognitive and developmental psychologists, who were independently examining the development of children's memory abilities.

Within the present decade, however, some notable changes have become evident in both fields of memory and developmental research. Although these changes were, for the most part, independently generated, it will become apparent that the foci of interest appear markedly complementary. Hence, the following discussion will concentrate on a brief outline of contemporary approaches to memory which have been cultivated from within a general theory of cognitive development.

Contemporary Developmental Approaches to Memory

Piaget. Piaget's theory of memory development (Piaget & Inhelder, 1973; Piaget, 1968) is incorporated within a general theory of cognitive development. In brief, Piaget's theory focuses upon human adaptive processes that are evident in one's interaction with the environment. Assimilative processes are operant when a person utilizes prior knowledge to cope with one's environment, and accommodation processes occur whenever a change in behavior results from interaction with the environment. In essence, the impetus for development is a function of organism-environment interactions, which results in disequilibriums that are monitored through the assimilative and accommodative processes. Thus, the growing child undergoes progressive maturation through a series of invariantly ordered stages (i.e. sensorimotor, preoperational, concrete operational, and formal operations), each of which is qualitatively discontinuous from the others.

With respect to memory development in particular, Piaget and Inhelder (1973) assert that "the development of the memory with age is the

history of gradual organizations closely dependent on the structuring activities of the intelligence, though regulated by a special mechanism,
namely, the structuring of the past or of past experiences" (p. 380).

The memory-knowledge orientation is further differentiated into
memory in the strict sense (i.e. a type of spacial-temporal account of a
specific event) and memory in the wider sense (i.e. the organism's entire
knowledge or cognitive network). "The schemata used by the memory
are borrowed from the intelligence, and this explains why they follow
one another in stages corresponding to the subject's operational level"
(Piaget & Inhelder, 1973, p. 382). These schemata, which operate
during encoding, retention and recall, are primarily facilitative in the
organization, interpretation, and reconstruction of memory. As a result
of this close interaction between memory and knowledge, any developmental changes in the cognitive system similarly lead to developmental
changes in what is stored and retrieved. As an example, an infant (i.e.
1.5 years) may demonstrate an ability for recognition memory and yet
be unable to recall or reconstruct a prior event, since the latter requires
mental imagery or language. As Flavell (1977) notes, in recall "the subject unconsciously experiences an internal representation (e.g. an image, an idea) of something experienced earlier" (p. 186).

In summary, Piaget's assertion that understanding, knowing, and remembering are inseparable facets of intelligence implies that as the
child's general operational level undergoes change due to maturation
and experience, he will demonstrate qualitative differences in his ability
to perceive and remember orderly relationships and meaningful events
(Brown, 1975). It is Piaget's unique perspective on children's cognitive
development that has been the most widely accepted and influential for
our present-day understanding of children's memory and cognitive development.

Flavell. As it will shortly become apparent, Flavell's approach to
memory development represents an elaboration and extension of
Piaget's (Piaget & Inhelder, 1973; Piaget, 1968) theory, and therefore the
notions outlined in the previous section are similarly applicable here.

Flavell (1977) has identified four categories of phenomena for his
model of memory development. The first of these is referred to as basic
processes. These processes are in essence the child's memory capacities
and, according to Flavell, undergo very limited developmental change
after the age of two. Since the child under 1.5 years of age relies solely
on perception and sensori-motor schemes, these basic processes are
commonly associated with recognition memory.

The second category represents a person's acquired knowledge and is synonymous with Piaget and Inhelder's (1973) "memory in the wider sense." Flavell (1977), however, has expanded this category to include the notion of constructive memory. In addition to an emphasis on the interaction of the subject's general knowledge and cognitive activities with respect to memory acts, the constructivists assert that individuals are continuously involved in a process of internal conceptual representations of their environment, in the form of spontaneous inferences and interpretations. In other words, an individual translates those features of interest in the input, into a form that is congruent with one's internalized semantic system. Hence, that which is retrieved or reconstructed constitutes something quite different from the original stimulus input. Flavell (1977) emphasizes the point that the processes which constitute constructive memory are by far more sophisticated and complicated than the traditional information-processing model has led us to believe, and this assertion has been supported by an extensive body of independent research (Bransford & Franks, 1971; Paris & Lindauer, 1976; Bransford & Johnson, 1972; Paris & Carter, 1973). Moreover, there is some evidence to indicate that instructions to intentionally utilize constructive processes (i.e. imagery instructions) can facilitate semantic integration (Paris, Mahoney & Buckhalt, 1974).

The third and fourth categories of memory phenomena of relevance to developmental investigations, strategies and metamemory have been pioneered and extensively explored by Flavell and his associates. On the basis of a number of studies of memory strategy usage in young children at encoding (Flavell, Beach & Chinsky, 1966; Keeney, Cannizzo & Flavell, 1967) and retrieval (Ritter, Kaprove, Fitch & Flavell, 1973), Flavell and his associates have distinguished two major deficits that differentiate the memory performance of the young child and the adult. The first is a mediation deficiency, apparent when the subject is unable to employ a potential mediator (i.e. verbal), even when one is specifically instructed to do so, or when the subject is trained to produce the required strategy, but this does not mediate performance. In contrast to this, a production deficiency, the second form of memory deficiency, can be remediated through training. Brown (1974) equates mediational deficiency with a developmentally related structural limitation and further suggests that, "If, however, performance is mediated appropriately once the strategy is produced then the initial deficiency is termed a production deficiency. Therefore, if the training works, the initial deficiency was one of production" (p. 63).

This distinction suggests important ramifications of interest to both diagnostic and remedial specialists working with children. Whereas the diagnostician would be concerned with the identification of specific memory strategies that are acquired at each stage of development, the remedial specialist would be more interested in the kinds of training programs or procedures that promote the production of different memory strategies. For example, since organization, clustering and elaboration strategies have been found to be consistently superior to simpler rehearsal strategies, the need to emphasize training in the utilization of the former is implied.

The final category relevant to differences in child and adult memory, first introduced by Flavell (1971), is described as metamemory. Metamemory refers to one's self-knowledge about: one's own memory capabilities, the mnemonic requirements of different tasks, potential strategies for meeting task demands, and strategies for capitalizing on one's own capabilities (Flavell & Wellman, 1976). In regard to child/adult memory performance differences, it is the young child's lack of knowledge about one's own memory processes and capabilities that results in inferior memory performance. Conversely, the adult characterically demonstrates an ability for the careful self-assessment of strategies available for task execution, as well as the astute intuition to select the strategy that is most appropriate and maximally efficient. This component will be discussed further in the ensuing chapter on metacognition.

In general, Flavell's approach to the study of memory in children is similar to Piaget's in terms of an emphasis upon both the qualitative differences of levels of memorial abilities, and yet distinguishable with regard to his emphasis upon the kinds of processes, strategies, and memorial self-awareness that lead to improved memory performance. Flavell's approach represents a dynamic, versatile view of memory development and, as such, has been widely accepted by cognitive psychology researchers and practitioners, as well as educators.

Soviet Psychology of Memory Development

The essence of Soviet research into memory development is well exemplified by Yendovitskaya (1971), Meacham (1972), and Smirnov and Zinchenko (1969). Similar to Piaget, Soviet memory research is couched within a more general theory of the basic principles of the ontogeny of human psychology. Bronfenbrenner (1971) suggests that in contrast to Western European and American psychologists who attribute the psychological development of a child either to innate capacities or strictly environmental adaptation, Soviet theory is based upon the philosophical propositions of Marxism-Leninism. The translation of the Marxist-Lenin philosophy into propositions to account for the psychic development of the child was initially advanced by Vygotsky. Essentially, the Soviets believe "that the socialization process not only enriches the knowledge and skills of the child; it precipitates essential changes in various psychic processes and engenders a genuine development of the child's psyche as well" (Bronfenbrenner, 1971, p. xviii).

With respect to Soviet investigations of memory in particular, research "rests upon an explicitly stated developmental theory of dialectic interaction between the individual and the social-historical milieu" (Meacham, 1972, p. 218). The direction of change is multiform, in that the society provides the conglomerate of abilities and human achievements (most important of which is verbal concepts or language) and in turn the child exerts one's influence to create a new environment, hence new conditions for development.

The central theme of Soviet investigation is based upon the distinction of voluntary and involuntary memory. The latter refers to situations in which memory is subordinated to the fulfillment of a meaningful activity, whereas the former refers to the situation in which memory is a goal in itself (Smirnov & Zinchenko, 1969; Yendovitskaya, 1971). Although the dichotomy has been associated to the Western concepts of incidental (i.e. voluntary) and involuntary (i.e. intentional), Smirnov and Zinchenko (1969) point out that the distinction for Soviet psychology involves a much closer association with the cognitive influence on memory than implied by Western definitions.

At the preschool age, memory formation and cultivation occurs within the context of activities, which are characteristically directed toward some immediate and concrete goal. As such, that which is remembered is that material which the child considers necessary and interesting (Yendovitskaya, 1971). Mnemonic competence as the child enters grade school transforms to a level in which the child can use previously learned activities (i.e. naming or labeling) as a means for achieving a new goal, such as intentional remembering. The final stage of mnemonic competence is described by Meacham (1972):

> After an activity (action) such as rehearsing, classifying, labeling, etc., is comparatively well formed, it can then be subordinated as a means (operation) towards achieving a new goal, such as that of voluntary memory (action). Periods of production deficiency, therefore, refer to the time period

during which an activity is well formed but not yet subordinated to the goal
of remembering (p. 216).

Each subordinated operation makes more complex actions possible,
and ultimately a hierarchy of operations ordered in complexity is developed. Reese (1976) suggests that the source of the sequence of new goals
is the integration of the individuals and their social-historical context.

In summary, Soviet psychologists distinguish between memory as a
means or an end. The ability to subordinate an activity to the goal of remembering (i.e. characteristic of school activities) is a somewhat artificial situation, and the ability to spontaneously distinguish situations that
require the employment of memory tactics or strategies, only begins to
emerge at the upper-elementary grade levels. It is of considerable interest to note that the Soviet perspective has been especially predominant in recent Western studies of memory development (Brown,
Bransford, Ferrara, & Campione, 1983; Wertsch, 1979).

Some Common Themes Uniting Information Processing and Developmental Memory

In general, the above summary of approaches to memory suggests a
sharp contrast to earlier memory research. Unlike the passive, robot
analogy of yesteryears, the individual is now seen as an active participant in the "process" of memory. In reference to this emergent view,
Jenkins (1974) admonishes that we can no longer be comfortable with a
definition of memory that constitutes a series of boxes in a flow diagram;
rather, we must acknowledge that memory demands an understanding
of all higher mental processes, since all of these are interrelated in the
construction and reconstruction of events. Indeed, all of the memory approaches outlined here specify a close relation between memory and
knowledge (i.e. semantic memory or memory in the broad sense).

The importance of the notion relating to the indivisibility of memory
and intelligence is most crucial when one considers that the differences
that have been observed at different levels of development relate to
qualitative changes in the memory code itself. By assuming this point of
view, contemporary theorists have eliminated a major problem inherent
within a mechanistic point of view (i.e. memory constituting a mere
copy of information present at storage, which is simply reprinted for retrieval purposes). Moreover, the progressive changes in the cognitive
structures as one matures can account for the fact that knowledge or
LTM changes and improves over the years. In a similar vein, this
further suggests how mental processes, such as inferential reasoning,

generalization, application of rules, are necessarily dependent on a semantic memory system. Within a levels-of-processing context of memory, the knowledge/memory interrelation is accounted for in terms of the semantic memory component. Incoming information is transformed in order that it becomes consistent or compatible with the analyzing structures (i.e. general knowledge system).

A theme which is central to each of the above developmental memory approaches is that concerning the developing child's gradual accumulation of a versatile repertoire of memory strategies and plans. Whereas Flavell discusses the acquisition of such strategies and plans in terms of mediation and production deficiencies, Soviet psychologists refer to a process by which a learned activity eventually becomes subordinated as a means (operation) towards achieving a new goal such as intention to remember. Even though the levels-of-processing model represents a general model of memory and as such does not specifically deal with such aspects, the concept might easily be interpreted within the context of vertical and lateral depth of processing. For example, visual information (physical level of processing) that has been categorized and rehearsed would be more "deeply" processed (and therefore better remembered) than information that has merely been observed. In other words, such lateral depth of processing would very clearly be contingent upon the individual's repertoire of memory strategies.

A final theme that characterizes contemporary memory investigation is the acknowledgment that the processor is actively involved in the memory process, and brings to bear on a task one's individual sensitivity to assess the need for elaboration of input, as well as an intuitive awareness of the variables (personal, task, and strategy) which collectively affect one's memory performance. Such metamemory development is predominant throughout the child's school years and clearly recognizable throughout adulthood.

In summary, contemporary approaches to memory development favor an organismic as opposed to mechanistic theoretical approach (Lerner, 1976). This implies that the development of memory proceeds through a hierarchical series of levels, each of which is qualitatively distinct from those preceding it. Furthermore, in contrast to the additivity assumption of earlier models of memory, current memory approaches necessarily propose an interactionist viewpoint in which: "Memory encompasses many cognitive processes and cannot be considered either an isolated mental faculty or a passive storehouse of experience" (Paris & Lindauer, 1977, p. 35).

In the following section, we will examine some of the recent developments in the study of memory and how these abilities develop and change in school-age children.

How is Memory Studied?

Present-day study of children's memory reflects the recent advances in both information-processing theory and cognitive development research. It is now well recognized that the study of memory must be viewed within a much broader perspective than that of traditional studies which focused upon the basic processes relating to the child's capacity to encode, store and retrieve information. Within the last two decades, there have been important advances made to suggest that while these basic processes are an important element in memorial ability, these aspects can only be meaningfully examined in relation to the child's learning and understanding. In essence, the emphasis for child development research has shifted from the concentration of how changes in the environment affect the child's recognition or recall of information, to an emphasis upon how the child actively processes material to be remembered. Traditional research questions such as "How many items can the child retain in short-term memory?" have been replaced by questions concerning the types of strategies used by the child, the effects of the task demands and materials in relation to the cognitive abilities of the child; how the child's background knowledge affects recall; and how memory performance of mature, older, or expert learners differs from that of young, inexperienced or exceptional learners.

A number of contemporary experts in the memory and developmental fields have suggested that the crucial elements for consideration of the child's memory and learning can be depicted within a tetrahedral model (Jenkins, 1979; Brown, Bransford, Ferrara & Campione, 1983). The model includes four factors which are necessary to the examination of the "learner-in-context." These include (1) the learner's activity, (2) the characteristics of the learner, (3) the nature of the materials to be learned, and (4) the criterial task. Even though specific studies may focus upon a single dimension (i.e. systematic manipulation of materials to be learned or the examination of differing ages of experimental subjects), the interactive effects of the other dimensions must be taken into consideration. More importantly, the model allows for the reorganization of the voluminous research that has been generated in this area and helps to clarify our understanding of memory, not only in terms of basic processes, but also in terms of the important interactive association with knowledge and learning. A brief discussion of each of these four factors and how these are presently being studied will provide a suitable compendium of our current means of understanding of children's memory and development.

The Learner's Activity

The activities or strategies that a person utilizes within the context of a memory task have been shown to be highly significant with respect to subsequent retention and retrieval of information. Research in this domain has focused upon the identification of types of strategies; whether these are spontaneously applied or need to be deliberately activated by the self or some external person; whether strategies used effectively in one situation are generalized for use in other appropriate situations; and how the development of the child's repertoire of skills and strategies progresses. A typical research study examining children's utilization of memory strategies would begin with the exposure of a series of words or pictures that the child would be instructed to remember. Observations of how the child approached the task and subsequent performance would be made to ascertain whether a child would utilize rehearsal or other information-reduction strategies such as clustering by association or categorization, visual imagery, chunking, natural language mediation, or even subjective organization. Central to this type of investigation is the question of spontaneous use of task-appropriate strategies and, in the event of observed failure to spontaneously use these strategies, whether such children can be induced or trained to adopt these strategies. Studies of this sort have consistently demonstrated marked performance differences favoring those children who apply strategies to the task. More importantly, there is ample evidence to show that such strategies can be taught to substantially increase memory recall or recognition ability (Brown, 1975).

Along with this recent interest in the use of strategies and how this affects the developing child's memory capabilities, there has been a notable tendency to move the research context out of the traditional experimental laboratory to the natural learning contexts of the child. Researchers have increasingly become interested in how the child utilizes memory strategies to approach school-related activities such as reading, mathematics, writing and studying. Even though these investigations are relatively new to the field, early results show considerable promise and relevance for those associated with the teaching profession (Brown, Bransford, Ferrara, & Campione, 1983).

Characteristics of the Learner

Memory performance differences between the young and the old, the naive and the expert, and the average and the exceptional have long been documented in the memory literature. We know that different groups faced with an identical memory task will show marked differences in the amount and quality of the subsequent recall or comprehension of the task. Whereas earlier studies of this sort were primarily conducted to demonstrate that such differences do exist, contemporary researchers are now actively searching the question of what it is that the learner brings to the memory task and how this interacts with the ability to do well on it. Along with the repertoire of strategic skills the child may or may not have access to, the importance of one's background knowledge and experience as well as one's working memory capacity have been shown to be the critical factors here.

As an example, consider the situation in which a 10-year-old child who has been, for several years, involved in the hobby of collecting butterflies is asked to read a passage concerning the discovery of a new species of butterfly. It would be expected that the child's recall would be significantly better than that of same-age peers who have not been involved in this hobby. Alternatively, we might consider the results if a naive 18-year-old student was given the same passage to read. Likely, we would expect the recall to be better than that of the naive 10-year-old but possibly not as good as that of the 10-year-old butterfly expert. What is it that can account for these performance differences?

On the basis of the current literature in this area, it is reasonable to hypothesize that the 10-year-old expert brings to the reading task an extensive and elaborate semantic knowledge based on understanding of butterflies in general. While reading the passage, it is very likely that the child can integrate this new information into well-established patterns of knowledge about butterflies in general (i.e. citing patterns, color differentiations, association with similar species). Thus, the 10-year-old may be able to improve recall by relying on semantic networks related to the study of butterflies. On the other hand, the 18-year-old brings to the task the advantage of, perhaps, a more efficient repertoire of memory-enhancing strategies and certainly more school-related experience in terms of ability to read informational material to acquire new knowledge. Thus, in this situation it is clear that performance will ultimately depend upon knowledge base as well as the ability to effectively utilize one's limited information-processing capacity to acquire new knowledge.

Here again, these recent investigations concerning the characteristics of the learner have important implications for teaching. It is clear that educators need to consider both the developmental limitations that characterize the young child's capacity to process and acquire new information, and also the knowledge base that the youngster brings to the learning situation.

The Nature of the Materials

Recent research has advanced another area of inquiry which was for the large part only incidentally considered in traditional memory studies. The nature of the materials to be learned can have a significant effect upon the ease or difficulty one experiences in performing a memory task. If we consider a traditional list learning memory task, the actual items in the word list are critical to predicting performance outcome. For example, consider two 30-word lists, one which contains the first thirty names on a given page in a telephone directory and another list of food items including vegetables, fruits and meats. It can readily be predicted that presentation of the latter list will result in better recall performance. The greater ease of recall can be attributed to three primary factors which have been delineated in this line of investigation. First, the items to be remembered have distinct similarities, in that they all belong to a general category of foods. Next, the food items would likely be well-familiar to the list learner and thus could be easily related to the person's knowledge base and background experience. And finally a list which say contains 10 vegetables, 10 fruits, and 10 meats can be strategically clustered into these three broad categories and thereby further facilitate the person's ability to recall the items in the list. Out of these factors, we can pose three questions concerning the nature of materials that can be usefully employed by memory researchers and educators alike.

1. Are the materials to be learned, adequately organized and/or presented to maximize the student's opportunity to process and retain the information?
2. Are the materials to be learned relevant to the child's current knowledge base and level of understanding?
3. Do the materials to be learned faciliate or allow for the active, strategic processing of the information?

Studies which have systematically explored these questions have resulted in some intriguing insights into some of the major shortcomings of curriculum materials currently being used in the schools. For example, detailed analysis of elementary and secondary school texts have shown marked differences with respect to conceptual level of presentation, organization of information, and readability, and other factors have been shown to have differential understanding and retrieval effects upon students (Tierney & Pearson, 1985). Researchers are currently searching out new methods of analyzing textbook and school-related materials, and this work will no doubt have an important impact upon the nature and presentation of curriculum materials in the future.

The Criterial Task

The final dimension that has been explored and defined as important to the young child's learning and memory is the question of the criterial task. How is the child's memory to be assessed after exposure to a learning situation? Traditional memory studies have primarily relied upon recognition and recall tests to assess the amount of information that is remembered. A typical recognition memory task would involve exposing the child to a large number of pictures and later presenting these and other distractor pictures. The child's task is to indicate those pictures which have been previously viewed. The number of correctly identified pictures would be totalled to assess recognition capacity. Recall tasks differ in the sense that items or materials to be remembered are presented and then withdrawn prior to the child's being asked to remember or recall the information. Whereas these types of studies have generated important insights for our general theories of memory, the nature of the criterial task has only recently been recognized as having important practical significance. Correspondingly, the way in which we view and investigate the criterial task has undergone considerable alteration.

Most important is the recognition that the way in which a person approaches a learning task has a great deal to do with one's knowledge (or lack of knowledge) as to how the learning is to be assessed. For example, if a 10-year-old is given a word list and told that he will be asked later to recall the words, the child will no doubt approach the task with more effort and concentration than he would have without the knowledge of the post-recall requirement. Similarly, the directive from the teacher to study a particular chapter from a textbook as opposed to reading a chapter signals to the student the likelihood of such material being covered in a subsequent class test and thus the need for a careful and effortful learning of the specific material.

It is clear from the recent research in this area that the students' perceived goal of the task will have a significant influence upon the effort that they will commit, the degree of memorization that will be attempted, and the type of strategies they will bring to bear upon the task. It is important here to note that the student's perceived goal in any given task may or may not be the same as that supposed or intended or even requested by the experimenter or, for that matter, the teacher. However, we do have evidence to demontrate that those learning activities that are more directly compatible with the criterial task will result in the best performance. It therefore follows that researchers and teachers alike need to explore new ways of ensuring that the learner is aware of the learning goals in presenting new material, and that the material is compatible with the intended assessment of learning outcomes. A final point in this regard is the recognition that a clear understanding of the concept of the criterial task is only the first step to the much larger concern of generalizability of learning. In other words, the question of ultimate importance for future study of memory and learning concerns the determination of those learning and memory activities which yield the maximal generalization to related and new learning pursuits.

In summary of this section, a tetrahedral model has been used to describe the dimensions that developmental and memory researchers have determined to be most useful for our current understanding of how the youngster's memory abilities develop and how these factors ultimately influence learning. The following section will include a selective review of specific studies of children's memory development.

The Development of Children's Memory

Memory Strategies. There is an abundance of theoretical and empirical investigation to support the notion of improved memory performance with increasing age. Early studies in this vein were directed toward the elucidation of the kinds of strategies and processes the young child brings to bear on different memory tasks.

The studies by Flavell, Beach and Chinsky (1966) and Keeney, Cannizzo and Flavell (1967) dealt with rehearsal as an organizational process. The results of the first study revealed that with increasing age (subjects were grades kindergarten — six), there was greater recall and evidence of a greater amount of rehearsal. The second study utilized a similar experimental paradigm to examine the memory performance of three groups of first graders. One group consisted of children who rarely or never rehearsed, whereas children in the other two groups usually rehearsed. For the first ten trials all children were instructed to rehearse, and subsequent recall was found to be similar for all groups. There were no instructions to rehearse given on the second battery of trials. The results indicated that the majority of the nonrehearsers had dropped their rehearsal activities and, correspondingly, their subsequent recall performance was dimished. In contrast, all of the usual rehearsers maintained their previous level of high recall performance.

Another type of memory strategy, clustering criteria, was examined in a developmental study carried out by Denny and Ziobrowski (1972) with first graders and college students. It was found that young children tended to cluster material according to complementary relationships (e.g. pipe and tobacco), whereas adults tended to organize material according to similarity relationships (e.g. king and ruler). The authors concluded that "it cannot be assumed that because children categorize according to different criteria than adults they therefore lack the ability to use criteria adults use" (Denny & Ziobrowski, 1972, p. 281).

The development of memorization strategies was examined by Niemark, Slotnick and Ulrich (1971) utilizing subjects from grades one, three, four, five, six and college age. All subjects were given 24 pictures to memorize for free recall during a three-minute study interval. During this study period an "organization rating" was determined. This rating assessed the extent to which the subjects rearranged the pictures into categories. The minimum possible rating was zero which reflected no systematic rearrangement of the pictures, and the maximum three-point rating reflected a completely categorized rearrangement of the pictures. The ratings reflected organizational increases from .10 for grade one subjects, .30 for grade three subjects, .70 for grade four subjects, 1.0 for grade six, to 2.2 for college students. The older subjects made more frequent use of memory strategies than young ones, and those who used more strategies remembered more than those who did not. Similar developmental related differences in the utilization of categorical cues were reported by Halperin (1974) who examined the recall and recognition abilities of samples of six-, nine- and twelve-year-old children.

In an examination of retrieval cues used by children in recall, Kobasigawa (1974) hypothesized that as children mature they are increasingly likely to make efficient use of accessible retrieval cues. The samples of children, from grades one, three and six, were given a task in which recall items (e.g. bear) were presented with conceptually related cues (e.g. zoo). Kobasigawa (1974) found that the number of subjects who spontaneously used these pictures cues to retrieve target items increased as a function of age, and that when older subjects used these picture cues, they tended to recall more items that younger spontaneous cue users. Whereas a highly directive cueing procedure was needed for cues to be facilitative at grades one and three, the mere availability of the cues during retrieval was sufficient to enhance the grade six subjects' recall scores. Similar findings reported by Ritter, Kaprove, Fitch and Flavell (1973) led these authors to suggest that the development of retrieval skills in children may parallel the development of storage skills.

The Soviets have also generated substantial research to add to our understanding of this developmental sequence. Smirnov (1948), cited by Smirnov and Zinchenko (1969), attempted to assess the extent to which grades two, four, and six students could rely on semantic grouping and semantic relationships when remembering written material. In this study the following findings were evident:

1. The children did not consciously group the items.
2. The higher grades relied on minimal text organization to plan the order of memorization.
3. All groups did not comprehend the various degrees of structure in the text. For the most part, the subjects only became aware of the structure when carrying out a special assignment such as breaking the text down into parts.
4. The children were aware of the structural differences between texts, and identified the structurally well-formed texts as easier texts.
5. The extent to which the subjects could rely on this strategy in a special assignment was a function of age. The older the subjects, the more likely they could divide the text into organized sections.
6. During the initial stages of grouping for grade two subjects, phrases similar in context were not considered as common.
7. In all grades, if the child was unable to find a heading independently, the child would accept the correct heading suggested by the experimenter.
8. During retrieval, recall more frequently involved grouping than did recognition.

These findings suggest that there is a developmental increase in the extent to which individuals can rely on an organizational strategy for purposes of text processing. There also appears to be a significant discrepancy between the child's conscious knowledge of organizational strategies and unconscious application, as well as between what pupils do and what they are able to do. Even though semantic grouping is within the capacity of school children, these children do not rely on this strategy as a conscious technique for retrieval. As it has been hypothesized in a more general theory of memory, semantic grouping appears to be performed as a special action and is not subordinate to some more complex intellectual activities (Smirnov & Zinchenko, 1969). As young readers become more sophisticated, they rely more on focusing and search strategies to identify the story structure, central theme, inference, nuances of meaning, and logical and causal relationships. The extent to which the individual can identify and focus on the relevant cues and relationships to elaborate and process written information is dependent upon the developmental level of the individual.

In summary, the literature supports the notion that efficient memory performance is the result of optimal usage of memory strategies and processes available to the processor. This applies to both encoding and retrieval operations. Whereas more mature subjects may spontaneously adopt these strategies during task performance, younger subjects may require cueing or instructions to elicit the employment of these strategies. The apparent success of these initial studies in demonstrating and distinguishing a number of memory strategies used by children led to the logical successive question of "At what age are these strategies normally employed and under what conditions?" The studies of incidental and intentional learning have been especially useful in addressing this question.

Intentional Learning

Hagen (1972) utilized incidental and intentional learning procedures in the examination of selective attention in children of varying age levels. In a typical experimental task, the subject was shown pictures of two items belonging to two separate categories. In a given series of these pictures, the subject was instructed to remember only the items from one category. It was found that with increasing age, subjects intentionally attended only to the items required by the task. Younger subjects were inclined to attend to both items on a card regardless of instructions. These results would suggest that subject awareness and usage of intention instructions is more efficient in old subjects. Similar results were apparent in the investigations reported by Wheeler and Dusek (1973) and Hale and Piper (1973).

The developmental aspect of memory efficiency in terms of an intentional or incidental experimental condition has been widely explored in Soviet psychology. Smirnov and Zinchenko (1969) summarized an experiment carried out by Zinchenko with subjects aged three-and-one-half years, five-and-one-half years, eight-and-one-half years, eleven-and-one-half years and one group of adults. Different subjects of each age level were tested under involuntary (incidental) and voluntary (intentional) conditions. The incidental condition required the subject to view 15 pictures of familiar objects and name them. In the second condition the subjects were asked to name the pictures and remember them for subsequent recall. All subjects were later requested to recall and name the objects that were represented to them. The results showed that under both the incidental and intentional conditions, the number of objects correctly recalled improved with increasing age, stabilizing at eleven-and-one-half years. For the adults and eleven-and-one-half-year-olds, recall was greater under the intentional condition, whereas the recall for the eight-and-one-half-year-olds was similar in both conditions, and the incidental condition was superior for the three-and-one-half and five-and-one-half-year-olds.

A plausible explanation for these results has been advanced by Flavell, Friedrichs, and Hoyt (1970), who suggests that the young child does not differentiate "mere perception" from deliberate memory, even though exhibiting the ability to remember. Flavell et al. (1970) hypothesized that "the deliberate intention to memorize perceptual inputs for later recall only gradually emerges and articulates itself from the less deliberate intention just to recognize and contemplate them" (p. 338).

This hypothesis was examined in a study by Appel, Cooper, McCarrell, Sims-Knight, Yussen and Flavell (1972). Subjects included children from preschool, grade one and grade five. Two experimental tasks were employed including the two conditions of "look" and "memory." The first task allowed subjects simultaneous access to all the object pictures for one-and-a-half minutes, during which time they were free to inspect and manipulate the pictures as they chose. For the second task, subjects viewed the same items through slide projections, one at a time, on a screen. Subjects in the "look" condition were told to look at the items carefully, while "memory" condition subjects were instructed to remember the names of the objects. The findings of both experiments indicated that under both conditions, the percentage remembered increased with increasing age. There were no performance differences between the look and memory conditions for the four-and-one-half-year-olds. For the seven-and-one-half-year-olds there was no difference in conditions in the first task, but the memory condition resulted in greater performance in the second task. Performance in both tasks was greater under the memory condition for the eleven-and-one-half-year-olds. The authors concluded that differential instructions were only beneficial for older subjects.

Although the results of the Appel et al. and the Zinchenko study differ somewhat, both would strongly suggest that the intention to remember, as a useful differentiated state of an individual's memory, doesn't start to emerge until about age seven; by the age of 11 this state is fairly well-incorporated into the child's repertoire of memory plans and strategies.

Meacham (1972) adds further insight to the notion of intentionality in his review of American and Soviet research. He suggests that Flavell's production deficiency hypothesis could be reformulated on the basis of certain Soviet discussions, in stating, "The effect of intention is that the subject chooses from among the mnemonic activities which are currently available, that which he thinks is most appropriate for the material and then engages in that activity. It is important to note that this effect is not upon the mnemonic activity, per se, but rather upon the choice of a particular activity in which to engage" (Meacham, 1972, p. 214).

In concluding this section, it would seem apparent that conditions of intentional learning constitute an integral function with respect to the increased efficiency of the memory ability of the growing child. It is important to point out that the results of these intentional learning studies reveal an obvious age parallel with formal school years. More importantly, the bulk of the recent research in the area of memory and children's learning has been focused upon the examination and extent of the complex interrelationships between memory, learning and schooling. The profusion of studies in the area of reading comprehension and text recall have been particularly instrumental in highlighting the importance of background knowledge or LTM in regards to memory proficiency. Some of the major work in this area will be reviewed in the following segment.

Background Knowledge

If it is accepted that memory and comprehension are inextricably tied to cognitive development (as has been theorized by cognitive psychologists), then it seems reasonable to expect that children who have prior experiential knowledge concerning a prose passage will be able to retrieve that information more readily than if presented with a passage containing totally unfamiliar information. Accordingly, the reliance upon logical operations in prose recall would be exemplified by the child relying on these operations to organize the perceived relationships and experiences.

Piaget and Inhelder (1973) noted that in the context of lecture and passage recall, individuals can reconstruct certain connections through continued reflection and processing. This has been reported in the literature as early as 1932 when Bartlett examined narrative recall in adults. He found that exact recall of prose information occurred only if the information was sufficiently bizarre or if the information was crucial to the main theme. Otherwise, subjects usually relied upon contextual inferences, embellishments, presuppositions and personal likes and biases to reconstruct the gist of the passages. Studies such as these strongly suggest that information processed in the past can gain greater significance through elaboration by added experiences and updated contexts.

Although several investigations have demonstrated the same outcome as that described above, few researchers have attempted to establish a theoretically based procedure which can be utilized to assess the extent to which individuals rely on their knowledge to process and elaborate information from prose. However, Kintsch (1974) has formulated a theoretical procedure based on modern linguistics and logic to account for the structure of narrative prose, and to explore the nature of the knowledge utilized by children and adults to process prose.

Kintsch (1974) proposed that the basic units of meaning are propositions in which a one-word concept serves as a predictor and the remaining ones are arguments. Each argument fulfills a unique semantic role within the proposition, while the predicate specify the relationships among the arguments. The arguments are concepts, not words, and are stored in the individual's semantic memory. These concepts are defined by the proposition in which they are used. The connected, ordered list of those propositions, generated through propositional analysis, represents the meaning of the text and is considered the text base, or microstructure. These propositions can also be ordered in a subordinate-superordinate relationship. Essentially, a proposition is subordinated by a prior proposition if the subordinated proposition contains an argument that also appeared in the higher proposition (Kintsch, 1975). This procedure generates clusters or propositions which represent the theme or themes of a passage.

Beyond this level, these chunks of propositions or macropropositions are formed through four macro-operators, or rules. The first rule deletes irrelevant, nonpresuppositional material, and while the second operation removes redundant material, the substitution of category names for category members is performed by the third rule — or the generalization rule. The construction rule summarizes a sequence of actions or events by introducing a term that refers the sequence as a whole (e.g. reading a book) (Kintsch, 1977a). The resulting macropropositions generated by these rules represent the macro-structure of the text. More operationally, the macro-structure is a formal representation of the theme and the exposition, complication, and resolution frames of a story (Kintsch, 1977a, 1977b).

In an attempt to test the model, Kintsch (1977a) presented two groups of mature subjects with a series of stories. One group received scrambled stories and the other group received the ordered stories. The group instructed to read the scrambled stories took significantly longer than the group that was presented with the unscrambled stories. After reading each story, the subjects were required to write a brief summary of the story. These abstracts were then organized into propositional units, and analysis revealed that the quality of the abstracts were independent of the input order. Furthermore, Kintsch (1977a) found that with these two groups (scrambled and unscrambled), given unlimited time, raters could not distinguish the stories in terms of the two modes of presentation. These findings suggest that subjects rely on similar "schemes" for story recall and that these can be represented through formal propositional analysis.

In an attempt to assess the extent to which children could rely on a schema to facilitate story recall, Kintsch (1977a) presented 16 four-year-olds with a series of ordered and scrambled pictures within the context of a narrative. Analysis of the recall data, in the form of storytelling, revealed that the group in the normal presentation condition was able to recall 77 percent of the propositions, while the group in the scrambled condition was able to recall only 26 percent of the propositions. These findings were interpreted as showing that when children have access to a story schema, the reliance on this schema can aid recall.

In summary, the above findings and other research carried out by Kintsch and his coworkers (Kintsch, 1977a, 1977b) suggest that in processing stories, individuals rely on a story schema as a means to organize information. It is further suggested that if the proposition is old, the individual can just refer to the original memory trace and process the information to a deeper semantic level. Through additional elaboration, the individual can also improve the quality of the memory trace. However, if the proposition is new, the reader must store the proposition in memory as part of a developing text base, and deeper processing and elaboration are far more difficult.

On a less formal basis, other research using a variety of techniques of prose analysis has tended to support the findings of Kintsch (1976, 1977a, 1977b). Several studies have supported Kintsch's notion of story scheme in particular. For example, Brown and Murphy (1975) presented four-year-olds with sets of four pictures either as a logical narrative or a random sequence. The findings indicated that children presented with the randomized sequence performed significantly more poorly than children presented with a logical sequence. Futhermore, second grade children's recall and reconstruction performance was appreciably better than kindergarten children's recall and reconstruction performance. These findings lend support to the notion that young children are able to benefit from the presence of a unifying connective logic or schema to aid recall (Brown & Murphy, 1975).

In a follow-up study, Brown (1975) presented kindergarten and second grade children with logical experimentor-imposed, self-imposed, or arbitrary sequences. In support of the previous findings, the logical- and subject-imposed sequences were retained far better than arbitrary-imposed sequences.

In his discussion of the development of memory, Yendovitskaya (1971) notes that the effectiveness of remembering in preschool children is in direct relationship to the meaningfulness of the presented material. Korman (1944) as reported by Yendovitskaya (1971) found that preschool children aged 4 to 5 could remember and produce, with sufficient logical sequences, complex prose material. Children did not appear to restate the material in a meaningful manner but, rather, tended to rephrase the material in a meaningful context. However, it was noted that the quality of this reproduction was a function of age; whereas four- to five-year-olds will only recall the basic episodes of a fairy tale, the six-year-olds will recall more of the precise and detailed information (Yendovitskaya, 1971).

Recent studies have shown that the structure of the plot of a story also affects subject recall. Thorndyke (1977) found that the closer the story (presented to the subjects) matched the standard well-learned structural hierarchy of goal-directed episodic sequences, the better was subject recall performance.

Other studies have presented evidence to support the notion of a levels-of-processing effect on prose recall. For example, Schallert (1976) attempted to assess the effect of induced processing of prose. The continuum of depth processing from shallow to deep was induced by having subjects either count the number of four-letter words, count the number of pronouns, rate passages for degrees of ambiguity, and rate each paragraph for the degree of difficulty to learn. As postulated, depth of processing appreciably affected subject-recall performance.

In considering the developmental nature of memory and comprehension, it seems axiomatic to expect that differences in the performance of adults and children in prose recall would be evident. This premise was explored by Mandler and Johnson (1977), who indeed found qualitative differences in children's and adults' recall. In general, the results suggested that children's memory is less determined by encoding and is more determined by the operations the child can bring to bear during the recall process.

A couple of studies by Paris (1975) and Paris and Upton (1976) shed some light into the specific nature of such differences.

Paris (1975) attempted to assess the extent to which kindergarten and fifth grade children could recall inferential and verbatim information from prose. The fifth grade children performed significantly better than the kindergarten children in the recall of both inferential and verbatim information.

These findings were supported by a later study (Paris & Upton, 1976) in which kindergarten, second grade and fourth grade children were presented with stories. In a delayed free-recall situation, the children recalled 1.9, 4.4 and 9.3 semantic units, respectively. In the aided-recall situation in which the subjects were presented with both verbatim and inferential questions, fourth grade performance was significantly better than kindergarten or second grade performance. From this it would appear that as children develop they become increasingly able to rely on semantic knowledge to make inferences as they read passages, thereby enhancing their later retelling.

In summary of the research presented in this section, it would appear that the prior knowledge of the subject can significantly affect the extent to which the individual can process and elaborate information from prose for purposes of future retrieval. This knowledge is comprised of logical operations (inference, classification, seriation), story structure or schema (story organization, level or propositions, and number of arguments) and personal experience related to story content. Preschool and early elementary level students demonstrate limitations in all of these areas. However, if cues such as a well-formed fairy tale structure or directive questioning is employed, then performance is improved. It is only in the upper-level grades that students are able to apply their own knowledge schemas to interpret unordered text and to utilize such aid in their recall.

Metamemory

The final area of investigation which has recently been determined as a critical factor in the development of children's memory is the area of metamemory. This concept was briefly alluded to in the previous discussion of Flavell's approach to memory and essentially refers to everything a person knows and understands about one's own memory capabilities and how one regulates these during memory tasks. Since the research in this area is now more closely associated with generic study of metacognition, it will be discussed in the ensuing chapter on metacognition.

In summary of this segment, we have presented some of the relevant findings of four major research areas relating to our current understanding of the development of children's memory. These include memory strategy development, intentional learning, background knowledge, and metamemory. The following segment will deal with the practical applications of models of memory.

PRACTICAL APPLICATIONS OF MODELS OF MEMORY

This section addresses the question of how knowledge of memory acquisition and memory development might be applied to practical problems confronting children and educators. Specifically, three special issues of this knowledge are considered in their application to children's information processing, education and therapy. In all sections, the skills and abilities of younger children are contrasted with those of older children to give parents, teachers and educators an applied and developmental perspective. Because of current interest in information-processing models of memory, the practical applications of two models are considered: the multistore model and levels of processing models. Also considered are the practical applications of the developmental model advanced by Piaget and Inhelder.

APPLICATIONS OF THE MULTISTORE MODEL

In the course of our experience with young children, we as parents and teachers have probably noticed that they do not remember very well. The explanation most frequently given is that children do not voluntarily use a variety of strategies or tricks to better retain and retrieve information from memory. This particular explanation is a developmental adaptation of the multistore model of memory. An earlier section of this chapter dealing with the multistore model of memory distinguished between **structural** (or invariant) systems of memory and **memory control processes,** suggesting operations which can be learned or developed in order to alter the way that memory functions. As discussed earlier, those who assume a multistore model of memory believe that memory consists of three discrete storage systems: (1) a sensory register, (2) a short-term store, and (3) a long-term store. All information passes through this system and is either held temporarily for incorporation into the system before it decays or is forgotten, or it is held in consciousness for mental work and retained for use at some later point in time (see Fig. 4-1 on page 73).

According to the **sensory register** concept, all information coming from the external world enters the information-processing system through the senses. This information is believed to be temporarily registered in some large-capacity register from which we selectively process some of it. The initially large register system shrinks regularly and promptly, and revives again. The sensory register is generally believed to hold large quantities of information. However, this is for extremely brief periods of time, often less than a second (Colehart, 1975), after which the iconic (visual) or echoic (auditory) image fades away. The learner, whether as a young child or as an adult, must selectively process some of this information if it is to be transferred into short-term storage in consciousness for the mental work of further interpretation and processing. Unless this information is scanned and transferred to short-term storage, it will be forgotten completely (see Fig. 4-1 on page 73).

Representing To-Be-Remembered Information Through Diverse Modalities

Data provided by Sheingold (1973) concerning the amount of information that can be held in the sensory register confirm that the capacity of this system is quite large and that the capacity estimates are similar for all age levels and are unaffected by the type of information (visual, auditory, single-item, multiple-item display) being processed. It is generally believed (Broadbent, 1958) that the modality in which information is stored in the sensory register is similar to the sensation that gave rise to it. In other words, if information is presented through the visual mode, it is represented in the sensory register iconically, or if auditorily, then it is represented echoically and so on. Although it is generally accepted (Case, 1974; Pascual-Leone, 1980) that there are age-related restrictions on processing capacity, much of the research in the Piagetian and neoPiagetian framework has revealed that both the very young and older children are responsive to various dimensions of their sensory world. Children are capable of representing a variety of information in the sensory register in a manner similar to adults.

Overall, however, it is important for parents and teachers to observe that the amount of time that information resides in short-term storage, without some active externally imposed attempt to prolong its duration, is about 10 to 30 seconds. Although the duration of unprocessed information seems to be about the same for children and adults, it is important to note that young children are especially deficient in their ability to prevent the loss of information from the sensory register. Therefore, frequent and prolonged exposure to a few selective stimuli may strengthen the memory trace of these stimuli in the sensory register.

The Visual-Iconic and Echoic-Auditory Sequence in Information Coding

Parents and teachers need to note that children are capable of representing information in a variety of ways—visually (Paivio & Csapo, 1969; Proctor, 1978), auditorily-verbally (Conrad, 1971), and semantically (Wickens, 1970). Although older children prefer the visual-iconic representation, and their information-processing and memory functioning may be filled with pictorial representations, there is good evidence to indicate that young children prefer to represent information iconically. An important implication of these notions is that if young children's information processing and recall is to be strengthened, it would seem reasonable to help them initially code information through the visual-iconic form and subsequently to recode the same information in an alternative form, often an echoic-auditory one.

Thus, the parent or teacher who uses the visual modality of the TV screen to present information to the young child can predict that it is the visual message that will be first processed and remembered. The saliency of the visual field on the TV screen may serve as the unique attentional device directing children's attention to key aspects of information that will be remembered at a future date. Parents and teachers must note, therefore, that the visually presented information may perhaps be the more conspicuous component of the audiovisual information that will be better remembered by young children. The pictures will be more powerful than the sounds and words that accompany them (Hayes & Birnbaum, 1980). However, this is not to imply that auditory information is an insignificant source of information to younger children, only that young children seem to comprehend and retain the visual information more spontaneously than they do the auditory information and appear to have better factual memories for visually presented materials (Beagles-Roos & Gat, 1983; Pezdek & Hartman, 1983).

In assessing children's general tendency to process information initially within a visual modality, teachers and parents should note that although children prefer visual representation in their coding strategies, it is to the children's advantage to receive early encouragement for adapting their coding strategies to task demands requiring attentiveness to the auditory facets of the information-laden situation. In presenting to-be-remembered information to the child, teachers and parents would do well to remember that the visual modality alone may not be sufficiently effective in promoting information processing. Following Calvert, Huston, Watkins and Wright (1982), teachers can expect salient auditory features (vocalizations and sound effects) to serve as additional attentional devices in enhancing children's comprehension and retention of the programs. By encouraging multi-modal (visual, tactile and audio) representations, teachers and parents reinforce the notion that sound serves as a salient attentional cue for bringing children's attention back to the visual setting and helping them to process the information in a variety of codes (Anderson & Levin, 1976).

Developmental improvement in memory functioning would appear related to the better use of control processes such as selective attention in rehearsal, chunking, imagery, subjective organization in the short-term store, and the organization of information in the long-term memory store. Changes believed to occur in the use of control processes allow for a more efficient use of memory.

Educators and practitioners who assume a multistore model of memory have generally concluded that after age four when the structure of memory is completed, the one feature that distinguishes the young child from the older child or adult is the improvement in children's ability to use control processes (Ornstein, 1977). By about age 12 or 13 years, it is argued that children have acquired or developed a variety of perceptual, mnemonic or conceptual strategies that equip them to alter the ways in which they remember.

Control Processes

Rehearsal. It has been believed for a long time that rehearsal is an important process for transferring information to long-term or more stable memory (Atkinson & Shiffrin, 1968). It is suggested that although children do not rehearse spontaneously (Rundus, 1971), the more rehearsal an information receives, the longer it will reside in short-term storage and the greater is the likelihood that it would be transferred to the long-term store. Although the precise role of rehearsal in children's long-term memory has not been clearly established, it is generally believed that by rehearsing or by repeating the information over and over again, the child can delay the loss of the to-be-remembered information from the memory. The more the child rehearses the information, the more resistant it becomes to forgetting. Thus, it is suggested by several researchers (e.g. Asarnow & Meichenbaum, 1979; Ornstein, Naus & Stone, 1977) that children as young as five years of age may be encouraged to rehearse single-item and multi-items sets as a means of improving short-term memory.

Naming, Pointing and Haptic Manipulation

Primitive precursors of rehearsal which can be encouraged at the preschool level are the toddler's sporadic attempts to retain and maintain material via naming, pointing or eye fixation (Wellman, Ritter & Flavell, 1975). Labeling becomes well established during the early grade school years and is a prime example of what has been called maintenance rehearsal (Cuvo, 1975; Ornstein & Naus, 1978). Multistore proponents argue that the more frequently an item is looked at fixedly, labeled, touched or handled, the more likely it will be transferred to the memory store or be accessible for recall at a future date. Structured opportunity for cumulative rehearsal, "show-and-tell" exercises, naming, pointing and haptic manipulation of objects in the environment are processes that strengthen retention of information in children.

The prototypical pattern of rehearsal among third graders is a rote repetition of single items. The amount of information that can be retained by older children in short-term store has been estimated to range between four and nine items (Mandler, 1967; Miller, 1956). In comparison to older children, young children have a much smaller capacity. However, children can be trained to include more items in their rehearsal sets by a continual refinement of rehearsal strategies (Butterfield, Wambold & Belmont, 1973). Generally, these strategies reflect both voluntary and coached attempts by the learner to consolidate and organize information entering and residing in the multistorage system (Rundus, 1977).

Chunking

One strategy often used by teachers to increase the capacity of short-term store involves grouping (chunking) bits of information together to form larger units which may themselves become single-item or unitary bits of information. For example, in helping the young child to memorize the sequence of a series of numbers 4032880390, the teacher would probably have considerable difficulty, as the span grossly exceeds the capacity of most children's short-term memory. In order to simplify the child's task, the teacher might combine the digits into larger but fewer units or items. Thus, a child who is being urged to memorize her telephone number may be encourged to group the information as follows 403-288-0390. By chunking the information in this manner, fewer units of information need to be remembered by the child, although in a practical sense more information is retained. In essence, chunking involves finding some higher-order category to which several of the items belong and helping children organize their storage and retrieval of information according to these categories. Children may not be able to generate categories for chunking spontaneously. If they are helped to do so, their memory scores may improve considerably. Moely, Olson, Halwes and Flavell (1969) demonstrated that even kindergarten children could be trained to chunk items either while examining the stimulus items or later during recall. Let us say, for example, that a child needed to remember the following list: horse, cow, dog, lion, pig, balloon, ball, kite, car, train, bus, boat, plane. Left to their own resources it is not likely that the children would be able to recall more than 5 to 9 words, the limit imposed by short-term memory. However, if the child were helped to formulate an organizing principle that enabled him or her to recognize the presence of five animals, five toys and five vehicles, the child might succeed in remembering 12 to 15 words.

For the most part, chunking instructions facilitate the retention of item information for older-age children more so than younger children, suggesting that mnemonic strategies involving categorization and stimulus consolidation may be difficult for young children. Prior to five years of age, children have been perceived to be passive, nonstrategic and nonplanful in memory tasks. Recent evidence suggests, however, that in many domains preschool children have more strategic competence than was initially supposed (Gelman, 1978).

Using Visual Imagery

A technique for facilitating the elaboration of interactive visual images, called the key-word technique (Raugh & Atkinson, 1975), seems to support the notion of the superiority of children's visualizing abilities. This memory technique based on high imagery consists of transforming important and to-be-remembered words into visual images consistent with the meaning of the word(s). Therefore, by instructing children to produce visual images of to-be-remembered information, teachers can often assist children in remembering foreign vocabulary, difficult sounding technical terms and recalling historical events and places (Jones & Hall, 1982; Shriberg, Levin, McCormick & Pressley, 1982), and remembering faces and names (McCarty, 1980).

Making Memory Tasks Goal-Oriented

Currently much attention is being given to other elaborative processes and strategies for facilitating efficiency as related to recall and recognition. Istomina (1975) has argued that efficiency in memory can be generated if the **goal** of the memory activity and the **setting** of the activity makes sense to the child. Types of strategies explaining why certain things should be remembered and how they can be remembered are becoming parts of pretraining programs in most preschools. Whereas a significant aspect of memory functioning entails knowing what is to be remembered, an equally important aspect is knowing the end result of the remembering and understanding the **objective** underlying the memory activity. Thus, teachers can be instrumental in generating sets of memory protocols which abandon the traditional free-recall tasks in favor of more goal-oriented recall tasks. For example, for preschoolers recall tasks could be set up around specific items to be purchased at a grocery store (e.g. apples, bread, butter, potatoes), items to be stocked in the cupboard (toilet paper, soup cans, soap, toothpaste), items for cool storage in the refrigerator (e.g. milk, juice, cool-aid), ingredients necessary for making cookies (flour, butter, chocolate chips, nuts), or ingredients necessary for making a painting.

Subjective Organization of Stimuli Materials

Another process for facilitating the operation of memory which is more amenable to training in somewhat older children (ages 7 and over) is known as subjective organization. This process suggests that with a view to promoting memory efficiency, children could be coached to pair information with specific locations and specific settings. For instance, children can learn to associate specific to-be-remembered information items with places along paths that they frequent regularly. Associations may also be encouraged with people and objects they encounter frequently. For example, information which may have to be recalled at a later date can be paired with shops, school buildings, TV shows, TV characters, names of teachers, etc., i.e. places and persons that are salient in the child's experience. Such locational and organizational cues can often assist children in recalling important but otherwise difficult-to-remember items of information. The use of locational cues may subsequently help the child to retrieve the important information from the short-term memory store. This technique implies the imposition of order upon a stimulus or set of stimuli as it is being entered into the memory system.

In brief, teachers should note that recent concentration on preschoolers' memorization has revealed that gradual progression to competency is more likely to occur if the precise goal of the memory activities is made clear to the child, and if the setting for the memory activity is made as concrete as possible.

Enhancing the Salience of Category Clusters

What has been stressed in the preceding section is the use of a number of control processes or strategies for delaying the loss of information from the short-term memory store. Another equally important strategy for improving the child's retention is one which is aimed at enhancing the salience of category clusters for recalling items. For example, if the child is helped to construct categories of conceptually similar words or items of information, the organization of information under different nodes can allow children to recover information quickly. Kellas, McCauley and McFarland (1975) have suggested that even young children are capable of storing information under familiar categories such as tex-

textures (rough, smooth, soft), **temperatures** (cold, hot, warm), **locations** (near, far, high, low), **sounds** (loud, quiet, talking, singing, music), **tastes** (sweet, sour, salty, bitter), **shapes** (round, square, 3-sided), and so on.

One idea of how information is organized in long-term storage is proposed by Collins and Quillian (1969), who suggest that children can recall more information that is organized in terms of nodes (see Fig. 4-2).

FIGURE 4-2

Illustration of the memory structure for a three-level hierarchy

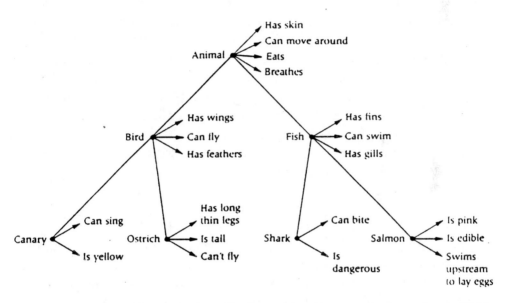

Source: Collins, A. M., & Quillian, M. R. (1969). Retrieval time from semantic memory. *Journal of Verbal Learning and Verbal Behavior, 8,* 240-247.

Later, with the development of memory abilities, these organizational structures can be differentiated on the basis of more and more advanced hierarchies of nodes. At the lowest level of the hierarchy, information stored at each node is specific to things defined by that node. At a higher level of the hierarchy there may be a node for general properties (including temperature, color, texture, etc.) and there could be a node for general functions (for example, fly, cut, chop, run, bounce, etc.). If such subjective and objective organization is reinforced in children, it is expected that with increasing practice children will become more adept in storing information under salient categories, clusters and structures.

Thus, for example, in Figure 4-2 there is in the hierarchy a node for birds in general, and a node for specific types of birds (canary, ostrich). A child associating with the node for birds would recall information unique to all birds, i.e. wings, flying, feathers. A child associating with the node for specific types of birds would recall information unique to specific birds, i.e. canaries are yellow, small and singing birds; ostriches are tall, have long and thin legs, and cannot fly.

Organizing for Primacy Versus Recency Effects

Although there is little evidence that young children spontaneously rehearse information (even if it is presented to them as being very important for future recall), it is important for teachers assisting children in subjective organization of memory tasks to note the differential effects of "primacy" and "recency" in children's recall of information. Children's recall shows more recency effect (which involves recall from short-term memory). Parents and teachers both need to be aware that in giving instructions to children that must be implemented almost right away, children will remember more of the instruction words and information presented at the end of the communication. Therefore, the most important components of the communication or instructions must be presented toward the end rather than the beginning of an interaction.

Organizing for High-Saliency and High-Specifity Effects

In elaborating the idea of subjective organization of materials, Anderson and Bower (1973) have proposed the saliency model which assumes that words and sentences are linked in semantic memory on the basis of association, and contents of memory are highly organized around associative dimensions. It is important for teachers to know that children's response latencies can be expected to be shorter to sentences and phrases that have **high saliency** and **high specificity** as opposed to low saliency and low specificity. For example, recall and memory can be expected to be better in the case of high saliency and high specificity recall information such as "a zebra has stripes" as opposed to "a zebra has feet." "A canary is a yellow bird" has higher saliency than "a canary is a singing bird." Similarly, a category or conceptual differentiation such as "a peacock has a crest" has higher saliency and higher specificity than a sentence such as "a peacock has a tail." It can be reasoned that if children are encouraged to organize recall tasks in terms of high saliency and high specificity, it can be expected that their recall responses would be faster at least to the high-saliency and high-specificity inter-item associations.

One further extension of the saliency model suggests that semantic memory can be strengthened on the basis of high-saliency associations. Consider, for example, that a child is presented with a pair of sentences: "The parent praised Tommy" and "The boy hit Tommy." Suppose that the student is given a fill-in-the-blank exercise which requires him to remember the person who praised and the person who hit. For accurate recall of the specific action by the parent and the boy (praising and hitting), it is important that the student has some strong retrieval cues. Young children may not be able to formulate their own retrieval cues. However, they can be quite effective in using retrieval cues if these are given to them as part of a strategy control procedure. Thus, a high-saliency association with "parent praising" and "boy hitting" can be established in the mind of the student if the teacher suggested, for example, that "A parent is always kind and praises a child" or "A boy is sometimes naughty and can hit a child." Thus high-saliency associations can be drawn between elements of the sentences in such a way that the parent's action will be linked with praising, and the boy's action will be linked with hitting.

Organizing for Integration Effects

Operating simultaneously with the differentiation process in organization is the concept of integration. This position (see Rosner & Hayes, 1977) holds that while young children are less capable of generating and sorting out irrelevant and inappropriate items in conceptual groups and categories necessary to effective recall, they do not necessarily lack the ability to use some of the more sophisticated general and specific categories of items and contents if these are prepared for them and explained to them at their level of understanding. With a certain amount of assistance from teachers and parents, most young children are capable of differentiating the animal category (dogs, cats, horses) from the not-animal category (birds, spiders, snakes) and the nonanimal category (clothing, blankets). These examples are explanations of how children come to organize information in a way that helps them to form categories in which irrelevant items are gradually excluded. As children grow older, formerly fragmented categories become more integrated and represent more adult-like conceptual groupings. Children are therefore able to store information in short-term storage using integrating categories. Using the same differentiation and integration categories, they are also able to retrieve information from the short-term storage system. With

greater memory development and early practice in strategy development and control processes, children can subsequently store a variety of
information in the long-term memory system and are able to do it in a
highly organized fashion.

Intentional Versus Incidential Memory Activity

Most studies (Craik & Tulving, 1975; Nelson et al., 1979) have reported better recall of information under intentional compared to incidental memory conditions. Intentionality is important in children's
approach to memory tasks. Instructing children to "remember" something as opposed to "looking at it" produces much better recall
(Wellman, Ritter & Flavell, 1975; Yussen, 1975). Teachers can facilitate
acquisition, recall and retention of information in children by directing
attention to the significance of remembering the information. For example, a reminder that the information will be vital in a class test or that
certain instructions will have to be followed in using the home computer,
that certain rewards can be obtained for remembering the information,
and certain penalties will have to be paid if the information is forgotten,
are examples of intentional memory conditions that teachers can introduce. Under intentionally informed conditions, preschool children have
been known to recognize and recall more visual material from a television program than did children who viewed the program in an incidental memory condition (Hayes, Chemelski, & Birnbaum, 1981).

Explanations that have been offered for this superiority of the intentionality effect are vague, but the message is very clear in its prescription
for improving children's memory performance. If we wish to help children remember their lessons, as teachers we must provide incentive for
intentional learning and provide intentional learning conditions. By doing so, teachers can promote conditions that motivate children to consolidate information that has already been committed to short-term
memory in such a way that it facilitates long-term retention. Under
intentional-recall conditions, preschool children may indeed be more
motivated to use some additional elaboration procedures in processing
important information (Hayes, Chemelski & Birnbaum, 1981).

APPLICATIONS OF THE
LEVELS-OF-PROCESSING MODEL

One of the novel features of the levels-of-processing approach to
memory is that memory is a by-product of perceptual analysis (Craik &

Lockhart, 1972). Craik and Lockhart (1972) propose that stimuli entering the information-processing system are processed in a hierarchial fashion — in a series of processing stages and are analyzed to varying degrees giving rising to short-term or long-term memory trace. It is assumed that retention is a direct function of the depth to which information is processed. For example, a visual stimulus such as the word **car** can be perceived at a sensory level, dealing with its physical properties such as contour, shape, etc. At deeper levels of processing, the meaning of the word may be evoked (e.g. a vehicle moving on wheels, a carriage, cart, motor car) producing a more durable memory trace of the meaning extracted from the stimulus. It is reasoned that sensory memory traces are fleeting because the perception of the physical properties does not require a deep analysis, whereas the deeper semantic analysis produces a more durable memory trace of the meaning extracted from the stimulus.

Semantic Versus Nonsemantic Encoding

It is obvious that words and phrases that are processed at a shallow level (Does the word begin with a capital or small letter? Does the word car rhyme with **jar** or **lay**?) will likely not be recalled as often as words that have been analyzed more deeply at the semantic level (e.g. analysis about semantic properties of the words — Mummy drives a car; The car takes me to school; The car is parked on the street or in the garage). Generally speaking, semantically encoded words and phrases are remembered better than those nonsemantically coded (Craik & Tulving, 1975; Till & Jenkins, 1973). Thus, asking the child questions requiring deeper semantic analysis such as, "Is the word a farm animal or is it a zoo animal?" "Would it live in a shed or in a pool?" would facilitate retention more than other types of nonsemantic encoding. Research from both the intentional and incidental recall and recognition tests supports the notion that semantic coding accompanied by elaborative rehearsal facilitates retention more than nonsemantically coded information characterized by rote repetition.

A number of authors (e.g. Fisher & Craik, 1977; Geis & Hall, 1976; Ghatala, Carbonari, & Bobele, 1980) advocate **obligatory semantic encoding** across age levels, arguing that children have a growing appreciation of the semantic features of items and they do not resist pressure for obligatory semantic encoding. Encoding is obligatory in the sense that the teacher may draw the child's attention to specific semantic features of the stimuli by nature of the questions asked about the to-be-remembered items of information. Therefore, the greater the amount of semantic elaboration that the teacher forces upon the child's learning situation (for example, orienting questions such as "Was it a part of my body?" "Was it supposed to hurt?" "Would it fit in my desk?"), the greater is the skill with which children are able to generate suitable and compatible cues for retrieving information or the contents of memory.

Spread of Semantic Encoding Versus In-depth Semantic Encoding

Craik and Tulving (1975) suggest that it may be appropriate for teachers to stress the **spread of encoding** in addition to the **depth of encoding**. The depth of encoding concept suggests that some continuous hierarchical set of analyses be conducted on the information to be recalled or recognized. By contrast, the spread of encoding concept implies that teachers may develop a more durable memory trace by including additional information within the dimension of orienting activity as well as information from other dimensions which would activate associations with other both semantic and nonsemantic features. The spread-of-semantic-encoding theorists (Geis & Hall, 1976; Hunt, Elliott, & Spence, 1979) support the usefulness of generating both semantic and nonsemantic encoding. With older children the use of encoding nonsemantic and semantic features of the memory stimulus would likely activate richer networks of associations including other semantic and nonsemantic features. In other words the greater the dispersion or elaboration of the encoding along semantic and nonsemantic dimensions, the greater is the meaningfulness of the encoding, and the better is the retrieval of memory contents in both the incidental and intentional-recall conditions.

It is important for teachers to note that spontaneous elaboration occurs more frequently with older than younger children. Older children (grades 7, 8, & 9) are more likely to elaborate stimulus information to a degree that it becomes resistant to forgetting (Ghatala, Carbonari, & Bobele, 1980), whereas younger children (grades 1, 2 & 3) may need much more assistance from teachers and parents in elaborating stimulus information enough to recall it in the intentional-recall conditions.

Semantic conditions can be effected by the teacher in the following ways.

Development of Semantic Themes

Preschoolers have better memories for pictures and sentences when they are presented for learning in a semantically organized manner

(Emmerick & Ackerman, 1976). Thus, having children verbally con-struct relationships between pictures and the constructs they portray, or having children verbally construct relationships between nouns and be-tween nouns and actions, can produce heightened levels of recall in chil-dren across age levels (Chi & Koeske, 1983). Generally speaking, older children (more than younger children) are able to profit from their abili-ties to form a theme. However, significant gains can also be made by young children in information recall if teachers can help them to or-ganize recall materials in the form of theme-related sets. For example, an explicit thematic elaboration such as "the farmer's wife sat on the stool to milk the cow" may help the child to recall subsets of items such as cow, stool, pail, and woman, which are not explicitly organized. Figure 4-3, adapted from Baumeister and Smith (1979), illustrates this point quite well.

FIGURE 4-3
Examples of items used in Lists (a) and (b)

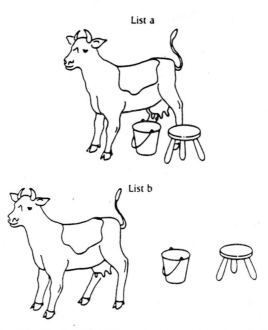

Source: Baumeister, A. A., & Smith, S. (1979). Thematic elaboration and proximity in children's recall, organization, and long-term retention of pictorial materials. *Journal of Experimental Child Psychology, 28,* 132-148.

Referring to Figure 4-3, for example, the teacher can arrange learn-ing conditions in such a way that List A is presented before List B. The three objects in List A—a cow next to a bucket and a milking stool—form a semantic theme which is more likely to be remembered by the child than when the three objects are spatially blocked but not explicitly organized in terms of a semantic theme.

A teacher's assistance to the child in developing an organized theme around the unrelated items could serve as an excellent retrieval cue and improve a child's subsequent recall. For example, a young child may see a number of unrelated objects in a picture—dog, chair, bone, table, child—and may fail to develop a memory trace for the objects in the picture or for the theme depicted unless a teacher or parent helped the child to form a theme such as "the dog is under the table and wants to chew the bone, but the child won't let him." In the earlier stage the child may need external help to develop semantic themes for objects and events that need to be remembered. However, with advanced age the child will be able to develop independent thematic elaborations and strategies focusing on meaningful semantic features of the information to be memorized.

Even in conditions where subsets of objects or information items that appear to be thematically unrelated items are presented, the teacher can help to improve the child's recall by offering inducements to elaborate semantically and to develop meaningful relationships between a number of items (Buss, Yussen, Mathews, Miller, & Rembold, 1983).

Multiattribute Encoding

The effectiveness of the teacher's effort in improving memory is believed to depend on how well the child can be taught to anticipate retrieval cues for recalling items of information. A number of research findings (e.g. Thomson & Tulving, 1970; Ceci, Lea & Howe, 1980; Ceci & Howe, 1978) address the issue of information retrieval offering cues that teachers may use with children. The more closely the retrieval cues reinstate the context in which the children learn something, the more effective they will be in helping the child to recall the learned information. If, for example, children associate a word in a list (trailer) with a cue, "It's a form of transportation," the statement, "A form of transportation," would be a more effective retrieval cue than would the statement, "Rhymes with 'sailor.' " Higher levels of recall are maintained when children are given retrieval cues that remind them of the context i.e. This word applies to gardening—it is a kind of root—it is a seed—it rhymes with bead.

In formulating retrieval cues for memory tasks, teachers can be facilitative by (a) directing attention to the semantic, phonetic and physical properties of the words to be remembered, and (b) by reinstating the context in which the information was processed.

If children remember an attribute of the item (meaning, color, or location of "trailer"), it is likely that information about other attributes associated with it will also be remembered (Ceci, Lea & Howe, 1980). The message of the levels-of-processing research is very clear in its prescription for teachers: In improving children's memory performance, multiattribute encoding would appear to be useful to students over a wide age range. Although the levels-of-processing experimentalists have not established clearly whether processing invariably proceeds from physical to semantic attributes (see Craik & Lockhart, 1972, p. 676), one of the most useful notions advanced by the levels-of-processing theorists is the idea that a variety of features (semantic and physical) can be used to represent information in memory and to fix the level at which the information is processed.

If we, as teachers, wish to help children remember their lessons, we must encourage them to relate their lessons to a network of associations and experiences that they have already acquired. Since young children cannot be expected to engage in contextual associations and semantic elaboration spontaneously, the teacher will need to provide more individual help to the younger child in encoding specific semantic and non-semantic properties to represent the information in memory and to develop retrieval cues for memory tasks. The teacher must not lose sight of the encoding-specificity principle which prescribes that, at all age levels, the more multiattribute the encoding (whether semantic or physical), the more effective is the acquisition, retention and retrieval of the information represented in memory.

The Role of Cumulative and Elaborative Rehearsal

The role of cumulative or elaborative rehearsal (in conjunction with the use of physical and semantic associations) for the long-term retention of information in memory cannot be denied (Postman, 1975).

Teachers must not overlook the effect of cumulative rehearsal in making semantic associations. Long-term retention of information, such as telephone numbers, addresses, teachers' names, classroom number, locker combinations, is very important to the child's survival in the context of the school and community. Unfortunately, such information does not lend itself well to any elaborative semantic associations. In such cases, perhaps the best way to commit this information to memory would be through cumulative rehearsal or practice.

In brief, teachers have the responsibility for making information more resistant to forgetting over a long period of time by encouraging the child (a) to engage in both nonsemantic and semantic analysis of information, (b) to formulate effective retrieval cues, and (c) to commit information to memory through cumulative rehearsal.

A DEVELOPMENTAL MODEL OF MEMORY: EDUCATIONAL APPLICATIONS

From a Piagetian view, memory is predominantly an interpretation of experience rather than a clear and accurate detection and representation of the stimulus itself. In other words, memories do not necessarily represent aspects of the stimulus event, but are constructions and reconstructions of the event. This view of memory has important developmental consequences for the young learner, as the child's constructions are based on the child's knowledge state or the way in which the child perceives reality. Obviously, one of the most important implications of this view is that the products of the child's memory change with age just as the child's perception of reality changes with a stage-related change in cognitive structure. Because intellectual structure changes during the developmental years, it is also believed that the content of memory changes. Furthermore, the Piagetians believe that three qualitatively distinct memories exist: recognition, reconstruction and recall. It is believed that these memories have different figurative components and different developmental onsets.

Memory in a Broad and Narrow Sense

Contrary to the traditional notion of memory which argues that children's long-term memory is poorer than their short-term memory, Piaget and Inhelder (1973) contend that memory in the broadest sense improves over time — that is, specific memories of past events are actually better over some period of time rather than worse. As the child's conceptual understanding of the world improves with age, so children's memory, in the broad sense, also improves with age. For the teacher, then, this signifies that improvement in recall is specific to stimuli incorporating some operative feature. Memory for information that has no operative feature declines with age. In other words, Piaget believes that children's recall corresponds closely with their level of operational development. Mnemonic activity or elaborative encoding strategies for assisting children in improving long-term memory must correspond with the child's level of operational development.

Piaget (1968) has stated that the memory trace is a construction rather than an exact copy of reality. The traditional notion that memory trace can be strengthened in children by helping them with encoding devices and strategies (narrow memory sense) is viewed rather skeptically within a Piagetian framework of memory development. Memory traces will not conserve information about operative properties of objects and events unless children have within their intellectual structure some corresponding operational scheme that can assimilate this information. If, for example, children have not developed a concept of seriation, no amount of elaborative strategies or mnemonic devices to recall seriation will help children to conserve this information, or to reproduce a figurative image of a set of seriative sticks.

However, the Piagetians have proposed three distinct types of memories (recognition, reconstruction and recall or evocation) which can be strengthened during strategy training.

Recognition is inherent in every sensory-motor habit of the child and is the earliest memory to develop. It is also important in promoting an accommodation of mnemonic schemes used in traditional memory improvement. Much of the representation of information will be at the level of recognition memory. Therefore, children of any age should find recognition easier than tasks requiring reconstruction, and reconstruction easier than recall. Teachers can expect to observe a reliable sequence of recognition, reconstruction, and recall in children's memory performance activity. Teachers must accept that this progression from recognition to reconstruction to recall reflects the basic nature of the child's intellectual development and that without the corresponding intellectual maturity children are unable to use more sophisticated types of memory. The child's ability to represent actions of others (imitation) is the basis of reconstruction, and mental imagery, i.e. the child's ability to remember both objects and relationships between them, is the basis of recall. Teachers must accept that the developmentally more advanced forms of memory (reconstruction and recall) may not be observed in the early preschool child. Thus, external inducements or strategies for promoting this type of memory will be ineffective. With respect to the general pattern of memory development, the sequence evolves much as described by Piaget, and parents and teachers can do little to modify or change it. On a more positive note, however, the transition from recognition to reconstruction memory can be facilitated by teachers and parents who reinforce children in assimilating action schemas (cf. Liben, 1977). Reconstruction is a kind of recall by action and involves a form of imitation. Since children learn to manipulate objects at an early age, the manipulation of materials assists memory by reactivating action schemes that can be applied to the objects.

Summary

Three different modes of memory functioning have been considered in this chapter: Retrieval stratagems, control processes, and devices for strengthening short-term and long-term memory. With the acquisition of improved retrieval strategies children may gain access to more information about the memory trace. The three modes of memory functioning are concerned with the process by which information is assimilated into memory. In this regard each model has distinct views and accounts for how memory changes vary between the approaches.

The multistore model specifies a processing system that is accompanied by a variety of control processes that can make the basic system operate better. In this approach the teacher can serve as an active contributor to the process by which information is encoded in the memory through rehearsal, chunking, etc.

Although the multistore information-processing position proposes a system or structure that remains basically invariant with age, the teacher can still feel like an active contributor to the extent that this position suggests that improvement in children's memory comes from learning to make better use of the system or structure of memory. The more diligent the teacher is in helping the child to organize information, the better will be the child's retention of the information.

The levels-of-processing model proposes that information is evaluated in a series of processing stages, and deeper levels of processing facilitate retention. In this approach, too, the teacher can help in children's memory performance through effective nonsemantic and semantic representation of information.

The levels-of-processing model proposes that older children are better able to elaborate memory traces (i.e. enrich the trace with semantic information) and use retrieval processes that serve to facilitate memory performance. Although the capacity to understand physical properties and semantic properties of objects remains basically invariant with age, teachers can assist older children in elaborate semantic encoding and fixing of information at a deeper level. In this way older children are better able to elaborate memory traces. With the assistance of the teacher and parent, older children can enrich the fund of memory by means of strategies for semantic elaboration.

In the position advocated by Piaget, however, there is the belief that the memory structure changes with age and that the child's progress through the developmental sequences of recognition, reconstruction and recall cannot be facilitated as a function of external inducements, reinforcement or discriminative learning. Each phase of memory has different figurative properties which define the evolution of memory in the child. There is little external help the teacher can give to alter the stage-like developments. However, Soviet psychologists, such as Vygotsky (1978), argue that such mediation is critical to learning and development.

It is of significance for the teacher to note that in the multistore and levels-of-processing approach the child encodes information in terms of a cluster or memory attributes about the stimulus event or object. The individual child can be assisted by the teacher to develop a bundle of memory attributes by selectively attending to and coding information about one or several attributes. The older child can be helped and encouraged to develop a more durable memory trace by going beyond the simple structural and perceptual features of a stimulus event to processing information semantically and coding it in terms of multiattributes. The levels-of-processing approach proposes that the child's attention to the perceptual features contributes to short-term memory only, whereas the semiotic function, i.e. the semantic elaboration of information by the child, can make the memory of the stimulus event more permanent. In the Piagetian model, however, the semiotic function has little contribution to make to the child's more or less permanent retention of information or the progression from recognition to reconstruction to recall. The Piagetians do not focus on the value of providing a retrieval environment for the child, or assisting the child with retrieval cues that will serve to facilitate recall by strengthening the memory trace. Nor do Piagetians maintain conclusively that memory improves as a consequence of operant development. Nonetheless, Piaget and Inhelder have contributed greatly to our thoughts concerning the notion of the stage-related changes in children's knowledge base and the corresponding developmental sequences (recognition, reconstruction, and recall) which characterize the evolution of children's memory.

If the work in children's memory over the last decade is any indication, it is researchers like Flavell, Brown and Wertsch, who have worked at combining the views of information processing, Piaget and Soviet psychologists, who will have the greatest impact for future practical models of memory.

REFERENCES

Anderson, D. R., & Levin, S. R. (1976). Young children's attention to "Sesame Street." *Child Development, 47,* 806-811.

Anderson, J. R., & Bower, G. H. (1973). *Human assertive memory.* Washington, DC: Winston.

Appel, L. F., Cooper, R. G., McCarrell, N., Sims-Knight, J., Yussen, S. R., & Flavell, J. H. (1972). The development of the distinction between perceiving and memorizing. *Child Development, 43,* 1365-1381.

Asarnow, J. R., & Meichenbaum, D. (1979). Verbal rehearsal and serial recall: The mediational training of kindergarten children. *Child Development, 50,* 1173-1177.

Atkinson, R. C., & Shiffrin, R. M. (1968). Human memory: A proposed system and its control processes. In K. W. Spence and J. T. Spence (Eds.), *The psychology of learning and motivation: Advances in research and theory,* Vol. 2 (pp. 89-195). New York: Academic Press.

Atkinson, R. C., & Shiffrin, R. M. (1971). The control of short-term memory. *Scientific American, 225,* 82-89.

Baddeley, A. D. (1976) *The psychology of memory.* New York: Basic Books.

Bartlett, F. C. (1932). *Remembering.* Cambridge: Cambridge University Press.

Baumeister, A. A., & Smith, S. (1979). Thematic elaboration and proximity in children's recall, organization, and long-term retention of pictorial materials. *Journal of Experimental Child Psychology, 28,* 132-148.

Beagles-Roos, J., & Gat, I. (1983). Specific impact of radio and television on children's story comprehension. *Journal of Educational Psychology, 75,* 128-137.

Bransford, J. D., & Franks, J. J. (1971). The abstraction of linguistic ideas. *Cognitive Psychology, 2,* 331-350.

Bransford, J. D., & Johnson, M. K. (1972). Contextual prerequisites for understanding: Some investigations of comprehension and recall. *Journal of Verbal Learning and Verbal Behavior, 11,* 717-726.

Broadbent, D. E. (1958). *Perceptions and Human Communication.* New York: Pergamon Press.

Bronfenbrenner, U. (1971). Preface to the English translation. In A. V. Zaparozhets & D. B. Elkonin (Eds.), *The psychology of preschool children.* Cambridge, MA: MIT Press.

Brown, A. L. (1974). The role of strategic behavior in retardate memory. In N. R. Ellis (Ed.), *International review of research in mental retardation,* Vol. 7 (pp. 55-111). New York: Academic Press.

Brown, A. L. (1975). The development of memory: Knowing, knowing about knowing, and knowing how to know. In H. W. Reese (Ed.), *Advances in child development and behavior,* Vol. 10 (pp. 103-151). New York: Academic Press.

Brown, A. L., Bransford, J. D., Ferrara, R. A., & Campione, J. C. (1983). Learning, remembering, and understanding. In J. H. Flavell & E. M. Markman (Eds.), *Handbook of child psychology, Vol. 1: Cognitive development* (pp. 77-168). New York: Wiley.

Brown, A. L., & Murphy, M. D. (1975). Reconstruction of arbitrary versus logical sequences by preschool children. *Journal of Experimental Child Psychology, 20,* 307-326.

Buss, R. R., Yussen, S. R., Mathews II, S. R., Miller, G. E., & Rembold, K. L. (1983). Development of children's use of story schema to retrieve information. *Developmental Psychology, 19,* 22-28.

Butterfield, E. C., Wambold, C., & Belmont, J. M. (1973). On the theory and practice of improving short-term memory. *American Journal of Mental Deficiency, 77,* 654-669.

Calvert, S. L., Huston, A. C., Watkins, B. A., & Wright, J. C. (1982). The relation between selective attention to television forms and children's comprehension of content. *Child Development, 53,* 606-610.

Case, R. (1974). Structures and strictures: Some functional limitation on the course of cognitive growth. *Cognitive Psychology, 6,* 544-573.

Ceci, S. J., & Howe, M. J. A. (1978). Semantic knowledge as a determinant of developmental differences in recall. *Journal of Experimental Child Psychology, 26,* 230-345.

Ceci, S. J., Lea, S. E. G., & Howe, M. J. A. (1980). Structural analysis of memory traces in children from 4 to 10 years of age. *Developmental Psychology, 16,* 203-212.

Chi, M. T. H. (1976). Short-term memory limitations in children: Capacity or processing deficits? *Memory and Cognition, 4,* 559-572.

Chi, M. T. H., & Koeske, R. D. (1983). Network representation of a child's dinosaur knowledge. *Developmental Psychology, 19,* 29-39.

Colehart, M. (1975). Iconic memory: A reply to Professor Holding. *Memory and Cognition, 104,* 268-294.

Collins, A. M., & Quillian, M. R. (1969). Retrieval time from semantic memory. *Journal of Verbal Leaning and Verbal Behavior, 8,* 240-247.

Conrad, R. (1971). The chronology of the development of covert speech in children. *Developmental Psychology, 5,* 398-405.

Craik, F. I. M. (1973). A "levels of analysis" view of memory. In P. Pliner, L. Krames, and T. Alloway (Eds.), *Communication and affect: language and thought* (pp. 45-65). New York: Academic Press.

Craik, F. I. M., & Jacoby, L. L. (1975). A process view of short-term retention. In F. Restle, R. M. Shiffrin, N. J. Castellan, H. R. Lindman, and D. Pisoni (Eds.). *Cognitive Theory: Volume 1.* New York: Erlbaum.

Craik, F. I. M., & Lockhart, R. S. (1972). Levels of processing: A framework for memory research. *Journal of Verbal Learning and Verbal Behavior, 11,* 671-684.

Craik, F. I. M., & Tulving, E. (1975). Depth of processing and the retention of words in episodic memory. *Journal of Experimental Psychology: General, 104,* 268-294.

Cuvo, A. (1975). Developmental differences in rehearsal and free recall. *Journal of Experimental Psychology, 19,* 265-278.

Denny, N. W., & Ziobrowski, M. (1972). Developmental changes in clustering criteria. *Journal of Experimental Child Psychology, 13,* 275-283.

Emmerick, H. J., & Ackerman, B. P. (1976). The effects of pictorial detail and elaboration on children's retention. *Journal of Experimental Child Psychology, 21,* 241-248.

Eysenck, M. W. (1978). Levels of processing: A critique. *British Journal of Psychology, 69,* 157-169.

Eysenck, M. W., & Eysenck, M. C. (1979). Processing depth, elaboration of encoding memory stores, and expanded processing capacity. *Journal of Experimental Psychology: Human Learning and Memory, 5,* 472-484.

Fisher, R. P., & Craik, F. I. M. (1977). Interaction between encoding and retrieval operations in cued recall. *Journal of Experimental Psychology: Human Learning and Memory, 3,* 701-711.

Flavell, J. H. (1971). First discussant's comments: What is memory development the development of? *Human Development, 14,* 272-278.

Flavell, J. H. (1977). *Cognitive development.* Englewood Cliffs, NJ: Prentice-Hall, Inc.

Flavell, J. H., Beach, D. R., & Chinsky, J. M. (1966). Spontaneous verbal rehearsal in a memory task as a function of age. *Child Development, 37,* 283-299.

Flavell, J. H., Friedrichs, A. G., & Hoyt, J. D. (1970). Developmental changes in memorization processes. *Cognitive Psychology, 1,* 324-340.

Flavell, J. H., & Wellman, H. M. (1976). Metamemory. In R. Kail and J. Hagen (Eds.), *Perspectives on the development of memory and cognition* (pp. 3-33). Hillsdale, NJ: Lawrence Erlbaum Associates.

Geis, M. F., & Hall, D. M. (1976). Encoding and incidental memory in children. *Journal of Experimental Child Psychology, 22,* 58-66.

Gelman, R. (1978). Cognitive development. In M. R. Rosenzweig & L. W. Porter (Eds.). *Annual review of psychology,* Vol. 29 (pp. 297-332), Palo Alto, CA: Annual Reviews.

Ghatala, E. S., Carbonari, J. P., & Bobele, L. Z. (1980). Developmental changes in incidental memory as a function of processing level, congruity, and repetition. *Journal of Experimental Child Psychology, 29,* 74-87.

Hagen, J. W. (1972). Stategies for remembering. In S. Farham-Diggory (Ed.), *Information processing in children* (pp. 66-78). New York: Academic Press.

Hale, G. A., & Piper, R. A. (1973). Developmental trends in children's incidental learning: Some critical stimulus differences. *Developmental Psychology, 8,* 327-335.

Halperin, M. S. (1974). Developmental changes in the recall and recognition of categorized word lists. *Child Development, 45,* 144-151.

Hayes, D. S., & Birnbaum, D. W. (1980). Preschoolers' retention of televised events: Is a picture worth a thousand words? *Developmental Psychology, 16,* 410-416.

Hayes, D. S., Chemelski, B. E., & Birnbaum, D. W. (1981). Young children's incidental and intentional retention of televised events. *Developmental Psychology, 17,* 230-232.

Hunt, R. R., Elliott, J. M., & Spence, M. J. (1979). Independent effects of process and structure on encoding. *Journal of Experimental Psychology: Human Learning and Memory, 5,* 339-347.

Istomina, M. (1975). The development of voluntary memory in preschool-aged children. *Soviet Psychology, 13,* 5-64.

Jenkins, J. J. (1974). Remember that old theory of memory? Well, forget it. *American Psychologist, 29,* 785-795.

Jenkins, J. J. (1979). Four points to remember: A tetrahedral model and memory experiments. In L. S. Cermak & F. I. M. Craik (Eds.), *Levels of processing in human memory.* Hillsdale, NJ: Erlbaum.

Jones, B. F., & Hall, J. W. (1982). School applications of the mnemonic keyword method as a study strategy by eighth graders. *Journal of Educational Psychology, 74,* 230-237.

Keeney, J. T., Cannizzo, S. R., & Flavell, J. H. (1967). Spontaneous and induced verbal rehearsal in a recall task. *Child Development, 38,* 953-966.

Kellas, G., McCauley, C., & McFarland, C. E. (1975). Developmental aspects of storage and retrieval. *Journal of Experimental Child Psychology, 19,* 51-62.

Kintsch, W. (1974). *The representation of meaning in memory.* Hillsdale, NJ: Erlbaum.

Kintsch, W. (1975). Memory for prose. In C. N. Cofer (Ed.), *The structure of human memory.* San Francisco: W. H. Freeman and Company.

Kintsch, W. (1977a). On comprehending stories. In M. A. Just and P. A. Carpenter (Eds.), *Cognitive processes in comprehension.* Hillsdale, NJ: Lawrence Erlbaum Associates.

Kintsch, W. (1977b). *Memory and cognition.* New York: John Wiley and Sons.

Klatsky, R. L. (1980). *Human memory: Structures and processes.* San Francisco: W. H. Freeman and Company.

Kobasigawa, A. (1974). Utilization of retrieval cues by children in recall. *Child Development, 45,* 127-134.

Korman, T. A. (1944). Odinamike myshleniya: Vosproizvedeniya. (Concerning the dynamics of thinking and recall.). *Doshkolnoye vospitaniye (Preschool Upbringing),* 3-4.

Lerner, R. M. (1976). *Concepts and theories of human development.* Reading, MA: Addison-Wesley Co.

Liben, L. S. (1977). Memory from a cognitive-developmental perspective: A theoretical and empirical review. In W. Overton & Gallagher, J. (Eds.), *Knowledge and development: Advances in research and theory,* Vol. 1 (pp. 149-203). New York: Plenum Press.

Lindsay, P. H., & Norman, D. A. (1977). *Human information processing.* (2nd edition). New York: Academic Press.

Lockhart, R. S., Craik, F. I. M., & Jacoby, L. L. (1975). Depth of processing in recognition and recall: Some aspects of a general memory system. In J. Brown (Ed.), *Recognition and recall* (pp. 75-101). London: Wiley.

Mandler, G. (1967). Organization and memory. In K. W. Spence & J. T. Spence (Eds.), *Psychology of learning and motivation,* (Vol. 1). (pp. 328-372). New York: Academic Press.

Mandler, J. M., & Johnson, N. S. (1977). Remembrance of things parsed: Story structure and recall. *Cognitive Psychology, 9,* 111-151.

Mazuryk, G., & Lockhart, R. S. (1974). Negative recency and levels of processing in free recall. *Canadian Journal of Psychology, 28,* 114-123.

McCarty, D. L. (1980). Investigation of a visual imagery mnemonic device for acquiring face-name associations. *Journal of Experimental Psychology: Human Learning and Memory, 16,* 145-155.

Meacham, J. A. (1972). The development of memory abilities in the individual and society. *Human Development, 15,* 205-228.

Miller, G. A. (1956). The magical number seven, plus or minus two: Some limits on our capacity for processing information. *Psychological Review, 63,* 81-97.

Moely, B. E., Olson, F. A., Halwes, T. G., & Flavell, J. H. (1969). Production deficiency in young children's clustered recall. *Developmental Psychology, 1,* 26-34.

Nelson, D. L., Walling, J. R., & McEvoy, C. L. (1979). Doubts about depth. *Journal of Experimental Psychology: Human Learning and Memory, 5,* 24-44.

Niemark, E., Slotnick, N. S., & Ulrich, T. (1971). Development of memorization strategies. *Developmental Psychology, 5,* 427-432.

Ornstein, P. A. (1977). Memory development in children. In R. Liebert, R. Poulos, & G. Mormor (Eds.), *Developmental Psychology,* (2nd edition). Englewood Cliffs, NJ: Prentice-Hall.

Ornstein, P. A., & Naus, M. J. (1978). Rehearsal processes in children's memory. In P. A. Ornstein (Eds.), *Memory development in children* (pp. 69-99). Hillsdale, NJ: Erlbaum.

Ornstein, P. A., Naus, M. J., & Stone, B. P. (1977). Rehearsal training and developmental differences in memory. *Developmental Psychology, 13,* 15-24.

Paivio, A., & Csapo, K. (1969). Concrete-image and verbal memory codes. *Journal of Experimental Psychology, 80,* 279-285.

Paris, S. G. (1975). Integration and inference in children's comprehension and memory. In F. Restle, R. Shiffrin, J. Castellan, H. Lindman, and D. Pison (Eds.), *Cognitive theory (Vol. 1).* Hillsdale, NJ: Lawrence Erlbaum Associates.

Paris, S. G., & Carter, A. Y. (1973). Semantic and constructive aspects of sentence memory in children. *Developmental Psychology, 9,* 109-113.

Paris, S. G., & Lindauer, B. K. (1976). The role of inference in children's comprehension and memory. *Cognitive Psychology, 8,* 217-227.

Paris, S. G., & Lindauer, B. K. (1977). Constructive aspects of children's comprehension and memory. In R. V. Kail, Jr., & J. W. Hagen (Eds.), *Perspectives on the development of memory and cognition.* Hillsdale, NJ: Erlbaum.

Paris, S. G., Mahoney, G. J., & Buckhalt, J. A. (1974). Facilitation of semantic integration in sentence memory of retarded children. *American Journal of Mental Deficiency, 78,* 714-720.

Paris, S. G., & Upton, L. R. (1976). Children's memory for inferential relationships in prose. *Child Development, 47,* 660-668.

Pascual-Leone, J. (1980). Constructive problems for constructive theories: The current relevance of Piaget's work and a critique of information-processing simulation psychology. In R. H. Kluwe & H. Spada (Eds.), *Developmental models of thinking* (pp. 263-296). New York: Academic Press.

Pezdek, K., & Hartman, E. F. (1983). Children's television viewing: Attention and comprehension of auditory versus visual information. *Child Development, 54,* 1015-1023.

Piaget, J. (1968). *On the development of memory and identity.* Worchester, MA: Clark University Press.

Piaget, J., & Inhelder, B. (1973). *Memory and intelligence.* New York: Basic Books.

Postman, L. (1975). Verbal learning and memory. In M. R. Rosenzweig & L. W. Porter (Eds.), *Annual review of psychology,* (Vol. 26), (pp. 291-335) Palo Alto, CA: Annual Reviews.

Proctor, R. W. (1978). Attention and modality-specific interference in visual short-term memory. *Journal of Experimental Psychology: Human Learning and Memory, 4,* 239-245.

Raugh, M. R., & Atkinson, R. C. (1975). A mnemonic method for learning foreign language vocabulary. *Journal of Experimental Child Psychology, 67,* 1-16.

Reese, Hayne W. (1976). Models of memory development. *Human Development, 19,* 291-303.

Ritter, K., Kaprove, B. H., Fitch, J. P., & Flavell, J. H. (1973). The development of retrieval strategies in young children. *Cognitive Psychology, 5,* 310-321.

Rosner, S. R., & Hayes, D. S. (1977). A developmental study of category item production. *Child Development, 48,* 1062-1065.

Rundus, D. (1971). Analysis of rehearsal processes in free recall. *Journal of Experimental Psychology, 89,* 63-77.

Rundus, D. (1977). Maintenance rehearsal and single-level processing. *Journal of Verbal Learning and Verbal Behavior, 16,* 665-681.

Schallert, D. L. (1976). Improving memory for prose: The relationship between depth of processing and context. *Journal of Verbal Learning and Verbal Behavior, 15,* 621-632.

Sheingold, K. (1973). Developmental differences in intake and storage of visual information, *Journal of Experimental Child Psychology, 16,* 1-11.

Shriberg, L. K., Levin, J. R., McCormick, C. B., & Pressley, M. (1982). Learning about famous people via the keyword method. *Journal of Educational Psychology, 74,* 238-247.

Smirnov. A. A. (1948). *Psikhologiya Pamyati. (The psychology of memory.)* Moscow.

Smirnov, A. A., & Zinchenko, P. I. (1969). Problems in the psychology of memory. In M. Cole & I. Maltzman (Eds.), *A handbook of contemporary Soviet psychology* (pp. 452-502). New York: Basic Books.

Tierney, R. J., & Pearson, P. D. (1985). Learning to learn from text: A framework for improving classroom practice. In H. Singer & R. B. Ruddell (Eds.), *Theoretical models and processes of reading.* (3rd edition). Newark, DE: International Reading Association.

Thomson, D. M., & Tulving, E. (1970). Associative encoding and retrieval: Weak and strong cues. *Journal of Experimental Psychology, 86,* 255-262.

Thorndyke, P. W. (1977). Cognitive structures in comprehension and memory of narrative discourse. *Cognitive Psychology, 9,* 77-110.

Till, R. E., & Jenkins, J. J. (1973). The effects of cue orienting task on free recall of words. *Journal of Verbal Learning and Verbal Behavior, 12,* 489-498.

Tulving, E. (1968). Theoretical issues in free recall. In T. R. Dixon and D. L. Horton (Eds.), *Verbal Behavior and General Behavior Theory* (pp. 2-36). Englewood Cliffs: Prentice-Hall.

Tulving, E. (1972). Episodic and semantic memory. In E. Tulving and W. Donaldson (Eds.), *Organization of Memory.* (pp. 381-403). New York: Academic Press.

Vygotsky, L. S. (1978). *Mind in society: The development of higher psychological processes.* (M. Cole, V. John-Steiner, S. Scribner & E. Souberman, Eds.). Cambridge, MA: Harvard University Press.

Waugh, N. C. & Norman D. A. (1965). Primary memory. *Psychological Review, 72,* 89-104.

Weiss, S. L., Robinson, G., & Hastie, R. (1977). The relationship of depth of processing to free recall in second and fourth graders. *Developmental Psychology, 13,* 325-526.

Wellman, H. M., Ritter, K., & Flavell, J. H. (1975). Deliberate memory behavior in the delayed reaction of very young children. *Developmental Psychology, 11,* 780-787.

Wertsch, J. V. (1979). From social interaction to higher psychological processes: A clarification and application of Vygotsky's theory. *Human Development, 22,* 1-22.

Wheeler, R. J., & Dusek, J. B. (1973). The effects of attentional and cognitive factors on children's incidental learning. *Child Development, 44,* 253-258.

Wickens, D. D. (1970). Encoding categories of words: An empirical approach to meaning. *Psychological Review, 77,* 1-15.

Wickelgren, W. A. (1981). Human learning and memory. *Annual Review of Psychology, 32,* 21-52.

Yendovitskaya, T. V. (1971). Development of memory. In A. V. Zaparozhets & D. B. Elkonin (Eds.), *The psychology of the preschool child.* Cambridge, MA: M.I.T. Press.

Yussen, S. R. (1975). Some reflections on strategic remembering in young children. In G. H. Hale (Chair), *Development of selective processes in cognition.* Symposium of the Society for Research in Child Development. Denver.

CHAPTER FIVE

PROBLEM SOLVING

NEWELL AND SIMON (1972), in their extensive treatise on human problem solving, were concerned with the complex relationship between learning and problem solving and a broader consideration of the question of how information is taken into the organism, interpreted, represented, transformed and acted upon. In the chapters on perception, memory, and attention, we considered a number of information-processing mechanisms and cognitive strategies by which information is recognized, acquired and stored. Children's learning activities and learning behaviors are indeed varied. However, if we are to study children's functioning in the real-life setting, we must proceed from the premise that they can use problem solving as a way of learning and functioning, and that they can be taught cognitive strategies as a way of getting them to solve problems.

Newell and Simon (1972) have defined a problem as a situation where the child wants something and does not know immediately what action or series of actions to take in order to get the desired object. The thing the child wants to acquire may be tangible (something to eat) or abstract (the solution of an equation). The things the child may have to do to solve the problem may be psychomotor (physical activity, like climbing on a stool to reach the cookie jar) or cognitive (involving conceptualizing, associating or relating). Children, in order to engage in problem-solving cognitive activity, may have to perform a variety of intellectual tasks such as identifying, categorizing and discovering concepts.

The Piagetian View of Problem Solving

According to Piaget, in order to understand how and why children solve problems in their own fashion, the teacher must consider the stage of the child's intellect, i.e. whether the child is able symbolically to represent his or her world and, second, understand something about various properties of objects and relationships that hold between them. This latter ability presupposes what Piaget calls the operationalization of thought. Consistent with this approach, all problem solving calls for mental manipulation of symbols that stand for parts of the problem. At all age levels, symbolic manipulation is required, whether the problem is to get the orange hanging on the tree or to find the best plan to solve a mathematical problem. The hallmark of the operationalization of thought concept is the child's ability to use symbols. In the Piagetian view young children may have difficulty in problem-solving responses because of the predominance of perceptual features in the child's intellectual base. Preschoolers may have difficulty in problems requiring analytical reasoning because the thought of the preoperational child is basically unidirectional, static and limited in operational structures. Only when children are able to accommodate the intellectual structure to include transformational schemes, i.e. operations which enable them to identify and appreciate the logical relationships between elements, are they able to internalize action schemes that help them to know what they want to do about a problem, and logical rules to follow in addressing the problem, in identifying the elements of the problem and in evaluating their own abilities.

It is Piaget's belief that a common set of operations — classification, conservation and seriation — permit the concrete operational mind of the child to reason about specific types of problems. Operations of classification, conservation and seriation are internalized schemes corresponding to understandings about how things can be related to one another. Before children are able to solve problems, classification, conservation and seriation operations underlying concrete operational thought are coordinated into cohesive and interdependent groupings allowing for a more or less synchronous emergence of problem-solving ability within each of these areas. Thus, according to Piaget the failure of the preoperational child to engage in the operations of classification or class inclusion is attributed to limitations of the preoperational mind. The preoperational child is incapable, for example, of considering two dimensions (e.g. color and composition) simultaneously and is therefore unable to solve problems requiring the child to classify objects (e.g. beads) by both color (red and blue) and composition (glass and wooden). The preoperational mind is unable to distinguish between subordinate and superordinate classification systems. Not only is the young child easily distracted by the most salient features of the perceptual field, more importantly the child cannot distinguish between the perceptual and abstract features of the stimuli, and cannot sort or classify stimuli along more than two dimensions.

Classification

Although there is increasing evidence (see Sugarman, 1981) to show that children are capable of using hierarchical classification systems much earlier than the age mentioned by Piaget and Inhelder, a question that teachers need to be concerned with is whether or not children actually have a logical understanding of class hierarchies. It is argued by some researchers (see Hooper, Toniolo & Sipple, 1978; Pinard & Laurendau, 1969) that structures, operations and groupings develop at different rates and in a much less synchronous fashion than was believed in earlier thought. A conservative position that teachers must accept, at least tentatively, is that preoperational children are unable to work their way up and down the classification hierarchy, and tend to use it as an abstract system for **manipulating** objects rather than for logically **grouping** objects.

It should be noted that the ability to classify implies the internalization of a system of operation or rules that will permit the child to infer relationships between objects in the enviroment. Piaget argues that until children are able to use the hierarchical classification structure they will not be able to organize and manipulate objects or information in problem-solving ways. Piaget notes the development of various groupment abilities the child must have in order to classify. Principal among these operations are the following:

- **Addition:** This operation implies that adding two elements in a hierarchy forms a new class of objects. For example, the preschooler may initially have difficulty understanding that the addition of two elements in a hierarchy forms a new class of objects. Combining red beads (r) and blue beads (b) forms a new class of objects, glass beads (g) or $(r + b) = g$.
- **Reversibility:** This operation implies that for every operation effected on the system there is another that reverses it; for example: $(b + r) = g$ and $(g - r) = b$.
- **Associativity:** This operation implies that there are a number of ways in which lower-level groups within a class of objects can be combined to form high-order groups, for example: $(b + r) + g$ (glass beads) + w (wooden beads) = Ab (All beads) or $(g + w) = Ab$.

- **Identity:** This is an operation that when added to or subtracted from anything else in the system leaves the system unchanged, for example: $(gw + o) = gw$, $(gw - o) = gw$, or $(gw - gw) = o$.

Two Piagetian principles that cut across the use of the above-noted operations and are integrally related to the use of class hierarchies require an understanding and knowledge of tautology and resorption. **Tautology** implies the knowledge that combining any class with itself produces itself. For example, combining red beads with red beads produces red beads. **Resorption,** by comparison, refers to the knowledge and understanding that a subclass added to a higher-order class is redefined in terms of the higher-order class. For example, red beads combined with blue beads are simply redefined in terms of glass beads.

An understanding of all these operations underlying classifications is necessary to using a hierarchical structure in problem solving. Furthermore, according to Piaget, to truly understand classification systems, children have to first understand class inclusion which, it would appear, is a type of knowledge and ability that develops relatively late. Markman (1978) directs the attention of teachers to the fact that, typically, this ability develops late in the concrete operational period; that is, no earlier than early adolescence. It was Piaget's belief that such operative knowledge enables older children, contrasted to younger children, more easily and accurately to organize, understand, classify, and use hierarchical structure in problem solving.

Conservation

Conservation, another classic benchmark of the operational structures necessary to problem solving, is not sufficiently advanced till the stage of concrete operational thought. Conservation implies the child's ability to conserve properties of objects and the recognition that certain object properties remain invariant despite superficial changes in the object's configuration. For example, does the child understand that his cotton candy doesn't weigh less when it is flattened into a pancake than when it is rolled into a ball? Does the child understand that the amount of juice in his glass is no more or less when it is poured into a cup?

As with understanding the usage of classification structures in problem solving so also with conservation, the child's ability to conserve for purposes of problem solving is contingent upon the availability of important logical operations. Principal among these are the following:

- **Identity** refers to the knowledge and understanding in problem solving that a property remains the same if nothing is added or taken away from it. For example, does the young child understand that his cotton candy remains the same whether it is in the form of a ball or a pancake if no more cotton candy is added to it?
- **Negation** is an operation that permits the learner in problem solving to reason that an alteration in one dimension can be reversed by an equal but opposite transformation.
- **Reciprocity** refers to the knowledge and understanding that changes in one dimension compensate for changes in another dimension. For example, does the child understand that the number of his toys remains the same if he gives away a toy dog but gets a toy cat of the same size in its place? The older child's understanding of reciprocity — i.e. "If something of a particular amount has been taken away from one dimension, an equal amount has been added to another dimension" — allows the older child to consider more than one dimension of any array simultaneously and to consider successive states of objects and changes occurring in them. Because the young child is incapable of using mentally reversible operations, the child cannot compare present and past states of objects and cannot, therefore, appreciate the operations involved in reciprocity.

It was Piaget's belief that the aforegoing group of logical operators underlies children's performance on conservation tasks. There is some evidence to suggest that conservation is related to general age ranges according to which we can anticipate in children certain kinds of knowledge pertaining to conservation of numbers, continuous quantity, weight, volume and area. Piaget's research indicated that teachers would be unlikely to find children younger than six or seven years of age conserving properties of objects. Although we now have some evidence for believing (see Gelman & Gallistel, 1978; Antell & Keating, 1983) that children conserve at a much younger age than was originally thought possible, nevertheless it is accepted that children's knowledge about the factors that precipitate the more advanced forms of conservation is very limited.

Seriation

As with conservation, research on children's relational knowledge — the ability to reason about relationships that exist between objects and items in a series — has shown that children seriate much earlier than was originally believed possible at six years of age. Bryant and Trabasso (1971) and Riley and Trabasso (1974) claimed that children as young as four years of age could make transitive inferences about a five-item series reasoning — for example, that if A is greater than B, and B is greater than C and D, then it follows that A is also greater than D. However, knowledge about the factors that precipitate and promote this competency demonstrated by some young children is very meager. Furthermore, children's ability to order items does not necessarily imply that this ability is based on an operative understanding of seriation.

Sometimes children may be able to work from side to side of the seriation operation and solve transitive inference problems. However, the question to consider is whether the children have the memory to remember accurately the premises used in the solutions of seriation tasks. Based on the current experimental findings, Trabasso and his associates believe that children have knowledge about transitive relationships and that their ability to reason with this knowledge and to arrive at solutions is much like that of adults. The only difference is that younger children are unable to abstract a rule system from the seriation operations.

According to Breslow (1981), children construct knowledge of seriation in a quantitative fashion and are able to reason about things in that series without an operative understanding of relationships outside the context in which the novice learner has learned the series. For example, children may be able to discriminate between the size of sticks shown in adjacent pairs $(A > B, B > C, C > D, D > E)$ but may be unable to discriminate if tested on their knowledge of all possible pairs.

However, the older children, at the level of concrete operational thought, are able to acquire an abstract rule system to reason. This is unlike preoperational children who rely on the appearance or perceptual features of objects. Concrete operational children learn a set of reversible operations (rules and logical operations) for working with elements in a problem-solving task. The child's acquisition of these abstract rule systems allows him to experiment with elements and to explore possible relationships between objects, their properties, and between higher- and low-level classifications.

While there is considerable improvement in children's reasoning between the ages of 12 and 14 years of age, it has to be remembered that this kind of reasoning is still at the concrete operational thinking level and does not allow the average child the capacity to make logical decisions about **hypothetical** situations pertaining to the future, or deciding upon various problem-solving alternatives and options with respect to abstract psychological dilemmas and conflicts frequently facing the adult.

In short, it can be argued that, like so many other apparent competencies demonstrated by children, the intellectual power that concrete operational children show in reasoning about conservation, seriation and hierarchical classification is generally quite impressive. Only with the advent of the formal operational thought, however, children acquire a set of formal operations that permit them to generate possibilities (hypotheses) and to operate on those possibilities in a manner that is quite abstract and freed from the constraints of the concrete world. Until children acquire this kind of elaborated set of logical operations with which to reason in an abstract and more flexible fashion, the problem solving of these children will often be quite incomplete. In each instance, formal operational children become much more agile in their judgments. Not only do they use abstract rule systems more effectively, they are also able to devise more complete logical symbols and combinational schemes in approaching a solution to their problems.

Rather than reviewing the extensive literature that exists on the significance of formal operational thought in the cognitive development of the child, the current discussion will focus primarily on the practical reasons and the theoretical implications for the attainment of formal operations in logical decision making and problem solving.

Compared to the reasoning of the concrete operational mind, the attainment of the formal operational thought suggests that with entry into the latter stage, there is some rapid improvement in the child's ability to solve formal operational problems. Piagetian theory suggests that by age 14 or 16 years, the logical structure of the child's thought approximates that of the adult. Consequently, it is presumed that children, by age 16, possess the same intellectual capacity that adults have to make better decisions after considering a variety of abstract materials and information about the consequences of alternatives and options available to them. In short, research evidence (see Martorano, 1977; Weithorn & Campbell, 1982) supports the notion that with the attainment of formal operational thought there is a rapid shift in reasoning ability which allows the adolescent-age child to solve problems more effectively in terms of (a) generating more choices and alternatives, (b) having more rational reasons for choosing and rejecting options, and (c) having a better understanding of the potential risks or consequences associated with each choice or combination of choices.

Recent research (see Martorano, 1977; Danner & Day, 1977; Stone & Day, 1978) has also confirmed that with the attainment of formal operational thought, the adolescent acquires several types of complex concepts requiring formal operational structure: combinational operations and the isolation of operations such as proportion, probability, correlation and chance. These capacities come into play to account for much of the improvement in reasoning, problem solving and decision making that we often see in adolescents as contrasted with younger children. Therefore, one of the benchmarks of entry into the period of formal operational thought is the adolescent's ability to work with numerous elements of the problem-solving tasks by apparently relying on more advanced operational skills and the ability to study relationships among a vast array of dimensions.

Combinatorial Operations

These operations imply the adolescent's ability to deduce sets of possible orderings or to derive a complete combinatorial scheme and to reason about these propositions. For example, by about age 15, most adolescents should be able to solve a problem requiring them to consider the relationship of their studying time and the effects upon their academic grades. Presented with this problem, concrete operational children are able to elaborate on four possible products of elements (i.e. increasing studying time by four hours a day and improving grades from B average to A average; increasing studying time by four hours a day and not improving grades; not increasing studying time and getter better grades of A average; not increasing study time and not getting any improvement in grades). The concrete operational mind is able to generate a set of four hypotheses to evaluate the problem. But it is only after the attainment of the formal operational thought that the late adolescent is able to understand the existence of a complete combinational scheme and to grasp that there are indeed 16 if not 20 possible outcomes to this problem. The formal operational mind develops a set of transformational rules with which to manipulate problem-solving operations at a more advanced level. With the advent of the formal operational mind, the problem solver can work out a complex combinatorial system involving complete affirmation or complete negation of the relationship. For example, the adolescent will also be able to reason that if the performance improves without adding to the study time, then the claim cannot be made that there is a relationship between increase in study time and improved performance, nor that increase in study time is related to a decline in performance. The problem solver may note that increasing study time may or may not lead to improvement in performance. This statement does not say anything about the consequences of **not** increasing study time, only what will happen if study time is increased. Thus, one of the statements that cannot be sustained is that increase in study time will lead to improvement in performance, or that improvement in performance is due only to increase in study time. The development of a completely elaborated combinatorial scheme is what gives the adolescent mind the required thoroughness in reasoning skills.

Other research has determined that after adolescents are able to elaborate complete combinatorial schemes, they are able to use the same set of possibilities to isolate variables **relevant** to a problem's solution from those that are **irrelevant.**

Proportion, Probability and Correlation

This implies the adolescent's ability to predict how certain operations will change or can be changed as a result of proportionality. One of Piaget's formal operational tasks requires the child to balance a tilting balance beam by determining the ratio between units of weight and units of distance from the fulcrum where weights are hung. In order to predict how the beam will operate, the child must determine a ratio between weight and distance and compare the ratios for both arms of the beam. This new set of transformational operations that the formal operational mind can use to manipulate operations is referred to by Neimark (1975) as INRC (identity, negation, reciprocal and correlative). For example, in the well-known Piagetian problem-solving task, the problem solver must return the balance to equilibrium and explain why the solution works. The following mental operations come into play for the child.

- The application of the **identity operation** shows the problem solver that no matter what transformations he implements (adding more weight to the side of the beam that was already tipped, or reducing the weight on the untipped side), no change is produced in the equilibrium.
- The **negation operation** demonstrates that the problem solver can restore equilibrium by subtracting the added weight or adding the weight that was taken away.

- The **reciprocal operation** suggests to the problem solver that equilibrium can be restored by the problem solver first observing the arm of the balance in which weight has been added or moved in distance from the fulcrum, and subsequently by implementing a change in weight or distance in the opposite arm, i.e. adding a comparable amount of weight or moving the weight an equivalent distance (reciprocity). By reasoning in terms of proportion and ratio, the problem solver should be able to work out a ratio between a specific unit of weight and an equivalent distance on the balance arm.
- Finally, the balance can be restored by using the operation of **correlativity**, i.e. by adding one unit of weight to the arm which may be comparable to moving the weight on the opposite arm one unit of distance away from the fulcrum.

Piaget argues that the concrete operational mind that cannot work out the ratios between weight and distance must restore the balance in the beam by actually manipulating the distance between where the weight is hung and the fulcrum. The formal operational mind, however, does not need to see the beam to reason about it. For the formal operational adolescent the problem can be solved simply by determining the ratios between the units of weight and the units of distance from the fulcrum where the weights are hung.

Knowledge of Probability

Other types of formal operational tasks require the child to predict the outcome of purely random events. These problem-solving tasks require the learner to have knowledge of probability and chance effects, and knowledge about correlated events; for example, the correlation between good health and certain types of nutritional ingredients in the diet. It must be noted by the teacher that, overall, correlations are apparently one of the easier formal operational problems to solve, whereas problems concerned with proportionality appear to be one of the more difficult formal operational tasks (Martorano, 1977).

Problem Solving and Other Underlying Subprocesses

Although Piagetian approaches to problem solving are quite different from other approaches (e.g. information processing), systematic attempts to evaluate their effectiveness have been few in number (Lawton & Hooper, 1978). Comparisons between information-processing approaches and Piaget's problem-solving tasks have found little evidence that one is better than the other. Piaget has argued that the synchronous development of operations at various stages of development organizes children's behavior across problem-solving domains. With age and stage development there is a change in children's processing and problem-solving power. Whether or not the child is problem solving in thought and behavior will depend upon the age and child's stage of cognitive development. Most children as they grow older will coordinate information relevant to the task and will produce information more effectively without being distracted by perceptually disorienting aspects of the environment. Children will normally succeed in problem solving if they are at a stage of cognitive development when their processing capacity is sufficiently, or at least marginally, above that required by the task. However, at all age levels four basic processes combine to produce the activity we call problem solving. These four processes (perception, memory, generation and testing of hypotheses and evaluation) develop to a greater extent as children get older, and therefore the reasoning and problem-solving capacity of the child varies with the unevenness of development within the concept domains. In other words, over time and with age, there are changes in how much information children can remember (**memory processing**), how much distraction by perceptually disorienting aspects (**perceptual processing**) they can avoid, and how much information they can consider or manipulate at any one time (**assimilation** and/or **equilibration**).

In order to understand the nature of children's problem-solving processes, it is important for teachers to recognize that, in order to perform a problem-solving task, the child must coordinate memory, attentional and executive strategy functions: Children must remember and recall information about the elements of the task, the relationship that exists between the elements of a task prior to transformation, and to predict the nature of the relationship after transformation. Therefore, cognitive strategies designed to facilitate problem solving in children must be consistent with the children's differential capacity to remember, attend and to coordinate all of the information relevant to the task.

As teachers, therefore, we must proceed from the premise that with increased processing capacity the older child will be able to consider the problem-solving task in several dimensions and to define the problem in terms of comparative steps.

The rigid way in which the intellect grows within Piagetian stages of development has given rise to some of the strong criticism directed against the Piagetian view of problem solving. The major point of criticism is that the rigid stage-like way in which development occurs does not contribute to a structure of problem solving that generalizes across tasks. NeoPiagetians (e.g. Pascual-Leone, 1980) believe, however, that not all problem solving occurs through the assimilation and accommodation of information into the permanent intellectual structures. There are performatory structures that cut across specific task operations and permanent operational structures. Performatory structures are situation-free, task-free, flexible and temporary constructions that are used by the young problem solver to assimilate information in a novel way. Through these novel but temporary syntheses, higher forms of problem-solving strategies are possible (Pascual-Leone, 1980).

Overall, advocates of problem-solving systems such as information processing have criticized the degree of rigidity, abstractness and generality with which the Piagetians specify the operations which are presumed to underlie logical task performance. Critics of the Piagetian position argue that good models of problem solving should be more precise, specific and structured and should demonstrate capacity to simulate problem-solving processes. Some pedagogical positions have therefore opted for the information-processing approach to problem solving as opposed to the cognitive development view formulated by Piaget.

Information-Processing Approach

Newell and Simon (1972) in their book on human problem solving present a basic structure that is involved in problem-solving behavior: They call it information-processing system, or IPS. The receiving systems of the problem solver (or receptors, i.e. the nerve endings and pathway by which senses travel to the brain) are connected to a processor, which in turn utilizes a memory. The memory also feeds information into the processor as well, which in turn feeds information to the effectors, i.e. motor processes that carry out decisions in the problem-solving process (see Fig. 5-1).

Much of the research in learning processes that has been done over the years has been based upon observations of children as they solve problems. Of primary interest to the teacher is the discovery of what children at any age already know about logical problem-solving rules. This area of interest is precisely the domain of the information-processing theorists who characterize problem solving as the sequential

FIGURE 5-1
Information Processing System

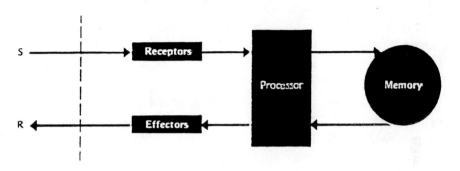

Source: Newell, A. & Simon, H. A. (1972). *Human problem solving.* Englewood Cliffs, NJ: Prentice-Hall.

application of a set of rules necessary to problem solution. It is assumed that if problem solving by children is to be rendered efficient and effective, the rules about problem solving must be both logical and precise, and necessary to the solution of the problem. One of the reasons why children, especially younger children, fail in using rules about problem solving is because of their inability to apply rules that are not logically and concisely laid out for them and, equally, because of their inability to sift out relevant from irrelevant rules that may be associated with a given problem.

For example, a young child who wants to find out why his toy car is not running may simply not have the subprocesses to isolate the factors that may be contributing to the problem (i.e. a broken part, a dead battery, a missing battery). Until the child gains information about rules that should be applied in order to isolate the number of factors that normally affect a toy car's operations, no amount of random manipulation of the toy on the child's part is likely to result in problem solution.

Just as solving problems is an important part of the child's daily activities, so teaching the child a cognitive strategy — a systematic plan for evaluating information pertinent to problem solution — is an important part of the education for problem solving.

The information-processing theorists are strong proponents of teaching children cognitive strategies for working out the step-by-step procedures for approaching problem solution. However, before it is possible for the child to implement a cognitive strategy reflecting logical rules, hypotheses testing, etc., it is important for the teacher to determine whether the child has acquired some of the basic perceptual, attention and memory subprocesses crucial to children's ability to integrate information from rule use.

Children vary in their ability to attend to a given stimulus in a focused way. They may have difficulty in attending to multidimensional features of a given object because of variations in their ability to avoid distractions from other multidimensional stimuli. Similarly, children may be inadept in strategies of rehearsing, organizing and storing information (mnemonic factors) as a result of deficits in their memory capacities. Because of limitations in those subprocesses believed to underlie problem solving, children may fail to apply logical rules of problem solving. They may be unable to assume either an analysis or synthesis approach to problem-solving tasks and activities until some of the basic subprocessing skills have been acquired. It should be noted that when problem solving is encouraged in children under conditions that minimize subprocessing demands (i.e. tasks not requiring increased memory demands or focused attention), logical rules would be used by young children more frequently and effectively. Similarly, it can be expected that children trained to use logical rules through systematic training will increase the frequency with which they will apply logical rules to problem-solving tasks. Support for both these positions is found in the research on children's problem-solving activities. With some interesting qualifications, the information-processing research on children's problem solving proceeds from the premise that problem-solving failures in children result from their ignorance of problem-solving rules, and that most problem solving in children is facilitated by specific assistance to children in cognitive strategies for remembering, organizing and storing information.

An Analysis and Synthesis Approach in Information Processing

Despite the diversity in the information-processing views of problem-solving, one premise which all information-processing theorists share is that problem solving of any kind is intentional rather than an incidental consequence of reinforcement history. It is presumed that the performance of the child in problem-solving tasks is influenced by (a) the interaction of a variety of structures corresponding to specific domains of cognitive activity (mnemonic, perceptual, and conceptual) and (b) the interaction of various stable characteristics of the problem solver (e.g. impulsivity and anxiety, or reflectivity and self-confidence). These enduring qualities of the learner produce individual variations and differences in the overall cognitive style which the learner brings to bear on the problem-solving task.

The information-processing view of problem solving is concerned with how information is taken into the organism, interpreted, represented, transformed, and acted upon in a problem-solving task or situation. This view of problem solving is characterized by two different but complementary frameworks: Analysis and synthesis. As implied in the decription, the analysis method involves an analysis of the components and basic processes or mental operations that are needed for problem solving and the cognitive activity (mnemonic, perceptual and conceptual) presumed to be underlying the problem solving.

By contrast, the synthesis approach to problem solving involves the consideration and knowledge of logical steps, decision-making rules, and sequences required to accomplish various problem tasks. Thus, the synthesis method or systems modeling method (as it is currently constituted) is directed toard synthesizing or constructing models that specify precise rule systems that illustrate the problem-solving process.

In summary, theorists and educators opting for studying the concepts and components of the information-processing model advance the notion that both the analysis and synthesis approach is necessary to effective problem solving.

The analysis approach proposes that the basic structures necessary to problem solving are developed relatively early in life (approximately by age five years). Greater development and effectiveness in problem solving is attributed to the acquisition of rule-system strategies that allow children to use their intellectual structure more efficiently. By contrast, the synthesis approach to children's problem solving attempts to synthesize models that simulate children's performance on specific conceptual tasks by appropriately rendering the synthesis to correspond to (1) the specific transformational skills of the children; (2) the amount of information that they can be expected to retain; and (3) the durability of that information.

Increasing integration of information and problem-solving acquisition takes place through:

1. The increased familiarity of children with the perceptual, mnemonic and conceptual structures made available to them through training in problem-solving tasks.

   On new tasks requiring an extention of rules learned earlier, the child's informal experience with the objects, apparatus (computer, push buttons) and visual materials (pictures, drawings) relevant to the solution of a problem may be most beneficial to the child at the **pretraining stage.** The research evidence shows that children who are allowed to handle problem-related materials prior to the problem-solving training solve the transfer problems more quickly and with fewer prompts and hints.

2. The application of logical and precise rules necessary to problem solution.
3. The acquisition of special cognitive strategies that allow children to use specific structures and operations with greater flexibility and efficiency (Ornstein, 1977).

It is presumed that the coordinated use of information gained from the application of these rules reflects a strategy, i.e. a systematic plan for evaluating the information leading to problem solution.

One important consideration in problem-solving strategy training is that preschool children are limited in their capacities to perform effectively because of the relatively greater influence of state or situation factors affecting their abilities. Young children's information processing, for example, is affected significantly by the degree to which environmental factors cause distraction and make them more prone to errors of haste and inattention. Older children seem better able to alert themselves to the requirements of the task as presented orally or visually to them and are able to disregard the distracting features of the environmental stimuli and the irrelevant variables of the conceptual task. Problem-solving programs, whether computer-assisted or teacher-directed, must ascertain the strength of the affective factors influencing the child's performance.

EDUCATIONAL AND CLASSROOM APPLICATIONS OF THE DEVELOPMENTAL AND INFORMATION-PROCESSING APPROACHES TO CHILDREN'S PROBLEM SOLVING

The information-processing view and cognitive development view of problem solving have a number of interesting implications and applications in the classroom. Some of the major ones are considered in this section.

Hypothesis Testing and Acquiring Rule Knowledge

The increased recognition that problem-solving behavior in children is strategic has led to a great deal of interest among teachers to study the types of rules that are used by children when solving problems. After a child recognizes that there is a problem to be solved, he or she can generate a set of hypotheses (possible solution). The size of this set and the adequacy of the hypotheses depend on the child's prior experience with similar problems. Children who have had prior experiences of problem solving may be able to draw on their knowledge base and formulate a set of possibly **relevant** answers to a problem, and to eliminate **irrelevant** information successively from that set as more information about the problem and its solution becomes available. We call this strategy focusing.

Younger children who have no experience of problem solving may generate trial-to-trial guesses about problem solutions and may not be able to capitalize from the outcome of past trials. At best, these children use a strategy that we call scanning. Eventually, focusing is the more efficient strategy which we want to encourage in our children. By teaching focusing strategies, the young learner can be helped to narrow the field of potentially correct alternatives very rapidly with each new item of information. After a child thinks of a hypothesis, he or she must acquire information to confirm or disconfirm it. As the child's experience accumulates, the expectation of correctness increases until the hypothesis is considered to be a rule. To date, problem-solving research shows that children do not spontaneously use hypotheses at above-chance levels until about second grade (Gholson, Levine & Phillips, 1972). In approaching problem-solving tasks, preschoolers and kindergarten children tend to apply nonhypothesis testing patterns or use hypotheses that are inappropriate to solution. Although most second grade children begin to solve problems by testing hypotheses, the frequency with which they use them may be increased markedly during the elementary school years if children are encouraged and trained via teacher-pupil interactions to use hypotheses and logical rules consistently and appropriately. At the very general level, this implies that children should be consistently required to volunteer hypotheses and to select some values and approaches that have relevance to solution. At the more specific level, teachers may assist pupils in formulating problem-solving hypotheses by means of the following mechanisms.

(a) **Using blank-trials procedure and feedback.** Teachers interested in teaching children to generate hypotheses and test them may first train children to work with artificial problems in the classroom which offer greater control of unwanted variations. Problem-solving tasks can be designed which require children to select from some teacher-given choices and alternatives. Following some choices, the young problem solver receives feedback (i.e. the child is told whether the choice is correct or not correct); however, on other trials the child receives no feedback (these are blank trials). The twenty-questions game (Bruner, Goodnow, & Austin, 1956) and the blank-trials procedure (Levine, 1966) are examples of procedures that can be used to assess and evaluate the child's ability to generate hypotheses and to develop simple logical rules for problem solution. These problem-solving games are played by children asking questions and receiving feedback from the teacher or another partner.

By using the blank-trials procedure with their students, teachers can examine whether or not the problem solver uses a variety of logical rules. For instance, in order to solve problems specified in Levine's (1966) deck of cards, the learner must test hypotheses that are consistent with the feedback provided for the preceding trial. If the learner is testing a hypothesis and receives feedback that confirms the hypothesis, then the teacher should teach the learner how to use the feedback to guide subsequent choices (win-stay). On the other hand, if the feedback is given that the learner's choice is incorrect, then the learner must decide to shift the hypothesis (lose-shift) and choose a new hypothesis from the alternative set which may contain the correct answer.

With the assistance of the teacher, children can be taught to play these games described above and thereby learn to generate hypotheses for problem solving.

(b) Dimension checking. In addition to the strategy of focusing and scanning described earlier, children can be trained in dimension checking. The problem solver retains a hypothesis until it is disconfirmed and continues to select alternative hypotheses until the correct solution is found. The teacher and student working together can help the problem solver identify a list of dimensions that could be relevant to problem solution. They could then proceed through the list, testing one dimension at a time and abandoning the dimension after it has been tested. For example, a six-year-old boy whose toy car has stopped working could be helped to identify the following dimensions that appear relevant to the problem formulation and solution.

- Is it the board on which the car runs?
- Is it a broken piece?
- Is it a broken motor?
- Is it a missing battery?
- Is it a dead battery?

Similarly, a ten-year-old boy faced with the problem of a study lamp which no longer works can be assisted in identifying a list of dimensions that are relevant to problem solution.

- Is it a faulty switch?
- Is it a broken bulb?
- Is it a damaged cord?
- Is it a fuse?

At the start, children can be asked to state what they believe to be the solution to the problem or the dimension which they believe to be most closely related to the solution: introtact probe solution.*

The experimental evidence to date shows that the gains from these type of manipulations such as blank-trials procedure, introtact probe procedure, and dimension checking are not very impressive with younger children's problem solving. Young children (preschool and kindergarten) do not seem to profit from these trainings because of deficiencies in the subprocesses of memory and attention, i.e. the requirement to retain information over a series of nonfeedback trials in hypotheses testing. However, with older children who are capable of using additional memory-recording aids and attentional devices, the gains from the preceding types of manipulations can be quite significant. Older children can be trained by the teacher in more advanced problem-solving rules and strategies. One method involves direct instruction in strategy development; the other uses indirect instruction through modeling.

(c) **Direct instruction.** The techniques of direct instruction have been very effective with children in the early and later elementary school years in teaching them to use developmentally advanced rules and strategies. Direct instruction in problem solving using an information-processing model has typically been more successful in improving the performance of children on sets of well-specified problem-solving tasks. Within the framework of the specific task, children are trained in how to use a hypothesis-testing strategy, i.e. how to use the win-stay and lose-shift rules, and how to persevere in generating alternative hypothesis if a previous set of hypotheses has been disconfirmed. A systematic training program which can be easily set up in the form of a self-directed computer-assisted program is developed to teach children:

---

*See Phillips and Levine (1975) for details.

- to identify relevant hypotheses
- to represent hypotheses visually
- to test each hypothesis one at a time
- to evaluate feedback provided by the teacher or computer

Using the training program described here, even young children can be trained to scan various elements of the problem and thereby reduce the number of random trials typically required by an untrained youngster. With the more advanced student, however, all elements of the training can be integrated or synthesized into one program, requiring the learner to use both a scanning and focusing strategy, and thereby both reducing the number of trials necessary to problem solution and increasing the frequencies of problem solutions.

(d) **Modeling.** Recently, a number of educators and researchers (e.g. Brown & Campione, 1977; Denney & Turner, 1979) have experimented with several types of cognitive strategy models which are presumed to improve problem solving by requiring children to observe an adult model using a similar strategy. In most cognitive models the following procedures are used by the adult model.

- Demonstrate the type of questions that are asked in the strategy.
- Verbalize the various steps that must be taken to use the strategy.
- Instruct how information gained from each question is recorded and evaluated.

At each step, the child observes the teacher who solves the problem (e.g. working out an equation) and explains each step in the analysis. The task of the child is to pay attention while the teacher goes through the analytical steps. The child rehearses the rules of the strategy, both overtly and covertly, and implements the rule for each step while solving an independent problem. Consider a teacher who presents an equation and asks the learner to observe while the teacher solves it by working out the steps of the equation.

$$\Box + 2 = 9$$
$$3 \times \Box \times \Box = 12$$
$$2 \times \Box \times \Box + \Box = 12$$

This problem-solving task calls for mental manipulation of symbols that stand for parts of the problem. The child also rehearses relevant rules (e.g. rules that dictate the order in which the addition and multiplication must be done).

With younger children, these types of modeling conditions provide encouragement to verbalize the various steps to be taken in using a strategy. However, most young children have limited ability to evalute what they have learned from the use of the steps and they are unable to derive maximum benefit from the feedback (i.e. you are right, you are wrong in your answer). In other words, young children may imitate adult behavior and rehearse the instructions given by the adult but fail to appreciate their significance. With older children, however, modeling conditions lead to more effective concept attainment.

The Rule-Assessment Approach to Children's Problem Solving

This approach represents an integration and synthesis of the Piagetian and information-processing viewpoints. According to Piaget cognitive development in children can be characterized as a range of situations in which the reasoning strategies are brought to bear on the skill with which children execute their reasoning. Piaget argues that on their way to mastering each of the variety of ideas, children are said to progress through a series of discrete knowledge states that reflect their general level of reasoning: first they reason in manner A, then in manner B, then in manner C. At each stage, there is a distinctiveness of the knowledge states within each concept. The existence of these distinct knowledge states and the invariant order of their occurrence suggests that there are several forms of reasoning competence which are inapplicable to younger children. For example, a large number of Stage II (transitional) reasoning problems and Stage III (concrete operational) reasoning problems cannot be mastered by younger children who are at the Stage I (preoperational) reasoning level. Stage I children cannot succeed on class inclusion, conservation, seriation, and transitivity problems because of their predisposition to error-prone forms of reasoning. From a Piagetian perspective, children progress through qualitatively discrete knowledge states on their way to mastering concepts and mastering the reasoning stages which are hypothesized to be mastered at about the same time. This had led to the serious question of whether there is any generality in the way that children of particular ages approach different problems. This question has been examined by using an information-processing approach to studying developmental sequences, the rule-assessment approach.

The basic assumption underlying the rule-assessment approach is that cognitive development can be characterized in large part as the acquisition of increasingly powerful rules for problem solving. Although this approach is somewhat similar to the Piagetian one, it differs from the Piagetian position in not presuming any necessary similarity in children's reasoning across different ages and concepts. A number of step-by-step procedures have been formulated by Siegler (1981) to orient teachers to the rule-assessment method.

The first step in using the rule-assessment approach is generating a series of alternative rules that children might use to solve a problem. Rational task analysis and a general understanding of the child's cognitive-developmental stage can make it possible for the teacher or guide to set up hypothesized rules for the child to follow in problem-solving tasks.

Second, a set of problem types is formulated that yields distinctive patterns of correct answers and errors for children following each of the rules.

Finally, if there are two or more tasks for which comparable problem types can be formulated, and if there is a theoretical prediction, either of developmental synchrony or of an invariant developmental ordering, rules can be formulated for studying the between-concept sequence.

Typically, the rule-assessment method characterizes the development of problem-solving ability as the progressive attainment of more powerful problem-solving systems (Siegler, 1981). These systems can be likened to the procedures used by a set of increasingly sophisticated calculators and computers. We begin with a simple model of a calculator that can perform only a limited number of memory functions. Over time, however, as we upgrade the calculators we are acquiring systems that can perform an increasing variety of sophisticated calculations and functions. These functions are flexible enough to enable us as problem solvers to succeed in solutions to a broad range of problem-solving tasks. Siegler (1981), for example, has proposed four rule systems that typify general changes in children's approach to Piaget's problems requiring a knowledge of equilibrium (see Fig. 5-2).

Children using Rule I make judgments about problems based upon one dominant dimension. In balancing the beam task, weight is characteristically the dominant dimension. Children approaching this task according to **Rule I** will predict that the balance in the beam can be restored by equalizing the weight on both sides of the balance. Teachers should note that children at this level of reasoning will pay little heed to the effect of modifying the distance of the weight from the fulcrum.

Children using **Rule II** reasoning will make judgments based on both the dominant (weight) and subordinate dimension (distance of weight from the fulcrum). Thus, if the weights on either side of the balance are equal, children will consider the effect of distance of the weight from the fulcrum.

FIGURE 5-2
Modal Rule Models

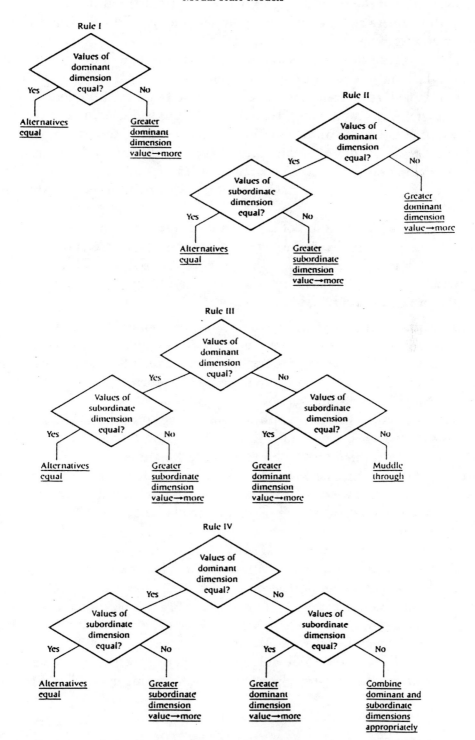

Children using **Rule III** reasoning will consider both the dominant (weight) and the subordinate dimension (distance), but if there is a discrepancy between the weights on either side, or if the weight is placed further from the fulcrum on one side of the balance, the child will not be able to reason on the basis of a ratio between weight and distance of the weight from the fulcrum. Teachers must be prepared for the probability that Rule III children may therefore decide to guess at the solution.

Finally, children using **Rule IV** reasoning will consistently consider both the dominant and subordinate dimensions. If the weight and distance are in conflict, the child using Rule IV reasoning will deduce some approximate ratio between weight and distance and will attempt to restore the balance on the basis of this knowledge of proportionality (see Fig. 5-2).

With the formulation of these types of rules, Siegler (1981) proposes that teachers can diagram the thought process of children operating under each rule system, given specific types of problems. To illustrate his procedure, Siegler proposes six modal problem types adapted from Piaget's equilibrium and balance task.*

1. **Equal problems,** with the same values on both dominant and subordinate dimensions for the two choices. Since weight and distance are equal on either arm of the balance, consequently children using any of the four rule systems should predict the correct solution. The tasks would be more suitable for young children.

2. **Dominant problems,** with unequal values on the dominant dimension (weight) and equal values on the subordinate dimension (distance). In this problem, obviously the weight is greater on one side, but the distance between the weight and the fulcrum is equal on both sides. The discerning teacher will note that children using any of the four rules will be able to predict correctly that the balance will tilt in the direction of the greater weight. Tasks involving dominant problems should be more suitable for young children.

3. **Subordinate problems,** with unequal values on the subordinate dimension and equal values on the dominant one. In this problem, obviously equal amounts of weight are placed on either side of the balance, but these weights on either side are placed at different distances from the fulcrum. Teachers must not expect children using the Rule I reasoning to be able to anticipate correctly how the equilibrium can be restored. However, children using Rule II, III and IV

---

*See Siegler (1981, p. 9).

systems will be able to predict that the beam will tilt in the direction of greater distance. Tasks involving subordinate problems should be more suitable for preadolescent-age children.

4. **Conflict-dominant problems,** with one choice greater on the dominant dimension, the other choice greater on the subordinate dimension, and the one that is greater on the dominant dimension being the correct one. As is implied, in this problem-solving task an unequal weight is placed at varying distances but in a direction of the greater weight. Again, teachers must anticipate that children using Rule III reasoning are likely to guess at the solution. Since there are three possible guesses — tilt right, tilt left, balance — the Rule III child's prediction will be no better than chance (33%). Tasks involving conflict-dominant problems may be more suitable for early adolescent age children at the concrete operational stage.

5. **Conflict-subordinate problems,** with one choice greater on the dominant dimension, the other choice greater on the subordinate dimension, and the one that is greater on the subordinate dimension being the correct one. In this problem type the weight and distances are confounded, with the balance tilting toward the greater distance. In solving these problems, children using Rules I and II reasoning will fail to predict correctly; children using Rule III reasoning will predict at a chance level. Only those children using Rule IV reasoning will predict accurately. Tasks involving conflict-subordinate problems may be more suitable for adolescents at the formal operational thought level.

6. **Conflict-equal problems** have the usual conflict, with the two choices being equal on the outcome measure. In this problem type, weight and distances are confounded, but counterbalanced, and equilibrim is restored by making the weights and distances equal. In this problem type, as in the conflict-subordinate problem type, we would anticipate that children using Rules I and II reasoning will fail to predict correctly. Children using Rule III reasoning will guess at no better than a chance level, and only those children using a Rule IV reasoning will predict accurately. Tasks involving conflict-equal problems are likely to be more suitable for adolescents at the formal operational thought level.

Siegler's experimentation with children grouped by rule use showed that there is a reliable age sequencing: Before the age of 3, children do not demostrate consistent rule use. By the age of 4 years, 50 percent of the children can be expected to use Rule I reasoning. The use of Rule I reasoning is perfected by about age 5. Older children between the ages of 8 and 12 years can be expected to use Rule II and III reasoning, whereas less than a third of 18- and 19-year-old students use the most advanced Rule IV reasoning. This knowledge of the approximately correct age sequencing in the implementation of the rule system can be of great use to the teacher who is formulating problem-solving tasks for rule-guided instruction with children of different ages. To the extent that age correlates with the sophistication of the rules that children are able to use, the descriptions provided by Siegler (1981) suggest distinct developmental patterns that can guide teachers and educators in designing specific problem exercises.

For the teacher an understanding of how these rules systems are adopted also allows an unambiguous prediction of the individual child's performance in specific problem tasks.

It may be useful to compare the rule-assessment approach to other strategies that have been discussed earlier in the study of cognitive strategy development. The rule-assessment approach is similar, for example, to the blank-trials procedure (Levin, 1966; Gholson, Levine, & Phillips, 1972) discussed earlier, in that both procedures are predicated on the assumption that learners, both young and old, follow rules (hypotheses) in solving problems, and that patterns of responding can reveal the nature of these hypotheses. Like other cognitive strategy training procedures, the rule-assessment approach has shown that children employ systematic strategies in problem tasks and show competence in doing so at a relatively early age. Implicit in the preceding discussion is the value of reinforcing strategy training among children over a wide age range. It seems clear from Siegler's (1981) experimentation that the rule-assessment approach and teaching of cognitive strategies can be useful in evaluating children's strategies from age four onward and also in assessing their knowledge of problems of time, speed, distance and fullness (Siegler & Vago, 1978).

For the classroom teachers, the implication is that they must have a sufficiently clear understanding of the children's knowledge base to specify two or more distinct strategies that they might bring to the task. The sense in which the strategies must be distinct is that they must yield different patterns of performance on specifiable types of problems. The fact that a child is using a systematic rule approach does not guarantee that it will be reflected in his performance. The problem type must be set up by the teacher or task designer such that it allows the child straightforward application of a rule.

The rule-assessment approach can assist the teacher to determine what rules children use when they perform various tasks. If the teacher monitors the child's responding closely enough, a great deal of information can also be obtained about what rules children do not use and in what context they do not follow systematic formulas. Although children may not clearly encode the relevant dimensions on many problems and although they might not place a high value on being consistent in rule usage early in childhood, still there is evidence to substantiate that the use of strategies begins early in childhood and that children can gain substantially from systematic strategy training.

The Production-Systems Approach

The rule-assessment strategy described above is also related to the production-systems approach used by Klahr and Wallace (1973; 1976). Taking a similar approach to that of Siegler, Klahr (1980) has designed production systems analyzing the various conceptual processes that would be involved in the implementation of any of the rules. Thus, according to Klahr, a problem-solving process is a set of productions, i.e. a condition and a corresponding action. The types of condition-action pairings that are the basic unit of production-system analyses are also basic to the rule models. Conditions represent momentary knowledge states which, when achieved, eventuate in some kind of action, which, in turn, adds to a new condition and leads to another production, and so on until a final goal is attained. The coordination of a set of productions—a condition and an associated action—is called a production system. In each production system, there is a prediction (P), expectancies (E), and changes in the contents of the short-term memory during task performance (SW). These changes occur as a function of the learner comparing expectancies with actual results and subsequently revising or retaining one's criteria for expecting certain results. For example, referring back to Siegler's (1981) basic rule models, the child is encouraged to consider the dominant and/or subordinate dimensions involved in the balance task. The child works through each production system, first predicting (P), then expecting and observing certain effects (E), and finally evaluating whether the expectancy was confirmed or disconfirmed. Let us assume that the child predicted wrong and the balance tipped in a way contrary to the child's specified expectancy. The child encodes this information in short-term memory and, in the next step, the child modifies the SW and makes corresponding changes in P and E.

By specifying the nature of the problem solving in such a precise manner, it is possible to embody the whole approach in computer-simulation programs such as those developed by Feigenbaum (1961) and Klahr (1980). The operation of these computer programs simulating Siegler's problem-solving sequences make it possible to test a wide variety of substantive statements about children's rules. The computer model generates a number of response patterns of P and E similar to those observed in children. These models simulate typical processes underlying children's problem solutions. These production system programs can be developed by the teacher around very specific problem tasks. It is believed that starting from specific tasks provides the teacher and the learner a basis for truly understanding any important aspect of the child's performance (Kail & Bisanz, 1982). It is presumed that by understanding the specifics of a child's performance on a particular task, we as teachers can coordinate and piece the specifics together to form an integrated understanding of the child's performance across a range of problem-solving (cf. Pascual-Leone, 1980).

Presumably, with increasing processing capacity the organism can include into the production systems a greater number of processing steps. These production systems may be thought of as rule books. Given a particular set of conditions, the child has a set of rules by which to play. Given certain conditions, a particular action is taken by the child toward an effective solution of the problem. For specific tasks it is possible to construct production systems reflecting how children of different ages solve problems. These production systems are often described with running computer programs that are taken as self-validating models of how problems are solved. These models propose sets of rules that activate cognitive activity in children. As children get increasing practice in solving problems with computer-assisted programs, they presumably become more aware of conditions not previously included in the production system, and this awareness leads to the inclusion of more new and complex conditions in the production system (Klahr & Wallace, 1976). In attempts to train children to develop more sophisticated solution strategies, early experience with relatively simple problem-solving tasks involving the execution of simple rules is very beneficial. Gradually, the inclusion of more complicated conditions in the problem-solving task may be useful to the older children in considering both the dominant dimensions and the subordinate dimensions. With an increase in the long-term memory capacity and the attentional span of the young child, there will be a corresponding increase in the capacity of the production system itself leading to a consolidation of the P and E skills. As Fischer (1980) has noted, older children having improved memory capacity use sophisticated computer strategies much more effectively. This may result from the increased speed with which they are able to process information (Kail & Bisanz, 1982).

Implementing Cognitive Strategy Training: Teacher Considerations

Both with younger and older children, the cognitive strategy is developed such that the following procedures are implemented (see Newell & Simon, 1972).

1. The teacher exposes students to problems that are very simple at first (e.g. leading them from a simple equation to a quadratic equation), guiding them through the various steps one by one.
2. Children rehearse various steps with the assistance and feedback of the teacher.
3. The teacher gradually makes the problems more difficult and requires children to engage in self-instruction of the rules.

Gradually, children should be led to develop more sophisticated solution strategies by encouragement to implement rules and strategies initially learned in a formal training program in more informal and naturalistic problem-solving contexts.

Advantages of Implementing Strategy Training

There are several reasons why teachers should attempt to implement cognitive strategy instructions in the classroom.

The first important point to be noted by the classroom teacher is that compared to groups of children receiving no strategy training; those who do receive some training invariably perform better. This knowledge suggests that the poor performance of the children on problem-solving tasks is not necessarily or entirely due to lack of competence but may result from lack of knowledge about the problem-solving process.

Second, cognitive strategies that direct the learner's attention to various steps to be taken in problem solving often shape the cognitive processes involved in changing hypotheses after a given solution process proves ineffective.

Third, cognitive strategies help the young problem solver to correctly interpret task requirements and to generalize knowledge obtained from problem-solving procedures used in one task to new tasks.

Fourth, cognitive strategy training procedures help to shape in the child behaviors that involve elements of persistence and perseverance which are presumed to be influential in problem solving in general (Meyers & Martin, 1974).

Finally, and perhaps most important, many students are passing through the educational system without learning the basic skills of problem solving or without motivation or interest in the types of informal learning-teaching tasks requiring problem solutions. Through cognitive strategy training the young learner recognizes that knowledge of specific procedures can be useful in the acquisition of problem-solving skills.

At the general level we would suggest that teachers and educators and other implementers of classroom strategy training should attempt to anticipate the nature of the problems that their students are likely to confront in the actual classroom setting. Subsequently, they should take the steps needed to develop cognitive strategies that will give greater structure to problem-solving procedures and will reduce the degree of trial-and-error problem solving. In other words, practitioners should consider the host of variables that are thought to be related to effective strategy across time and across problem-solving tasks.

As discussed earlier, the age of the problem solver is of crucial importance to the effectiveness of the cognitive strategy, just as is the influence of affective factors on the problem solving of children. The discerning teacher will note that at the general level the child's prior knowledge and experience in specific problems is most important to the type of cognitive strategy that the learner must use. However, it is not entirely true that lack of prior knowledge of the problem-solving process uniquely impedes children's capacity to use strategies. Certain children become better problem solvers than others because their educational background allowed them more effective problem-solving training and instruction and increased opportunities for practicing problem-solving strategies. Classroom teachers must therefore proceed from the premise that children's problem-solving performance can be improved by providing children: (1) training in more than one problem-solving strategy, (2) the presentation of numerous practice examples and nonexamples (Anthony & Hudgins, 1978), and (3) training in identifying the strategy that would be best for a given problem situation.

By having access to a wide variety of problems in the training, the student would have exposure to different problem-solving strategies requiring different heuristic procedures.

Principles Underlying The Problem-Solving Approach

Very few attempts have been made hitherto to train students in cognitive strategies for problem-solving tasks in the classroom. However, educators have made some start with attempts to develop a few specific principles that could guide the teacher in developing heuristic strategies for classroom implementation.

1. Breaking down interfering sets of functional fixedness. Functional fixedness implies the learner's difficulty in overcoming interference from previous problem solving.

Practically speaking, it should be obvious to teachers that a greater part of teaching learners to solve problems is getting them to examine the elements of problems from a different perspective and getting them to try to tackle problems in ways that are less conventional. This may relate to the idea of "brainstorming" in the classroom in which the objective for the group is to think up as many hypotheses as possible for a problem. Through brainstorming sessions, and the use of appropriate reinforcement strategies, the teacher may shape the students' hypothesis-forming ability and to create "alternative hypotheses." Brainstorming sessions represent an attempt to overcome conventional approaches to a problem by encouraging students to focus first upon the production of new ideas before evaluating the traditional suggestions available. It is hoped that by providing a permissive atmosphere, the teacher can encourage the exploration of original possibilities that might otherwise not be considered. Although there is limited evidence to support the optimistic claims voiced on behalf of the brainstorming strategy, it is nevertheless motivating for some types of students. "Brainstorming" does not teach students to recognize the best hypothesis or to confirm or to disconfirm the validity of each, but it would certainly generate some appreciation of cognitive strategies that are useful in problem solving.

2. Teaching problem solving through successive approximations. In order to teach students to solve a given type of problem, it is important that problem-solving responses be shaped by reinforcing students for solving very simple problems at first, where the solution is obvious. For example, to teach students to solve word problems in algebra, the teacher should give very simple examples at first where the translation into an equation is self-explanatory and immediately becomes clear to the problem solver. Subsequently, but gradually, the teacher presents the student with a similar sequence of experiences at a higher level of

equation complexity. This should be done by presenting numerous practice examples and nonexamples. For a nonexample, consider a teacher
who teaches students how to identify adjectives by requiring students to
name the adjective in a series of sentences. The teacher then gives the
learners immediate information on whether their choice is correct or not
correct. In all events, the problem-solving task is designed to be quite
"performable," meaning that the student can engage in the problem-
solving task with a relatively small amount of processing effort (Newell
& Simon, 1972).

3. **Presenting learning sets.** In order to teach through the problem-
solving approach and about the problem-solving process, it is important
that the teacher help the student to develop "a set for problem solving"
where the **set** is used to mean an attitude of a cognitive nature that leads
the learner to expect certain strategies to work and to facilitate performance in the problem solution. This implies that if the teacher gives a
problem to a group of students and then provides a set of subproblems
designed to help in the solution, the teacher is helping to teach and shape
problem-solving responses. This manipulation is referred to as a learning set.

The term "learning set" is sometimes used to include both **perceptual**
and **cognitive set** which refer to cognitive tasks in which previous experience with problem solving has an influence on the way present problems are solved. The teacher's function in the development of learning or
cognitive sets is to show how a previous mode of solution can be applied
even though it may not be the simplest solution to the present problem.

For example, in a problem called "Luchin's jars problem," children
are given jars with different capacities and are asked to pour water from
jar to jar to obtain a required amount of water. One jar might contain 15
units and another 2 units. To obtain 11 units you would have to fill the
larger jar and from it fill the smaller jar twice to leave 11 units in the
larger jar. In the problem task water is not actually poured from jar to
jar, because of the mess. Instead, students are instructed to pretend that
they are pouring. Thus, students are usually given the problems in word
form and are asked for a verbal solution.

Examples of the jar problems are show in Table 5-I. The first three
can be solved in only one way, and in the same way for all three problems. The largest Jar, B, must be filled, then poured once into Jar A and
twice into Jar C to obtain the required amount, D. The equation is:

$$D = B - A - 2C$$ (Equation 1)

The next three problems (4, 5, & 6) are examples of test problems. The first two test problems can be solved either by Equation 1 or by a simpler equation:

$$D = A - C \qquad \text{(Equation 2)}$$

The last problem (see Table 5-I) is an example of test problems that can be solved only by Equation 2. After solving the first three problems, subjects who use Equation 1 to solve the test problems are exhibiting cognitive set. The reason is presumably that this mode of performing is economical. It requires a minimum of mental effort to apply old solutions to new problems, in contrast to using the new equation. Despite the efficiency of this mode, the teacher's role is to take the student beyond the level of the learning set and to encourage the use of a newer mode of solution which should be more generally useful in problem solving. For example, if the teacher is teaching the use of equations and would like a pupil to **discover** their usefulness rather than being instructed about it, one could present problems like the Luchin's jars training problems. The student should soon discover the easier equation and, with suitable encouragement, he will verbalize it. The materials should be arranged so that first one equation works, then a different equation is required, then another is required. This process should continue until the student learns a very general cognitive set: equations are generally useful, but no one equation will always work (Reese, 1976).

Table 5-I

EXAMPLES OF LUCHIN'S JAR PROBLEMS

| | Capacity | | | Amount Required |
Problem	Jar A	Jar B	Jar C	(D)
1	14	163	25	99
2	18	43	10	5
3	9	42	6	21
4	23	49	3	20
5	14	36	8	6
6	28	76	3	25

Adapted from Reese (1976, p. 154).

4. Presenting an optimal discrepancy. In order to encourage the student to adopt a problem-solving orientation, it is important to arrange the problem situation in such a way that the problem is within the scope of "performability" of the learner and one can solve it with reasonable effort. In other words, the problem is so designed that it is not too difficult and yet difficult enough to be challenging and motivating. Berlyne (1966) suggests a number of strategies for keeping alive the curiosity of the learner enough that the learner is motivated to inquire about the problem. Berlyne suggests using "surpriseness" by arranging problem solutions which contradict the expectations of the students. Berlyne also suggests setting up a problem with several different answers, thus elevating the element of uncertainty in the problem solver. The learner is encouraged to relieve his uncertainty by selecting one of the answers as probably being the best. Independently, or with the help of the teacher, the learner is encouraged through a guided discovery method to check whether the chosen solution will work.

In formulating the problem situations, Berlyne stresses the significance of maintaining optimal discrepancy between the learner's existing abilities and potential ability for solving the problem. If the discrepancy between the two is too much, the risk is that the problem solver may not persist and give up the pursuit. However, if the task is too easy, the learner may lose interest and give up the chase. Thus, Berlyne is interested, at all times, to employ problem solving as a means of keeping the student motivated. He suggests that students can be motivated to learn problem solving through apparent contradictions as in the famous paradox of Zeno where Achilles can never catch the tortoise. (Achilles runs ten times as fast as the tortoise, and the tortoise goes ten feet while Achilles runs one hundred feet. If Achilles is one foot behind the tortoise, the tortoise covers one-tenth of a foot where Achilles covers no less than a foot. When Achilles covers that critical one-tenth of a foot, the tortoise is still one-hundredth of a foot ahead.)

5. Determining the scope of the learner's performability. The notion of optimal discrepancy when interpreted in the framework of information-processing theory implies that the learner will make little effort to process information unless there is already some suggestion that the quality of information processing necessary is within the learner's scope of performability. If there is too much doubt in the learner's mind about the capacity for effective information processing, the learner is not likely to even start on the information-processing task. On the other hand, some stimulation of doubt is motivating to the information-processing system. Doubt is relieved as the accumulation of successful information-processing instances convinces the learner that the task can be performed with a relatively small amount of processing effort. In this way, information processing becomes intrisically reinforcing to the student.

Teachers should note that if there is too much discrepancy between the learners' perception of the task difficulty and their assessment of their information-processing capacities, it may generate significant state-anxiety and affect problem-solving performance adversely. The disruptive effect of state-anxiety may occur at one of two levels: It may interfere with the operation of the conceptual system itself and may cause interference with the child's application of a particular set of problem-solving rules and strategies that the child had learned earlier. At a more basic level, it may interfere with the use of subprocesses (perception and memory) that support conceptual processes. Teachers should be alert to the fact that state-anxiety attenuates memory (Mueller, 1976; Sarason, 1972) and disrupts attention (Nottelmann & Hill, 1977), especially in problem-solving and information-processing tasks that have high memory demands (i.e. tasks requiring recall of factual information, and tasks requiring the information processor to keep touch of feedback information provided on a series of trials).

Monitoring Children's Affective States and Cognitive Styles

Teachers will no doubt discern the value of monitoring individual differences in children's anxiety states and how these might affect their performance in problem solving. The teacher's accurate manipulation of the child's "optimal discrepancy" critically influences the child's motivation and the child's persistence in problem-solving tasks.

Attentive teachers will easily discern that their high anxious students may fail to encode sufficient amounts of information about potential problem solutions and, consequently, are forced to rely upon less efficient solution strategies. High-anxious students, notwithstanding their competence in cognitive strategies for problem solving, may focus on one salient solution and may be unable to generate alternate hypotheses for problem solution. Similarly, they may be unable to profit from teacher feedback because of their high-tension state.

Considering the stress that many children feel within the home and school (see Fry & Grover, 1982), teachers would be well-advised to monitor closely the problem-solving performance of students with high-anxiety states and traits. In the event of complex problem-solving tasks by high-anxious students, it is suggested that reducing memory requirements (by providing memory aids such as open-book tests, accessibility to formulas and calculators) results in a reinstatement of more efficient problem-solving strategies (Gross & Mastenbrook, 1980).

Among the cognitive variables to be considered by the teacher, cognitive-style factors are recognized to be most important and relevant to problem solving. Considerable and specific attention is now being paid to the development of cognitive strategies consistent with the cognitive style of the learner. Two cognitive-style factors that have been implicated in children's performance in a variety of Piagetian and other information-processing tasks are reflexivity-impulsivity and field-dependence — field-independence. These cognitive-style factors are presumed to influence the type of perceptual processing that children use in task performance (Zelniker, Renan, Sorer, & Shavit, 1977). For example, reflectives may be impeded in a task that requires quick reactions and impromptu responses. Children who are reflective generally take more time in problem solving but will make fewer errors than impulsive children.

The teacher's objective in assessing impulsivity in children may be to formulate a cognitive strategy which counteracts the predisposing tendency of the impulsive child to scan the field as a whole rather than focus on parts of the stimulus field. If required to engage in complex problem-solving tasks, impulsive children may need training, for example, in the use of constraint-seeking strategies which require them to focus on a specific dimension. By contrast, cognitive strategies that train children to generate a number of hypotheses would be more useful for reflective children in order to help them counteract their predisposing tendency to focus on small parts of the stimulus field.

Knowledge of children's trait and state characteristics suggests that poor performance of young children in problem-solving tasks is not entirely due to lack of intellectual ability, but results often from the child's inability to modify cognitive-style patterns and deficits resulting from these which may interfere with a child's use of a particular strategy. In attempts to train children to develop more effective solution strategies, the teacher's function becomes twofold: (1) to teach children strategies, sets of rules and logical procedures that have particular relevance to problem solution; and (2) to teach strategies that enable children to overcome some of the deficits in their natural style of problem solving. As mentioned previously, these deficits may be inherent in their cognitive style and as a result interfere with the operation of the major conceptual system or the subprocesses of perception, memory and attention which support the conceptual processes. In either event, the child's problem-solving performance will continue to be adversely affected till such time as the teacher trains the child in the use of a specific cognitive strategy to counteract the negative predisposing tendency. Meichen-baum and Goodman (1969, 1971, 1975) have devised cognitive training procedures for use with impulsive children. These are discussed else-where in this chapter and in the chapter on metacognition (see Chap. 6).

Specific training in strategies to solve particular types of problems and structure children's interaction with the stimulus field are areas in which very little work has been done thus far. Such an oversight is parti-cularly curious, given intuitive and empirical evidence that children have little or no knowledge about rule-setting, hypothesis-seeking or dimension-checking strategies, and are therefore especially in need of techniques or mechanisms that will help them to acquire this knowledge. Efforts to remediate subprocessing deficiencies in young children also promote better rule use in strategy training.

General Problem-Solving Strategies for the Classroom

In addition to training children for specific cognitive strategies in problem-solving tasks, teachers need to teach them various other strate-gies that apply to problems in general. As students encounter different types of problems, they will spontaneously use certain strategies and processes they will have learned from prior knowledge and experience of solving problems. Certain teaching styles, if adopted by teachers, can also help to shape the problem-solving responses of their students. A few examples follow.

Teaching about expected results. For example, if the problem has to do with baking a cake, in order to be sure that a solution will be reached the students must have a clear concept of the desired result, i.e. they must know what are some of the distinguishing characteristics of a good cake. Subsequently, the students must identify knowledge, pro-cesses and procedures available to approach the problem.

Teaching requisite behaviors. In order to ensure that students will solve a given class of problems, it is important that students be taught behaviors or skills that are a requisite or prerequisite to problem solving. If the younger students do not already have some of the prerequisite level of cognitive skills to use a strategy effectively, then they may re-quire more extensive pretraining for the skill. For example, in order to perform a particular dance step, the learner may require a specific mo-tor coordination. Some younger students may therefore need more ex-tensive support by way of modeling and rehearsal in order to acquire the motor coordination necessary to perform the dance step. Strategies of modeling and direct instruction relevant to teaching requisite behaviors are discussed elsewhere in the chapter.

Working backwards. In order to reinforce problem-solving processes, teachers may often teach learners the process of beginning at a solution (by having learners state what they think the solution is) and then working back to the beginning. If the problem is to identify the number of odd-even numbers in a series, then the students can work their way back to the beginning (e.g. 39. . .9, 7, 5, 3, 1).

Substitutions. In some kinds of problem-solving tasks, teachers can encourage children to create their own practice exercises through substitution of numbers, words or phrases.

Use syllogisms to clarify the problem-solving process. Teachers can teach the process of using syllogisms to form chains of ideas from known facts to solutions. For example, "A soap film takes on a shape of minimum surface area." "The shape with the smallest surface area, enclosing a given volume, is the sphere." Hence, a soap bubble floating in the air, containing a fixed volume of air, has the shape of a sphere. (Soap films can be used to illustrate the solutions to many more complicated minimum-area problems.)

Another example of a syllogism useful in geometry is as follows: "If alternate interior angles are equal, then the lines are parallel," and "If lines are parallel then they do not meet." Therefore, if alternate interior angles are equal, the lines do not meet.

Restructuring the problem situation. Problems are often unsolvable to the student because of the teacher's inability to restructure the problem situation and present it to the student from a different perspective. It is hoped that if the problem is restructured, the problem elements will be perceived in a new and constructive light. One good example of restructuring has to do with the manner in which a problem is stated. Simple problems may turn out to be quite difficult for the student if they are posed ambiguously. For example, consider the following problem: How can a person build a house so that it has a southern exposure on all four sides? When stated in this form the problem has no solution, yet it may be made far simpler if restated with an emphasis on **where** one might build such a house (answer: at the North Pole) (Manis, 1966).

Problems can also be restructured by varying the order in which the problem elements are considered. For example, consider the following problem in which students are asked to pick out the one word that is unrelated to the other three: "subtract," "increase," "multiply," and "add."

This is an ambiguous item. From one perspective students might feel that "increase" is an unrelated word, since the other three words refer to some arithmetic operation. Judson and Cofer (1956) noted that ambiguous items of this sort were affected by the order in which the teacher presented the words. If the the words were presented in the sequence "multiply," "increase," "add" and "subtract," some students might feel that "subtract" is the unrelated word since each of the earlier words in the sequence implies increasing magnitude. Thus, teachers must be familiar with the students' interests and deliberations in order to restructure problem situations in such a way as to lead them to an accurate solution.

What are colloquially referred to as "hints" often provide another means for restructuring a problem situation. In a class of young children, teachers might very well hint at a particular object which is related to this problem solution. For example, "What is the purpose of these ropes hanging from the wall? Can these possibly be of help in solving the problem?"

Desensitizing children to their fears concerning errors or mistakes in problem-solving responses. Considering the stress that many children feel resulting from giving "wrong" answers, teachers can help to alleviate children's fears about giving wrong answers by suggesting that **no** answers are wrong. To illustrate the point, teachers should consider the attitudes of a well-known mathematics educator who adopted the position that there are **no** wrong answers, only correct answers to the wrong question. When a student gives an answer that does not fit a question, he or she is helped to formulate a question for which a given answer is correct. In this way the student is helped to see that the correct answer fits the second question and not the first. Thus, the student is persuaded to alter his hypothesis and solution to the problem.

In summary, teachers **teach** their students problem solving **by posing problems** and students **learn by solving problems.** The teacher's role is to present stimulating problems. The student's function is to discover the **combination** or **synthesis** of concepts or behaviors necessary to solve the problem. This "putting together" of old processes and concepts in a new way is closely related to the notion of insight in problem solving.

Attempts at problem solving are often unsuccessful because of the young learner's tendency to become fixated on some incorrect solution or approach. This is attributable to the fact that various problem elements may be perceived in a rigid manner quite ineffective for the problem at hand. This type of fixation can be overcome when the young learner is encouraged to approach a problem from a "discovery approach" rather than a rule-system approach.

Guidance and discovery in problem solving. This particular approach to problem solving stresses the importance of the teacher providing the learner with opportunity for discovery and self-direction. As an illustration of discovery learning, the learner is provided a series of example problem exercises and asked to discover and abstract the principle underlying the solutions. Alternatively, the learner is given a principle and asked to apply it to a number of problem exercises.

For example, in teaching the concept of "sonnet," the teacher might require the learner to identify the specific characteristics of a sonnet by giving a set of guidelines about rhyme schemes, number of lines, etc., and having the student apply the guidelines to a given series of sonnets. As another example, the teacher may want the student to discover what a "balanced meal" is by giving him a large variety of foods to select from, and also a set of rules or guidelines for a balanced meal, and ask the student to create his own balanced meal by checking it against the guidelines. This problem approach is likely to be more stimulating and challenging for the average student than would be the other approach of giving the student a number of examples and nonexamples of a balanced meal. The success of these approaches is contingent upon the degree of guidance and feedback provided by the teacher. The guided-discovery sequence is tried, revised and tried out again several times until it is so organized in the student's mind that he or she easily recognizes the sequential relationship and the guiding principles. Eventually, the student acquires competence in coding principles from given examples, and decoding examples from given principles.

The guided-discovery approach to problem solving has been the subject of debate for three or more decades. The significant question is whether the learning process is more stimulating and whether the learner retains for a longer period if given guidance or allowed to discover the problem solution for himself. The research evidence shows that a combination of guidance and discovery is the most effective approach to problem solving, but the degree of guidance necessary and the degree of discovery that should be reinforced is still a matter of considerable debate among educators. The success of the guided and discovery approaches is contingent upon the cognitive development stage of the learner, and the degree of interaction that is possible between the student and the teacher in reaching problem-solving solutions.

Summary

This chapter has discussed the Piagetian and information-processing approach to problem solving. Piaget's views of cognitive development have led to a consideration of a different set of issues and questions about problem solving than those studied in the information-processing model. Regardless of their particular theoretical orientation, teachers responsible for children's problem solving recognize the merit of Piaget's observation of how children use a variety of logical rules on problem-solving tasks. Looked at from a Piagetian perspective, children perform a variety of intellectual tasks (solve problems, discover concepts, classify and categorize) by attempting to understand the various properties of objects and relationships that hold between them. This ability to understand relationships and eventually to manipulate them develops through the attainment of operational structures. It presupposes the operationalization of thought at various levels of reasoning: preoperational, concrete operational and formal operational. Piaget's belief is that the most compelling evidence for cognitive development stages is in their invariant sequencing. All children develop through each of the stages in an orderly fashion. Because similar sets of operations are believed to underlie the various cognitive developmental stages, teachers can anticipate in children a synchronous evolution of problem-solving ability at each stage of thought. Because stages and their logical structures are dependent upon active assimilation and accommodation, the teacher's role in enlarging the problem-solving capacities of children lies in providing increasing opportunity for assimilation and accommodation and for gradual consolidation of experiences. Experimental research in this area has demonstrated that teacher-designed cognitive training programs and children's involvement in problem-solving tasks can effectively produce change in children's understanding of a variety of concepts leading to competence in problem solutions.

The information-processing model of problem solving, on the other hand, is more concerned with specifying rules and systematic processes associated with attaining problem solutions. The teacher's role in the educational process is to specify the problem-solving activity and problem-solving sequences in such a precise manner that the student will not only understand the specifics of the performance on particular tasks but will piece these specifics together to form an integrated understanding of how the problem can be solved.

Furthermore, specific cognitive strategies and training programs can be developed by teachers that would facilitate children's problem solving. Cognitive training programs for problem solving and strategies have been developed that can help children to modify natural cognitive styles which conflict with the requirements of the problem tasks. It is presumed by information-processing theorists that the poor performance of children on problem-solving tasks is not entirely due to a lack of ability (competence) but also results from lack of precise rules and cognitive strategies in their repertoire.

One implication of the foregoing discussion is that the student's ability to benefit from training in problem solving may depend on the student's achieving the prerequisite level of perceptual, mnemonic and cognitive skills necessary to the basic problem-solving process. The effectiveness of stimulus pretraining in inducing better problem solving in children seems marginal at best. However, some kind of pretraining involving familiarization with the materials to be used in task performance may be helpful in inducing children to generate a few simple hypotheses spontaneously.

One of the main contributions of the information-processing approach has been a production of the rule systems that are involved in effective task performance. Teachers and educators can help children working with specific kinds of problems to identify rule systems that govern their performance. These rule systems can be translated into more elaborate computer programs that simulate the performance of children on problem-solving tasks.

REFERENCES

Antell, S. E., & Keating, D. P. (1983). Perception of numerical invariance in neonates. *Child Development, 54,* 695-701.

Anthony, B., & Hudgins, B. B. (1978). Problem-solving processes of fifth-grade arithmetic pupils. *Journal of Educational Research, 72,* 63-67,

Berlyne, D. E. (1966). Notes on intrinsic motivation and intrinsic rewards in relation to instruction. In J. Bruner (Ed.), *Learning about learning: A conference report* (pp. 33-39). Washington, DC: U.S. Department of Health, Education and Welfare.

Breslow, L. (1981). Reevaluation of the literature on the development of transitive inferences. *Psychological Bulletin, 89,* 325-351.

Brown, A. L., & Campione, J. C. (1977). Training strategic study time apportionment in educable-retarded children. *Intelligence, 1,* 94-107.

Bruner, J. S., Goodnow, J. J., & Austin, G. A. (1956). *A study of thinking.* New York: Wiley.

Bryant, P. E., & Trabasso, T. (1971). Transitive inferences and memory in young children. *Nature, 232,* 456-458.

Danner, F. W., & Day, M. C. (1977). Eliciting formal operations. *Child Development, 48,* 1600-1606.

Denney, N. W., & Turner, M. C. (1979). Facilitating cognitive performance in children: A comparison of strategy modeling and strategy modeling with overt-self-verbalization. *Journal of Experimental Child Psychology, 28,* 119-131.

Feigenbaum, E. A. (1961). The simulation of verbal learning behavior. *Proceedings of the Western Joint Computer Conference, 19,* 121-132.

Fischer, K. W. (1980). A theory of cognitive development: The control and construction of hierarchies of skills. *Psychological Review, 87,* 477-533.

Fry, P. S., & Grover, S. C. (1982). The relationship between father absence and children's social problem solving competencies. *Journal of Applied Developmental Psychology, 3,* 105-120.

Gelman, R., & Gallistel, C. R. (1978). *The young child's understanding of number: A window on early cognitive development.* Cambridge, MA: Harvard University Press.

Gholson, B., Levine, M., & Phillips, S. (1972). Hypotheses, strategies, and stereotypes in discrimination learning. *Journal of Experimental Child Psychology, 13,* 423-446.

Gross, T. F., & Mastenbrook, M. (1980). Examination of the effects of state anxiety on problem-solving efficiency under high and low memory conditions. *Journal of Educational Psychology, 72,* 605-609.

Hooper, F. H., Toniolo, T. A., & Sipple, T. S. (1978). A longitudinal analysis of logical reasoning relationships: Conservation and transitive inference. *Developmental Psychology, 14,* 674-682.

Judson, A. I., & Cofer, C. N. (1956). Reasoning as an associative process: 1. "Direction" in a simple verbal problem. *Psychological Reports, 2,* 469-476.

Kail, R., & Bisanz, J. (1982). Information processing and cognitive development. In H. W. Reese (Ed.), *Advances in child development and behavior, Vol. 17.* New York: Academic Press.

Klahr, D. (1980). Information-processing models of intellectual development. In R. H. Kluwe & H. Spada (Eds.), *Developmental models of thinking.* New York: Academic Press.

Klahr, D., & Wallace, J. G. (1973). The role of quantification operators in the development of conservation of quantity. *Cognitive Psychology, 4,* 301-327.

Klahr, D., & Wallace, J. G. (1976). *Cognitive development: An information processing view.* Hillsdale, NJ: Erlbaum.

Lawton, J. T., & Hooper, F. H. (1978). Piagetian theory and early childhood education: A critical analysis. In L. S. Siegel & C. J. Brainerd (Eds.), *Alternatives to Piaget: Critical essays on the theory* (pp. 169-199). New York: Academic Press.

Levine, M. (1966). Hypothesis behavior by humans during discrimination learning. *Journal of Experimental Psychology, 71,* 331-336.

Manis, M. (1966). *Cognitive processes.* Belmont, CA: Wadsworth Publishing Co.

Markman, E. M. (1978). Empirical vs. logical solutions to part-whole comparison problems concerning classes and collections. *Child Development, 49,* 168-177.

Martorano, S. C. (1977). A developmental analysis of performance on Piaget's formal operational tasks. *Developmental Psychology, 13,* 666-672.

Meichenbaum, D., & Goodman, J. (1969). Reflection-impulsivity and verbal control of motor behavior. *Child Development, 40,* 785-797.

Meichenbaum, D., & Goodman, J. (1971). Training impulsive children to talk to themselves: A means of developing self-control. *Journal of Abnormal Psychology, 77,* 115-126.

Meichenbaum, D., & Goodman, J. (1975). The nature and modification of impulsivity. Paper presented at the first international congress of child neurology. Toronto, Ontario.

Meyers, J., & Martin, R. (1974). Relationships of state and trait anxiety to concept-learning performance. *Journal of Educational Psychology, 66,* 33-39.

Mueller, J. H. (1976). Anxiety and cue utilization in human learning and memory. In M. Zuckerman & C. D. Spielberger (Eds.), *Emotions and anxiety: New concepts, methods, and application* (pp. 197-229). Hillsdale, NJ: Erlbaum.

Neimark, E. D. (1975). Intellectual development during adolescence. In F. D. Horowitz (Ed.), *Review of child development research,* Vol. 4. Chicago: University of Chicago Press.

Newell, A., & Simon, H. A. (1972). *Human problem solving.* Englewood Cliffs, NJ: Prentice-Hall.

Nottelmann, E. D., & Hill, K. T. (1977). Text anxiety and off-task behavior in evaluative situations. *Child Development, 48,* 225-231.

Ornstein, P. A. (1977). Memory development in children. In R. Liebert, R. Poulos, & G. Mormor (Eds.), *Developmental Psychology* (2nd ed.). Englewood Cliffs, NJ: Prentice-Hall.

Pascual-Leone, J. (1980). Constructive problems for constructive theories: The current relevance of Piaget's work and a critique of information-processing simulation psychology. In R. H. Kluwe & H. Spada (Eds.), *Developmental models of thinking* (pp. 263-296). New York: Academic Press.

Phillips, S., & Levine, M. (1975). Probing for hypotheses with adults and children: Blank trials and introtracts. *Journal of Experimental Psychology: General, 104,* 327-354.

Pinard, A., & Laurendeau, M. (1969). "Stage" in Piaget's cognitive developmental theory: Exegesis of a concept. In D. Elkind & J. H. Flavell (Eds.), *Studies in cognitive development* (pp. 121-170). New York: Oxford University Press.

Reese, H. W. (1976). *Basic learning processes in childhood.* New York: Holt, Rinehart & Winston.

Riley, C. A., & Trabasso, T. (1974). Comparatives, logical structures and encoding in a transitive inference task. *Journal of Experimental Child Psychology, 17,* 187-203.

Sarason, I. G. (1972). Experimental approaches to test anxiety: Attention and the uses of information. In C. D. Spielberger (Ed.), *Anxiety: Current trends in theory and research* Vol. II (pp. 363-403). New York: Academic Press.

Siegler, R. S. (1981). Developmental sequences within and between concepts. *Monographs of the Society for Research in Child Development, 46,* (2, Serial No. 189).

Siegler, R. S., & Vago, S. (1978). The development of a proportionality concept: Judging relative fullness. *Journal of Experimental Child Psychology, 25,* 371-395.

Stone, C. A., & Day, M. C. (1978). Levels of availability of a formal operational strategy. *Child Development, 49,* 1054-1065.

Sugarman, S. (1981). The cognitive basis of classification in very young children: An analysis of object ordering trends. *Child Development, 52,* 1172-1178.

Weithorn, L. A., & Campbell, J. B. (1982). The competency of children and adolescents to make informed treatment decisions. *Child Development, 53,* 1589-1598.

Zelniker, T., Renan, A., Sorer, I., & Shavit, Y. (1977). Effect of perceptual processing strategies on problem solving of reflective and impulsive children. *Child Development, 48,* 1436-1442.

CHAPTER SIX

METACOGNITION

A LTHOUGH the term "metacognition" is relatively new to the general literature, the roots of this concept have been traced back to the beginning of this century. Cavanaugh and Perlmutter (1982), for example, refer to Baldwin's (1909) work using introspective question-naires to examine the study strategies of upper-level school-age children as an early precursor to today's emphasis upon a person's self-knowledge of thinking processes and performance outcomes. While several other early century theorists and researchers can be cited in this same vein (James, 1890; Kuhlmann, 1907; Huey, 1908; Thorndike, 1919), it is of considerable interest to note that these ideas have been essentially bur-ied for the greater part of the century.

Their recent reemergence has been attributed largely to the develop-ment of information-processing models of memory and new theories of cognitive development over the last decade and a half (Cavanaugh & Perlmutter, 1982). As memory models such as the levels-of-processing model (Craik & Lockhart, 1972) began to emphasize qualitative as op-posed to quantitative characteristics, interest shifted to the process and strategic aspects of information processing. At first, the work centered upon adult subjects, although developmental psychologists were very quick to recognize the potential of this approach for the study of young children (Brown, 1975). Such studies rapidly began to dominate the de-velopmental, psychological and educational literature, with a number of important features being incorporated into research investigations. What were these features which marked the foundation for the present-day concept of metacognition?

Most notable was the fact that this new emphasis on information processing began to broaden from the specific study of memory to many other learning-related areas such as attention, comprehension monitoring, studying, language, and social cognition. Along with this, children of varying ages and ability levels were examined. New experimental formats were implemented ranging from interviewing young children (Kreutzer, Leonard, & Flavell, 1975) to the training and generalization of strategies to improve performance (Belmont & Butterfield, 1977; Brown, Campione & Day, 1981). Emphasis further shifted away from the experimental laboratory to more naturalistic settings, and the recognized importance of both formal learning contexts and real-life contexts was acknowledged as centrally relevant to cognitive developmental issues.

All of these factors and resulting research findings led to the established conclusion that young children are markedly different from adults in the way that they take in information, retain and retrieve material to be learned. And, accordingly, as we have noted in the previous chapter, these recent studies have provided valuable insight as to the nature and type of qualitative changes that occur over the years, with the maturing child's task performance becoming increasingly more like that of an adult.

Probably the most important question to emerge from this work with respect to the present-day understanding of the concepts of metacognition and cognition is that concerning the mechanisms which promote these changes. Early explorations of this question have pointed to the importance of one's own understanding and knowledge of cognitive processes, and later how one's active control of these can affect task performance and outcomes. To date, there have been several views and definitions of cognition and metacognition advanced in the literature (Brown, 1975, 1977, 1978a, 1978b, 1980; Kail, 1979; Flavell, 1978, 1979, 1981; Flavell & Wellman, 1977; Forrest-Pressley & Waller, 1984; Baker & Brown, 1984; Forrest-Pressley, MacKinnon & Waller, 1985), and the major distinctions are apparent in the following definitions:

Cognition refers to the actual knowledge, goals, experiences and strategies that are utilized by the individual to further the acquisition of knowledge.

Metacognition refers to (1) the person's conscious knowledge about his or her cognitions and (2) the person's conscious control of these cognitions to assess and further cognition (Lupart, 1984).

Although many theorists and researchers have actively contributed to our current understanding of metacognition and the relationship to cognition and learning, it is the work of John Flavell and Ann Brown and their associates that has been most comprehensive and significant to this end. The following sections will provide a brief overview of their major contributions in this area.

Flavell

Since the mid-1970s Flavell and his associates have been actively researching, developing, and expanding the work on memory development and metamemory to the more general understanding of metacognition.

The first major study in this area was carried out by Kreutzer, Leonard and Flavell (1975). Kindergarteners, first, third, and fifth graders were all part of an intensive interview study to explore how able young children are at understanding their own memory systems. The collective findings revealed that signs of early developing awareness are apparent even at the kindergarten and grade one level. For instance, children at this age demonstrate the realization that more study time facilitates recall for a set of items, and they exhibit an ability to rely upon external resources such as peers or adults, external symbolic aids and external physical nonsymbolic aids to facilitate future retrieval.

Children in grades three through five appear to know the same things about memory as younger children, except they appear to know these things better. Moreover, these children have a better understanding that memory performance varies over occasions, types of data, and individuals and can better understand that the utilization of existing relations among test items can facilitate retrieval.

Kreutzer, Leonard, and Flavell (1975) also noted results suggesting awareness of how task variables can affect memory performance. Children as young as kindergarten age knew that individual test items previously learned would be easier to recall than unfamiliar items. Similarly, these children knew that task difficulty is a function of the number of the items to be remembered. However, only the older grade five subjects appeared to realize that retroactive interference (i.e. an imposed irrelevant activity) would effect retrieval.

On the basis of this and other related work, Flavell and Wellman (1977) have devised a classification system for metamemory development in children. It may be briefly summarized as follows:

Sensitivity — The child learns to identify which situations do and which do not call for intentional memory-related behavior.

Variables — The child develops intuitions about the variables which influence memory performance, as:

Person — performance-relevant characteristics of the information processor

Task — performance-relevant characteristics of the memory task or problem

Strategy — potential solution strategies (Flavell, 1978, p. 214)

Although the above components are specifically described in the context of metamemory development, these have subsequently become collectively known as components of metacognitive knowledge (Flavell, 1981).

The first component, sensitivity, has been a particularly useful concept, not only for the advancement of our understanding of this important aspect of children learning, but also for the reinterpretation of previous research results. For example, early studies have been carried out in an attempt to test or to clarify what Appel et al. (1972) called the "differentiation hypothesis." Essentially, this refers to the consistent observation that when young children are instructed to remember specific items or information because they will later be tested, they do not recognize this as an important cue for active or strategic memorizing. Studies to date have not confirmed that there exists, for any memory task situation, a point in the child's development when the child becomes clearly aware of this implication. Perhaps such a developmental point does not exist (Yussen, 1975).

Nevertheless, what is apparent is that as children increase their experiential and knowledge base, they begin to exhibit greater sensitivity to what Craik and Lockhart (1972) and Anderson and Armbruster (1980) suggest is cognitive processing which is appropriate in kind and depth to a variety of cognitive tasks. In other words, the child becomes increasingly able to flexibly control the ongoing cognitive processing to suit the self-determined requirements of the immediate task situation.

The second component of metacognitive knowledge—person variables—consists of the learner's sensitivity to intra-individual differences (e.g. I can remember more if I write down main points, rather than just repeat the main points as I read), interindividual differences (e.g. Some people may learn more through reading and notetaking rather than just reading) and universals. Universals refer to commonly held viewpoints, for example, by a community of readers. The belief that there are various kinds of understandings and that these kinds of understandings are interchangeably employed as a function of the purpose for reading is a commonly held view. Essentially, then, such intuitions assist in defining the reader's concept of him or herself as a reader.

According to Flavell (1981), the task variables, the third component of metacognitive knowledge, are concerned with the nature of the information in the cognitive activity (familiar, unfamiliar, well organized, poorly organized, presented under distracting conditions or not, etc.) and knowledge of task demands. Through knowledge of task demands, the learners become aware that they may process information differently depending upon the criterial task or response to text required.

The final component, strategy variables, refers to one's stored knowledge about the nature and utility of certain strategies which can be relied upon and utilized to interpret and understand a problem or learning activity.

More recently, Flavell (1979, 1981) has developed a global model of cognitive monitoring which includes four interrelated aspects: (a) metacognitive knowledge, (b) metacognitive experiences, (c) goal, and (d) actions.

The first component, metacognitive knowledge, essentially remains consistent with that described earlier (Flavell & Wellman, 1977), and therefore only the remaining three aspects and their interrelationships need be presented.

Metacognitive Experiences

This second aspect of the monitoring process, metacognitive experience, refers to the learner's conscious cognitive or affective experience (Flavell, 1981). Metacognitive experiences can have very important effects on the first component, metacognitive knowledge.

Metacognitive experiences and metacognitive knowledge are related to the extent that metacognitive experiences can develop and modify metacognitive knowledge. Experiences such as feelings of puzzlement or failure can lead to a change in cognitive goals and, as Flavell (1981) purports, a change in the nature of cognitive and metacognitive strategic intervention. For example, a reader may sense (metacognitive experience) that he does not understand a particular section in the text well enough to pass a subsequent examination. Consequently, the reader reads the selection through once more. This is an example of a cognitive strategy (cognitive action) aimed at the cognitive goal of **improving** knowledge. In this case, the reader is internalizing information from the text.

An example of metacognitive strategy aimed at the metacognitive goal of **assessing** knowledge and generating another metacognitive experience is illustrated in the following: A reader may wonder (metacognitive experience) if he understands a section of text well enough to pass an examination. To reduce the bewilderment, the reader decides to ask himself some questions (metacognitive strategy) and checks how well he answers them (metacognitive experience).

Essentially, the use of metacognitive strategies to assess knowledge leads to metacognitive goals and experiences, while the use of cognitive strategies to improve his knowledge leads to cognitive goals and experiences.

Goals

The third component of Flavell's (1981) framework of cognitive monitoring, cognitive goals, is the explicit or implicit objectives that instigate and maintain the cognitive enterprise. In a reading situation, particularly in a study situation, these goals comprise both the aim and purpose of the encounter and tend to be operationalized as a criterial task (Brown, Campione & Day, 1981; Rosenblatt, 1978). However, these goals will likely be less clearly defined if the reading situation is principally an aesthetic encounter, in which case the reader would be reading for pleasure or for pure enjoyment.

A further important factor to note here concerns the difficulty researchers may have in assessing how the learner views the learning goals or criterial tasks. One cannot assume that the purpose imposed by the researcher (or teacher) is synonymous with the purpose or purposes selected by the learner. Furthermore the learner's purpose for engaging in the cognitive activity may change throughout the duration of the activity. For example, comprehension failure occurring at different levels (word, sentence, intrasentence and passage) and the reader's sensitivity to factors which may contribute to comprehension failure (insufficient availability of prior knowledge and text ambiguity) may influence how a reader monitors his/her understanding of the text (Collins & Smith, 1980).

Actions

The final aspect of Flavell's model of cognitive monitoring, actions or strategies, is utilized to further and assess cognitive progress.

If the actions are used in the service of monitoring progress, they are viewed as metacognitive strategies, yielding metacognitive experiences and at times cognitive outcomes. However, if the actions are used to further cognitive progress, they are referred to as cognitive strategies and will yield cognitive outcomes as well as metacognitive experiences.

Several examples of such cognitive and metacognitive strategies have been reported in the recent literature. These include such activities as rereading (Garner & Reis, 1981), use of lookback (Alessi, Anderson & Goetz, 1979), looking forward to see if information will be consistent with or can be predicted by present understanding (Markman, 1981), formation of a pending question (Collins, Brown & Larkin, 1980), referring to an expert source (Collins & Smith, 1980), mapping (Geva, 1981) and note taking (Orlando, 1980). It is important to note that these actions are global procedures the learner may undertake to assess and further comprehension, and that they can differ qualitatively in their function and content. How these procedures are applied in the service of comprehension depends on the reader's metacognitive knowledge, metacognitive experience and how the critical task is viewed (Brown, Campione & Day, 1981). A final important factor in this area is the extent to which these strategies and others are involved in self-initiated and spontaneous monitoring of cognitive activities.

In summary, Flavell has been the leading pioneer in our present-day understanding of metacognitive processes and in identifying the importance of this development in young children's thinking. We will now review some of the work of Ann Brown, who has also played a critical role in this area.

Brown

Brown's early work focused upon the memory development of the mentally retarded child. Following Flavell's lead, Brown (1974) was able to demonstrate that those factors which characterize inefficient memory performance (i.e. production deficiency, mediation deficiency, metamemory abilities) are applicable to both developmental and mental retardation fields of investigation. Her work (Brown, 1973; Brown, Campione, Bray & Wilcox, 1974; Brown, Campione & Murphy, 1974, 1977; Brown, 1974) supported the notion of production deficiency in terms of the lack of rehearsal strategy usage in educable mentally handicapped adolescents, as well as demonstrated the successful training and long-term retention of this strategy over a six-month period. As a result of these series of experiments, Brown and her coworkers concluded that the difference between retarded and intellectually average children in

immediate memory tasks was not in the structures of the memory system per se but rather in the tendency to adopt the active rehearsal strategy.

In many ways, Brown's early work represents the corner stone of
what is regarded as her unique contribution to the development of metacognition theory. Brown and her associates have been variously credited
with the examination of metacognitive principles in relation to interventive procedures, the continued interest in examining children of differing age and ability levels, and the examination of metacognitive
processes in natural and school-based learning contexts.

Brown (1978) and Baker and Brown (1984) describe metacognition
as consisting of two parts (a) one's knowledge and (b) one's control of the
domain cognition. The first part, one's knowledge of the domain cognition, includes those factors important to one's knowledge of one's own
cognitive resources. Within the learning context, this essentially refers
to the level of compatibility one experiences between oneself as a learner
and the learning situation.

For example, we have no doubt all experienced the sense of frustration at being required to solve a difficult or complex problem in an area
we consider ourselves to be weak and/or have no interest or motivation
to carry through. We can talk about those aspects of the task that make it
difficult for us, such as the material being unfamiliar or too disor-
ganized. No doubt, too, we have all felt the surprise that results in certain situations when we are able to accomplish a perceived difficult task
with relative ease. Indeed, our initial apprehension for certain tasks
perhaps stems from a personal history of past failure in an area such as
math, mechanics or physics. In addition, most adults can quite readily
describe their learning strengths and weaknesses for a given area of
study. These examples include the three characteristics that Baker and
Brown (1984) have used to describe knowledge about cognition: (1) it is
stateable, (2) it is fallable, and (3) it is relatively stable.

Brown's (1975) review and examination of this first aspect of metacognition in children further suggests that this knowledge is late developing. In other words, the ability to realize one's own cognitive
limitations or the complexities involved in any given task is not readily
apparent until the mid- or even upper-elementary age level (Markman,
1977). The learner must be aware of one's own failures within given
learning tasks before taking steps to initiate a corrective procedure.

The second part of Brown's (1978) concept of metacognition consists
of one's control of self-regulation over one's learning enterprises. This

component includes any or all of the planning, monitoring, and check-ing processes that an active learner engages in to ensure optimal task performance. As Brown, Bransford, Ferrara and Campione (1983) and others using an information-processing approach describe it, metacogni-tive control is the responsibility of the central executive, which evaluates and guides one's cognitive operations.

The characteristics that Baker and Brown (1984) ascribe to this as-pect of metacognition are that: (1) it is not easily stated; (2) the control aspect is relatively unstable; and (3) the component is both task- and situation-dependent.

Brown and her associates have pioneered the work done in training children to utilize metacognitive control processes to improve task per-formance. Studies which have made the training goals clear to subjects and that have focused upon the task-general metacognitive skills have been successful, not only with young children, but with special learning needs children, as well. In addition, Brown and her colleagues have cen-tered their investigations in school-relevant areas such as study skills (Brown & Smiley, 1978), and reading comprehension (Palinscar & Brown, 1984).

Brown's emerging conceptualization of metacognition (Brown & French, 1979; Reeve & Brown, 1984) borrows in part from Vygotsky's (1963) theory of the zone of potential development. He notes that "We must determine at least two levels of a child's development, otherwise we fail to find the correct relation between the course of development and potentiality for learning in each specific case" (p. 28). At the first level, the zone of actual development represents those mental functions that have been attained due to a specific or already accomplished course of development. The second level, the zone of potential development, rep-resents a learning potentiality that may become actualized under the direction of adult guidance, demonstration or questioning. The basic thrust of Brown's current investigative approach to metacognition (Reeve & Brown, 1984) is captured in the following quote from Vy-gotsky (1963): "What the child can do today with adult help, he will be able to do independently tomorrow" (p. 20).

It is through the day-by-day interaction of children with adults in the social context that they begin to develop growing awareness of self-regulation of their own cognitions. At first, the child learns through con-scious other-regulation; for example, a parent's monitoring of a child's behavior on the playground, or a teacher's modeling of the correct solu-tion to a math problem. The child gradually begins to internalize this regulation process and assumes independent control over one's own cognition.

In summary of Brown's work in the area of metacognition, it is indeed apparent that her work in the training and self-regulation aspects of metacognition in average and special need students has important ramifications for teachers. As such, Brown's work will be referred to extensively in the applications segment of this chapter. The next section will briefly describe some of the current ways of studying metacognition.

How is Metacognition Studied?

Although the concept of metacognition, as it is presently developing, is a relatively new area of research investigation, a variety of methodological approaches have been implemented. These include ratings and predictions of understanding, measures of behavioral correlates, error-detection paradigms, and retrospective and introspective approaches. Each of these approaches will be described briefly with a relevant research example given.

Ratings and Prediction of Understanding

The rating of understanding paradigm involves the ability to predict accurately one's performance. By way of example, Flavell, Friedrichs and Hoyt (1976) found that nursery and kindergarten children tended to overestimate their recall ability, while Kreutzer, et al. (1975) found that young children had difficulty estimating the complexity of the tasks. These results evident in list learning tasks are also apparent in studies involving narrative text.

In a study by Brown and Smiley (1977), subjects ranging in age from 8 to 18 were asked to rate and recall selected folktales. Initially, the subjects listened to the story and read the stories simultaneously. One idea unit was presented per line. Following a second reading, the subjects were asked to rank the idea units into four groups, ranging from the least important to the most important. Comparisons with college student ratings (acquired in an earlier study) revealed a strong developmental trend (Brown & Smiley, 1977). While the 18-year-olds were able to distinguish all four levels of importance, the 12-year-old subjects demonstrated a great deal of difficulty differentiating the second and third levels. Furthermore, the 10-year-olds could only distinguish the highest level, and 8-year-old subjects were even less able to make distinctions. However, the insensitivity was not apparent in recall. A general pattern of results (level 4 > 3 > 2 > 1) was consistent across age levels.

Research of this type has suggested possible maturational and ability differences in children's ability to judge comprehension success. However, two limitations in using confidence rating techniques to assess children's metacognitive awareness must be noted. There is some evidence to suggest that young children tend to respond to questions affirmatively, regardless of the truth of the assertion (Brown & Lawton, 1977; Brown & Scott, 1971), and secondly, the learners' assessment of understanding or misunderstanding is typically made after, as opposed to during, a cognitive task.

Measures of Behavioral Correlates

Another source of information concerning children's developing metacognitive abilities is the measuring of visually identifiable behavioral correlates. A study which typifies this approach is reported by Patterson, Cosgrove and O'Brien (1980), who examined children in each of four age groups, 4, 6, 8, and 10 years, and presented them with oral messages differing in informational adequacy (information partially informative or uninformative). Although the nature of the criterial task was not clear, the children at each of the four ages differed markedly in their nonverbal behavior. Children at all ages showed more hand movement and longer reaction times when the messages were ambiguous. When coping with uninformative messages, four-year-olds made more eye contact with the speaker. However, body movement was unaffected. For six- and eight-year-olds, the reverse was true. In addition, the researchers found that when verbal responses were additionally requested, these responses were added to the established patterns of nonverbal behavior.

In summary, the above example study, as well as others in this line of research, give some clear evidence of nonverbal behavioral indicators of metacognitive monitoring. Along with the noted behaviors of look-backs, gestures, long reaction times, and different eye-contact patterns, the teacher could similarly explore long pauses, nods and frowns.

Error Detection Paradigm

In this experimental approach, errors or message inconsistencies are deliberately incorporated into the task and subject responses are examined to determine the effect upon the learner's processing and comprehension of the task. The particular advantage to the experimenter is in being able to control the task elements intended to confuse subjects and in consequently being able to examine the ways in which individuals monitor their comprehension. A classic investigation in the area is Markman's (1977) study.

Markman (1977) presented first, second and third grade students with instructions to complete a task. Some information was deliberately omitted; consequently, the criterial task could not be completed successfully. In the listening condition, all subjects required some probing before they noticed the inadequacy of the instructions. However, the extent of the probing differed for each grade group, with the third graders requiring the least probing, and the first and second grade subjects requiring the most. Interestingly, if demonstrations on the tasks accompanied the instructions, the children more readily indicated they had failed to understand. Markman (1977) suggests that this initial insensitivity to their own comprehension failure may be due to a lack of constructive processing. This would, of course, depend on the subject's perception of the criterial task. For instance, if the subjects based their understanding on the comprehension of the simpler structures that comprise the more higher-order structures, and if these simpler sentences contained the anomalies, then they would tend to overestimate how well they understood.

This was well exemplified in a later experiment in which third and sixth grade children were required to act as editors and listen to essays that contained both explicit and implicit contradictions (Markman, 1979). Although children were more likely to notice explicit than implicit contradictions, most of the children judged material as comprehensible even if the essays contained obvious inconsistencies. These findings suggest that children may tend to evaluate their performance in a piecemeal fashion, and focus on individual sentences as opposed to evaluating the higher-order relationships in text.

A number of studies of this type have been carried out in listening and reading contexts (Pace, 1979; Reis & Spekman, 1983; Garner, 1981) and the collective evidence has contributed to our knowledge of metacognition processing. It is apparent that learners can recognize errors in texts, for example; however this recognition is dependent upon maturational factors, reading competence and the reader's perception of the criterial task. However, Cavanaugh and Perlmutter (1982) and Winograd and Johnston (1980) have been critical of the design of error-detection paradigms and have recommended that these be used in combination with other approaches.

Retrospective Approaches

Numerous studies have utilized a post-task interview format in an attempt to assess the nature of the learner's metacognitive knowledge and their on-task regulation strategies. Questions, such as "Does the reason you are doing the task make a difference on performance?" or "What proportion of the story information can you remember?" or "What might you do differently on another trial of this task?" are typical of the kind that are used in this approach.

Forrest and Waller (1979, 1980) individually interviewed grade 3 and grade 6 children with a standard set of 13 questions about the reading skills of decoding, comprehension and advanced strategies. Analysis of performance indicated that knowledge in all areas assessed increased with grade level and reading ability. Of particular interest were the findings that young/poor readers gave little indication they understood how to monitor comprehension. Difficulty was evident in two areas: (1) ability to identify and select task performance clues which could be used as indicators to gauge test performance, and (2) remedial action that could be used to correct the situation.

In support, Myers and Paris (1978) found that eight-year-old poor readers were less aware of strategies that aid comprehension than their older counterparts. For instance, the older children appeared to know that the purpose for skimming was to pick out informative words. However, the younger children said they skimmed by reading the easy words.

In a subsequent study, Paris and Myers (1981), utilizing a similar post-reading interview procedure, instructed good and poor fourth grade readers to read and study a story so they could remember the information. Following the recall, the subjects were required to report on their reading activities. This consisted of rating the utility of 20 reading strategies on a nine-point scale. Analysis of the findings revealed that, compared to good readers, poor readers tended to give higher rankings to the strategies which had a detrimental influence on recall.

Studies of this type have been particularly useful in exploring the relationships between cognitive maturity, task proficiency and knowledge of factors and strategies related to monitoring of cognitive task performance. However, some critics (Nisbett & Winson, 1977; Cavanaugh & Perlmutter, 1982) have suggested that individuals may have little direct access to higher-order cognitive processes. Consequently, to use reading as an example, what readers say they do when they read and how they actually process print may be very different.

Furthermore, as noted by Hare and Pulliam (1980), good readers and certainly more mature readers may be more articulate and verbal than less mature and less proficient readers. This suggests that the apparent limited metacognitive functioning of the less proficient and mature readers may be more a reflection of their verbal ability than their metacognitive functioning. Essentially, the reader's verbalized metacognitive knowledge may be only partially related or may not be related at all to their personal metacognitive knowledge.

Introspective Approaches

The introspective approach is one which attempts to examine the metacognitive processing strategies during actual task performance. Subjects are typically given a problem to solve or a passage to read and are asked to "think aloud" as they perform the task.

A study by Olshavsky (1976-77) typifies the use of this paradigm. In an attempt to identify the type of strategies readers employ to comprehend an author's message, Olshavsky (1976-77) presented tenth grade good and poor readers with narrative passages. The subjects were required to think aloud each time the end of an independent clause was reached. This was signalled for them by a red dot. Subjects' comments were recorded, transcribed and analyzed, and Olshavsky was able to identify ten distinct types of strategies that subjects used to monitor their reading. For example, the two strategies related to monitoring of understanding included a statement of failure to understand a clause (recognition of comprehension failure) and a rereading strategy (remediation procedure). Although all the readers were found to use similar strategies, the more proficient readers used more strategies than the less proficient readers.

An interesting follow-up study by Olshavsky (1978) involved good and poor eleventh grade readers who were presented with narrative passages progressively increasing in difficulty. Contrary to expectations, the incidence of strategy usage decreased as the passages became more difficult. It is quite possible that when reading the initial less difficult passages, subjects were primarily reading for meaning. However, as the passages became more difficult, the reading purpose could have changed, consequently reducing the utilization of strategies to facilitate understanding. This finding would also lend support to the suggestion that readability is not purely a function of text but may be more a function of how the individual interacts with the text. This being the case, one could expect readers to select and apply different strategies and patterns of strategies to meet what they viewed as the critical task, particularly if the critical task was too overwhelming. This further suggests that passages used to assess monitoring should be difficult enough to ensure spontaneous monitoring but not so difficult as to result in frustration and a breakdown of strategy use.

These studies and others have presented the exciting possibility of examining ongoing strategic metacognitive monitoring during task performance. Lupart (1984) notes that the few studies conducted thus far have been promising, in that they have identified specific strategies for metacognitive monitoring. These studies have added considerable light into how individuals differ in their regulation strategies as well as explain the circumstances under which we can expect metacognitive behavior to be evident. However, it is not clear as to the extent to which the probing and think-aloud approaches interfere with the actual cognitive processing during task performance.

In summary, the brief review provided in this section makes it quite apparent that the recent approaches being applied to the study of metacognition are significantly different from the experimental laboratory-based studies that have dominated the literature for the greater part of this century. We are moving much closer to a research view that attempts to examine real-life thinking processes as they appear in the child's everyday contexts. For teachers and all persons associated with the education of young children, this research thrust has already yielded extensive implications for teaching applications. We will explore these first by reviewing some of the primary developmental considerations and then move to the section concerning educational practice.

The Development of Metacognition

Up until the last decade, models of information processing were developed on the basis of adult studies. When children or developmentally different groups were examined, these same models were utilized and, for the most part, discrepancies in performance between young children and adult were attributed to structural differences or capacity differences. For example, the inferior memory performance of young children was attributed to the overall smaller capacity to process information. However, the work by people like Chi (1976), Brown (1978), and Flavell (1976) and others who utilize a developmental psychological framework has been instrumental in demonstrating that these differences cannot be solely attributed to differences in storehouse capacity, nor can these differences by attributed to one component of the system such as memory or attention. The broader picture is described by Flavell (1976), who notes that "the growing child has much to learn about how, where and when to sort information and how, where, and when to retrieve it, as means to a variety of real life goals" (p. 233). Thus, it is important to consider both the structural and the control processing factors that are important to proficient cognitive processing.

Brown (1978) has outlined some of the primary limitations that are apparent in young children's memory as a direct result of a knowledge base that is considerably deficient in comparison to that of an adult. Given that the long-term memory houses all of the rules, operations, and strategies that optimize the capabilities of a limited resource system, it is logical to expect that the greater the experiential and knowledge base, the greater the information-processing proficiency will be. Young children are limited first by the amount of information contained in the long-term store, and further by the lack of internal organization of the information contained therein. Consequently, this results in less efficient means of information acquisition and information retrieval. The important question here then is: What are the factors that contribute to the growth of the child's long-term memory and the effective, conscious control of learning?

Wertsch (1979) has examined the development of thinking processes of preschool children and has suggested that what young children lack in the way of effective regulatory control of their cognitive experiences is provided for initially in the interactions with parents and/or older siblings. That is, the regulation aspects of all cognitive activity are taken on by the adult in a number of significant ways. Parents work with the child by helping to define and articulate the activity goal (e.g. "Go find the teddy bear, Johnny.") and by helping the child to monitor his progress toward that goal (e.g. "Did you find it in the toy box? No? Where did you play with it last?"). During the preschool developmental years, a tremendous amount of parental-child interaction is characterized by the parents' support in highlighting and arranging the perceptually or conceptually relevant aspects of the child's environment to induce information acquisition and learning. As children's knowledge and experiential base expands, so do their options for imposing self-control and regulation over information acquisition and retrieval.

The early years of a child's learning are no doubt dominated and perhaps limited by the type and quality of interaction that s/he has with parents and family. The importance of this stage of a child's development is in the fact that parents or the child's learning mediators are part of a long-term evolving, interactive social history. The learning emphasis is usually incidental and informal, and adequate communication and appropriate social behavior are the learning goals. However, when the child reaches school-age, the learning context of the child changes dramatically. Teachers assume the major responsibility for the development of the child's mental capabilities, and the learning goals are specifically organized and sequenced over the school years for a variety of subject matter. The context is very much formalized and group-based, and moreover the child will normally be with a given teacher for one year or less and then move on to a different class and teacher.

Hence, the relevance of these relationships can be understood if one envisages the metacognitive/cognitive development of a child as two conjoined triangles (see Fig. 6-1). The infant would be characterized by a minimal cognitive base and a maximal didactic other-regulation base whereas the thinking of an adult would be characterized by a maximal cognitive base and minimal didactic other regulation. It is the midsection which would encompass the traditional school-attending years of the child, which denotes the interactive nature of the learning that takes place at this stage. The teacher's function is not solely to transmit important facts or content to the child as it has traditionally been practiced, but rather the effective teacher is one who can assess the learning capabilities of the child and provide the relevant experiences to challenge that growth and promote the independent regulation of that process. In other words, the school takes over this important conscious other-regulation function to promote conscious self-regulation of one's mental processing (Reeve & Brown, 1984).

Interestingly, even though promoting self-regulation is no doubt one of the major implicit functions of the school system, we know surprisingly little about how this is accomplished. It is, however, only fair to comment that it has only been since the emergence of the recent cognitive and metacognitive literature that the relevance of this question has been recognized.

In essence, it was not until the last few years that we have had a clear idea of the cognitive/metacognitive distinction, and only from this have we come to realize the important implications for schooling. And, finally, as Flavell (1976) has noted, we have perhaps been incorrect in our experimental focus by selectively examining only the formal, most "internal, in-the-head storage and retrieval processes," whereas the "real world's tasks generally have the properties of an open-book take-home exam" (p. 233). In other words, our studies and assumptions about children's learning have been seriously incomplete because of our total attention to the internalized knowledge base of the individual without considering the multitude of resources, both **internal** and **external** (e.g. encyclopedias, almanacs, directories, experts, adults, etc.), that we all rely upon in our everyday thinking and problem solving.

FIGURE 6-1
The Development of Regulation in Children's Learning

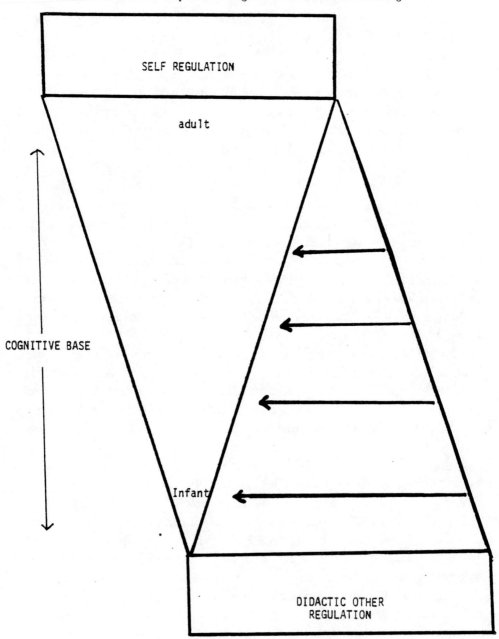

One of the promising areas of investigation of relevance to the question of how schools can promote the active self-regulation of the learner in the school classroom has been the intervention training research. The logical course for this line of research has been to identify the skills that older, more proficient performers demonstrate and to train younger inexperienced performers to use these skills.

Even though these type of studies have consistently demonstrated significant performance gains in children and special needs learners in several areas such as memory, reading comprehension and problem solving, the major limitation has been that these skills have not been generalized by these less proficient learners to other tasks or learning contexts.

As Reeve and Brown (1984) describe it, these studies have failed to incorporate the metacognitive elements necessary for the student to recognize the utility of the strategy or the need to plan and monitor the implementation of these techniques in similar problem situations. It has only been since the mid-1970s that educational researchers have recognized the need to inform and involve the learner in establishing the goal or purpose of the training, and to train micro-level metacognitive skills such as planning, checking and monitoring skills that could be applied to a variety of problem-solving situations (Reeve & Brown, 1984).

Another factor relevant to the teacher's role in promoting the active self-regulation of the learner is that of fostering metacognitive experience. As mentioned earlier, Flavell (1981) has utilized the term "metacognitive experience" to refer to the learner's conscious cognitive or affective experiences (i.e. ideas, feelings, sensations) related to any cognitive enterprise. More specifically, a metacognitive experience is one in which items of metacognitive knowledge have entered consciousness.

The linkage of metacognitive experience to the learning process is a direct and necessary one for proficient self-regulation of mental processing. The three major functions of metacognitive experience in this respect are described by Flavell (1981) as follows:

1. to lead one to establish new goals or to revise or abandon old ones,
2. to cause one to adjust the knowledge base by adding, deleting, revising or by assimilating and accommodating in the Piagetian sense, and
3. to activate cognitive and metacognitive strategies.

The teacher's role, then, is to promote the incidence of metacognitive experience within students. Students must first be made aware of the importance of careful, highly conscious thinking and then be given ample opportunity within the school context to experiment, examine, discuss and share their ideas about managing their own cognitive resources in relation to school tasks.

To date, the interventive training studies that have adopted these essential metacognitive principles have been successfully carried out with regular and special needs students in areas such as reading and writing, and the promise of such work is becoming widely recognized. However, as Reeve and Brown (1984) point out, these studies have been conducted under ideal training conditions, with a one-to-one student ratio. What is critical for future work of this type is to provide ways in which metacognitive training procedures that have been successful in ideal one-to-one tutorial situations can be applied to large groups or classrooms.

The last and perhaps most critical factor relating to children's classroom learning is that involving motivational and personality variables. Until very recently, this line of investigation has proceeded separately from research into metacognition. However, both Loper and Murphy (1985) and Cullen (1985) have presented cogent discussions to suggest a very close interrelationship between metacognition, learned helplessness and academic performance. Since it is anticipated that this will become a major research avenue in the future, this work will be very briefly discussed here.

Hagen, Barclay, and Newman (1982) were among the first to pose the argument that the crux of the learning problems characteristic of learning disability students was the combination of metacognitive deficits as well as self-schemata factors, such as the child's personal beliefs and motivations. Hagen, Barclay, and Newman (1982), similarly, issued the challenge for researchers to demonstrate that such internal self-awareness factors do in fact primarily affect school performance.

Loper and Murphy (1985) have taken up this challenge by first reviewing the literature relating to cognitive and metacognitive deficits of academic underachievers, and delineating the factors that primarily account for their learning failure. Major metacognitive deficiencies appear to include:

1. Evaluating their ability to successfully undertake a task.
2. Planning effective organizational schemes for approaching the task.
3. Applying successful strategies.
4. Monitoring their progress on an ongoing understanding of the task.
5. Identifying and correcting their errors or modifying their effort as they proceed.
6. Evaluating their overall performance when finished (p. 231).

Given this base, Loper and Murphy (1985) then reviewed all the intervention programs aimed at promoting self-regulatory behavior in both regular and attention-deficit children. Although they were clearly able to meet the Hagen et al. (1982) challenge by demonstrating that interventions to promote student self-awareness and regulation can improve academic performance, they caution that we need to know more about appropriate matching of task and learner characteristics. It is also important to point out that these studies are basically focused upon the individual child and, as Reeve and Brown (1984) have noted, we must eventually be able to apply these concepts to the teaching of large groups or classrooms.

The work reported in Cullen (1985) and Cullen and Carver (1982), which examined the influence of specific teacher behavior on the child's reaction to failure, has revealed a number of teaching practices which are likely detriments to student self-directed learning. The widespread use of stars or points to reward school work, for example, is seen to significantly detract the child's intrinsic interest in the task and tends to create inappropriate overemphasis upon the appearance of work.

Cullen (1985) and her colleagues have conducted an impressive series of such studies to investigate the relationship between metacognitive deficits and learned helplessness and they have concluded that metacognitive activity can be substantially impaired by the learner's affective state. Moreover, the degree to which the learner can achieve success in regulating learning behavior may be entirely contingent upon the teacher's ability to create a learning environment which supports both learning and affective needs. Future studies in the area of metacognitive development therefore will have to consider both variables.

In summary, it has become increasingly apparent that metacognitive principles are important to the learning and cognitive development of young children. The mediator role, which is initiated and largely dominated by the parents in the preschool years, is given over to the teacher when the child reaches school-age. We are only just beginning to identify the ways in which teachers can train and promote the incidence of metacognitive experiences in children, but the initial research in the area has been notably promising. It is also apparent that teachers will be major contributors to our general knowledge base in this area in the years to come for a number of reasons.

Notably, teachers have a long history of experience in helping young children learn, and as such have accumulated an in-depth knowledge of the kinds of appropriate learning tasks and practices for a given age level. Teachers have the advantage over researchers in their day-to-day contact with the child over a lengthy time period. And, finally, the teacher can be instrumental in pioneering ways to increase the quantity and quality of children's exposure to metacognitive experiences within group contexts. Overall, such teacher-based input will, as never before, have a significant impact on future theories of children's learning. For now, there are already a number of specific applications of metacognition for teaching practice which will be discussed in the following segment.

PRACTICAL APPLICATIONS OF METACOGNITIVE PROCESSES TO EDUCATIONAL PRACTICE AND CLASSROOM MANAGEMENT

If we want our children to perform well on any task, be it perceptual, mnemonic, or conceptual, it is important that we train them to be sensitive to their own cognitive state — that is, to know if or when they know something about the problem (Brown, Bransford, Ferrara, & Campione, 1983). A substantial amount of metacognitive research data suggests that the progressive development of children's knowledge of their own cognitive state, and variables affecting that state, can be facilitated and accelerated by the efforts of teachers, educators and parents.

In previous chapters, we have considered the performance of children on a variety of cognitive tasks — what children actually attend to and remember, or how the teacher can contribute (via strategems, devices and skills) to the child's attentional skills and memory enhancement. In this section we will consider the role and function of the classroom teacher toward a different type of cognition: children's awareness of their own cognitive processes, a body of knowledge that has come to be known as metacognition. We will primarily consider the teacher's function in facilitating the development of metacognitive skills in children and how knowledge of that acquisition could be useful in improving the confidence of children with low self-perception and evaluation.

METACOGNITIVE OPERATIONS

Metacognitive operations help the learner in a number of ways, principally as follows: (1) **predicting** the consequences of an action or event; (2) **checking** the results of one's actions to determine whether they worked and had the desired effect or did not work and had an unexpected or undesirable effect; **(3) monitoring** one's ongoing activity with a view to assessing how one is doing; **(4) reality testing** with a view to determining whether the activity makes sense to self and others in the immediate environment; and **(5) coordinating and controlling** deliberate attempts to learn and solve problems.

Brown and DeLoache (1983) argue that these metacognitive operations are the basic characteristics of efficient thought in the young learner, and one of their most important properties is that they are trans-situational and apply to a whole range of the young learner's problem-solving activities, from the highly structured settings of the classroom to the real world — everyday life situations of the home, playground, and on the street. Not only does a child have to learn the various skills of checking, monitoring, anticipating, reality testing, etc., but, perhaps of equal importance, the child has to learn that they are almost universally applicable; that, whenever faced with a new task, it will be to the advantage of the child to apply general knowledge about how to learn and solve problems. Despite the awareness that these metacognitive processes are fundamentally important to virtually all kinds of children's understandings and endeavors, the teacher's understanding of how the metacognitive systems operate is extremely limited. Also, as classroom teachers, we have only limited insights into how metacognitive processes can be stimulated. Our fundamental obligation, nevertheless, is to explore with children how basic rules, skills and strategies that apply to their functioning in the classroom can be integrated into their ever-evolving solutions to problems of play, social interactions and performance of nonschool tasks.

Teachers should be aware that, in regard to assessing metacognitive capabilities, children are often more in tune with their cognitive performance (what they do or are capable of doing) but lag behind considerably with respect to metacognitive knowledge (what they know or do not know). Similarly, children may be quite sensitively aware of variables affecting their performance negatively (such as noise, peer distractions, or failure to practice a task) or variables facilitating performance (such as a quiet setting, opportunity to rehearse a task, effort made to listen attentively to the speaker) but may be unable to manipulate the conditions affecting performance. Similarly, it is important for teachers to note that on metacognitive tasks employing performance measures, children's verbal competence (i.e. their conscious awareness that particular factors affect performance) may well give the false impression that these children have a sophisticated understanding of the metacognitive activity involved in the task. However, in actual situations requiring competent performance, children may not be able to use their cognitive knowledge on an actual task to facilitate or improve their performance. In other words, young children lack the relevant metacognitive knowledge and skills that would enable them to make a significant transfer from prior experience or to develop the necessary knowledge about how and what to think when confronted with a new problem. Young children do not know much about either their own capabilities on a new task or the techniques necessary to perform efficiently; they may even have difficulty determining what goals are desirable and certainly much greater difficulty in deciding what steps are required to get there. The teacher's task, therefore, in helping children with their generalized metacognitive deficits is three fold:

1. to consider with the child those self-regulatory metacognitive processing steps that are sufficiently general to apply to a range of different problem-solving situations.
2. to train children to become sensitive to their own cognitive states and thought processes by means of step-by-step instruction in the nature of the task and by means of teaching children how to self-monitor, self-interrogate and self-appraise in the task situation.
3. to provide children explicit instruction in self-mastery skills by using both reciprocal and direct teaching methods involving social interaction and exchange of ideas, demonstrations, rehearsals, modeling, explaining, questioning and feedback, etc.

What is being emphasized here is the teacher's major function in developing a teaching methodology and orientation that raises the children's cognitive consciousness, promotes the development of self-regulation and self-management skills, and provides explicit instruction for focusing the students' attention on relevant features of the task. Equally important is the teacher's function to explore with the children knowledge of the environmental factors influencing their perceptions (metaperception), and memory (metamemory) and habituation of attention (meta-attention). Each of these areas needs to be considered separately and at greater length for the benefit of the teacher.

METAPROCESSING KNOWLEDGE

At the level of broad generality, if the teacher wants the children to perform well on any classroom task, it is important that students be encouraged to become aware of their own thought processes. This involves the teacher providing the children opportunities to talk about and share ideas, feelings, and strategies that they use to remember things and to attend to important features of the task. Children may be encouraged, for example, to share ideas on what they do and say to themselves in order to resist temptation, how they avoid distraction, how they control their urge to act out, or how they suppress their emotions of anger or sadness. All these are factors that affect their task performance, selective attention, and sense of self-regulation. By making children more aware of their listening skills and their ability to alter their communications to make them appropriate to the task at hand and the situation (Wellman & Lempers, 1977), children can be made more cognitively aware of their perceptions and their ability to control and shape them. The teacher can contribute to the child's metacognitive awareness in a number of ways.

Impressing on the Child the Importance of Executive Control and Self-Mastery

Given the time constraints on processing and the large amount of information the child needs to process in the classroom, it appears that the child needs to be convinced of the proficiency of acquiring executive control as soon as possible in the learning process. It is important that the teacher make children as self-reliant as possible by teaching them appropriate metacognitive strategies that the child can easily learn to choose, apply, and revise rapidly in order to prevent information loss. We propose that, early in the learning and informational processing planning stages, teachers assess the metacognitive proficiency of their young learners and systematically teach them the basic principles of self-mastery in information processing. This can be done by encouraging children in a number of ways.

- Helping the child consciously select and apply a strategy relevant to the content of the information to be processed.
- Teaching the child to monitor the effectiveness of the strategy in the performance of the task.
- Encouraging the child to revise the use of the strategy, if necessary, and reapply the revised strategy in the time allowed by the teacher.

It is important for the teacher to recognize that in the early stages of learning there are likely to be major impediments to the effective use of these strategies. For example, there will be a major load on the young learner's processing capacity, such as difficulty in determining task requirements, expenditure of effort toward maintaining attention and motivation, and processing information within the time allowed by the teacher.

However, the teacher can facilitate the metacognitive strategy training process by strictly controlling and minimizing the processing load associated with the information to be processed. Considerable practice with individual strategies in those learning situations that do not overtax information-processing capacity should result in the automatization of the strategy. In other words, frequent utilization of an information-processing strategy and committing the steps of the strategy to memory so that it will require minimum mental effort should be encouraged by the teacher. If the child achieves some measure of self-mastery in processing information, this will increase the likelihood of the child using self-mastery strategies.

Stressing Self-Regulation

Self-regulation is the basis of self-mastery. As mentioned previously, children often fail to perform efficiently, not only because they lack certain skills, but because they are deficient in terms of self-conscious participation and intelligent self-regulation of their actions. We have as yet little developmental data to indicate whether young children are capable of self-regulatory behavior. However, based upon a considerable amount of research developed around the application of cognitive self-regulation or self-monitoring techniques in the treatment of a variety of behavioral disorders, we can predict that a progression of self-regulatory behaviors may be made to become a common feature of children's learning in many domains. The work of Luria (1982) and others such as Meichenbaum (1977), Hobbs, Moguin, Tyroler and Lahey (1980) support the promise of the self-regulatory approach for working with children across a wide range of behavioral demands (Kanfer & Zich, 1974; Fry, 1977), mental abilities levels (Gow & Ward, 1980), and age levels (Meichenbaum & Goodman, 1969, 1971, 1975; Goodwin & Mahoney, 1975).

The self-regulation mode of developing metacognitive knowledge is based on the principle that when children are involved in the induction of self-instruction, internalization of some verbal regulatory system begins to take place. Change in behavior occurs when children internalize the process of self-instruction, self-monitoring and self-assessment. Despite disagreement about how this process works, there is general optimism about the value of cognitive instructional techniques that encourage students to check and monitor their task performance and ongoing activity, to assess their satisfaction in task performance, and to plan their task performance in terms of specific goals, specific steps, and specific outcomes. All of this is very useful to the child with respect to metacognitive processing of the learning situation. The procedure itself is modeled directly after the steps believed to accompany the internalization of the self-regulatory self-guided system discussed by Luria (1982).

We propose that with young children the verbal self-instruction method of self-regulation be used more so than other self-control methods. Verbal self-instruction is one example of a type of cognitive strategy that might be implemented to promote self-regulation in the classroom, with few, if any, adjunct materials. Verbal self-instruction as designed by Meichenbaum and Goodman (1969, 1971, 1975) includes the following components: (a) questions concerning the nature and demands of the task, (b) answers to the questions in the form of cognitive rehearsal, (c) appropriate directive comments that specify steps for completing the task, (d) error-correction instructions, (e) coping statements, and (f) self-reinforcement.

As Peterson and Swing (1983) note, verbal self-instruction can typically be taught with minimal adjunct materials by using a sequential modeling-fading procedure in which the trainer performs the task while verbalizing aloud, and then the trainee both performs the task and verbalizes, first overtly and then covertly, following the trainer's example. The advantage of this self-instructional approach is that no further training or support materials are required once the young learner has mastered the self-instructional strategy. The learner simultaneously develops some skills for self-assessment of performance and self-reinforcement.

Since the self-instructional strategy can be used relatively independent of adjunct materials and external support, its use is recommended with students as young as those in the first or second grade. A verbal self-instruction strategy is potentially valuable for improving kindergarten and elementary students' performance in basic tasks in writing, arithmetic skills and oral communications. It seems reasonable to assume that young students have the prerequisite basic skills to benefit from training in self-instructional strategies, self-monitoring and self-reinforcement exercises along the self-guiding lines suggested by Meichenbaum and Goodman (1969, 1971, 1975).

Fostering Awareness of Problem-Solving Procedures

Metacognitive knowledge of problem solving is the first important step toward the reinforcement of self-mastery in the child. The point we wish to emphasize is that, in promoting self-regulation in children, teachers need to consider what the learner already knows about the problem-solving situation or task. At the general level, DeCecco (1968), Hayes (1981), and Wood, Bruner, and Ross (1976) contend that effective problem solving presumes an awareness of the specific steps which need to be taken if problems are to be solved. At a minimum level these steps include: (a) creating an awareness in the child that problems have solutions and that selective criteria must be established to solve a problem; (b) perceiving possible solutions to a problem by encouraging children to consider alternative ways of thinking about the problem and generating alternative solutions to the problem (Fry & Grover, 1982); (c) allocating study time effectively; (d) being sensitive to feedback and actively seeking feedback; (e) altering strategies to fit the task; and (f) evaluating information to arrive at a solution to a problem.

Two of the most important aspects of children's metaprocessing knowledge which has implications for the teacher are as follows: Is the child sensitive to task demands? Does the child have the ability to alter processing strategies to conform to the task demands? With young children, as compared to older children, the teacher needs to be aware that young children are not particularly sensitive to the information content that is gained through particular strategies, and hence they cannot make informative selections in assessing the requirements of the task. This makes it necessary for the teacher to assist the young children in the acquisition of metacognitive knowledge about the task. The teacher may help the process by frequently asking children to check, and subsequently to report on, whether they believe they have acquired enough information to solve the problem after each choice. Gradually, children coached to attend to critical information about the task, and about alternative solutions to the problem, will become more sensitive to feedback and will become more aware of the amount of information they need to gain about a task before a solution is possible. Children who are trained, via self-interrogation and self-monitoring strategies and skills, to discover solution-based criteria of a problem eventually discover for themselves what is to be learned and what active strategies they must use to retain the information. Gradually, children trained in self-monitoring become more adept in using self-testing and hypothesis-testing strategies for assessing the extent of their learning.

Providing Feedback and Reinforcement

Through training in self-interrogation, self-monitoring, and self-testing procedures, children can be made more sensitive to task characteristics and, therefore, more able to alter their selection strategies accordingly. The number of informative choices that children are able to make increases markedly after three years of age. However, there is relatively little spontaneous use of selective information about the task. In spite of children's increasing metacognitive awareness and knowledge of the task, they may not use the knowledge unless prompted to do so. In other words, children are not likely to use the metacognitive knowledge in a task situation unless they are helped with initial information about the task, and its demands and characteristics. The teacher needs to be aware that children's sensitivity to the value of information gained during a problem-solving task, and their strategic behavior in response to task characteristics can be increased through **intermittent feedback** and **reinforcement.** Gradually, children learn to make significantly more self-directive information choices regarding the problem-solving task by using processes of self-interrogation, self-monitoring and self-evaluation. Evidence of such metacognition awareness comes from studies in which children search for cognitive strategies in structured task-settings and are provided feedback and training in self-regulation. The metacognitive knowledge of these children is seen to be much more substantial when compared to subjects who function in free conditions and in the absence of any prompting and feedback from adults.

Flavell et al. (1970) have reported that children left on their own are poor at apportioning study time and using information. Teachers should therefore be aware that most children not trained in self-monitoring and skills for eliciting feedback do not easily discover what is to be learned. When faced with new information about a task, they will merely review the previously learned material. If children are exposed to new task demands and task characteristics, teachers can facilitate the child's discovery by explaining clearly and precisely the components of the new task, and drawing the child's attention to what is already known about the task.

Although the existing research studies provide little in the way of a coordinated understanding of how metacognitive knowledge develops or how this knowledge relates to the child's cognitive development or the child's actual task performance (Brown, 1978a, 1978b; Cavanaugh & Perlmutter, 1982), practitioners note that children are more aware of what they know or don't know about themselves than they are able to describe. It is the teacher's function to determine the extent to which the child already understands and the extent to which the child can be helped in metacognitive knowledge by certain types of teacher activities and classroom guidance. Cantor and Spiker (1978) and Steinberg (1980) recommend that by simplifying the task, instructing children thoroughly in the nature of the task, or by providing tasks familiar and relevant to children, it is likely that more advanced forms of metacognitive knowledge and processing can be fostered in children, especially with respect to metaperception and metamemory development.

METAPERCEPTION

Markman (1979) refers to the term "metaperception" as a two fold form of self-awarness: An awareness of information content (stimulus input) and a knowledge of factors that influence perception. Markman (1979) suggests that young children are not sensitive to the information content of messages as are older children. She notes that children are very sensitive about inadequacy of their listening skills and selective attention, and their inability to evaluate the informational adequacy of their messages. Being aware of their limited communication skills they may blame themselves for a failure to understand the message and may fail to realize that it is helpful to provide feedback to the speaker when they are in doubt (Ironsmith & Whitehurst, 1978). Children therefore are not likely to convey to the teacher their difficulty in understanding the referential communication. They will simply fail to respond to the teacher's inadequate messages. This knowledge about children's metaperceptions has a number of implications and applications for the classroom teacher. At the most general level it is important that the teacher assume more of the following types of functions.

(1) Encouraging Interrogation, Clarification and Summarizing in Children

When communicating messages to the child, teachers need to be aware that messages need to be given in very simple form so that the child is able to discriminate easily the informational relevant components of the message. When children receive a complex, uninformative or partially informative message, they are not likely to ask for clarification. Since children are known to underestimate their ability to evaluate the information content of messages (Miller & Weiss, 1982), it is encumbent on the teacher to encourage the children to ask questions and to seek clarification and feedback when they are in doubt about the information content of the message communicated. Unless the search for clarification and feedback is heavily reinforced by the teacher, children will simply fail to respond to ambiguous messages. It is unclear why children fail to request additional information. One possible explanation that is relevant for the teacher is that children are not able spontaneously to compare the message received to other alternatives available. Instead, they may simply choose the first referent that seems reasonable (Flavell, Speers, Green & August, 1981; Ironsmith & Whitehurst, 1978). The teacher can encourage the children to seek clarification of the communication by establishing a practice of asking them to decode messages and, thus, to ensure that the child has been able to discriminate the information-relevant from the information-irrelevant components of the message. The more often the child engages in the process of decoding messages and receives corresponding reinforcement and feedback from the teacher in the process, the more sensitive the child will become to the information content of the message. The increasing self-confidence to decode messages accurately will further encourage the child to attend selectively and to evaluate the extent of self-understanding.

(2) Using a Reciprocal Teaching Method for Metacognitive Skill Development

Consistent with the views of Luria (1976) and Vygotsky (1978), teachers need to be aware that the child's ability for self-regulatory activity can be enhanced mainly through social interaction with reasonably competent adults. Thus, teachers interested in having children take increasing charge of their own thinking behaviors need to be quite familiar with the learner's entering skill level and to help the child in the transition from the conscious **other-regulated** to conscious **self-regulated thinking** about the problem-solving task.

From a practical perspective, this engenders the need for teachers to resort to a reciprocal teaching method aimed at fostering a collaborative interchange between the young learner and a competent adult (Scardamalia & Bereiter, 1982). This is necessary to help the young learner to understand the cognitive goal to be strived for. Within a small-group reciprocal teaching environment, the young learner is regarded as a co-investigator.* Initially, the teacher takes more responsibility for

---

*Cf. Palinscar and Brown (1984) for details.

articulating the metacognitive awareness, often vocalizing plans and strategies, raising questions, and encouraging the child to monitor activities, and to participate in clarification and summarizing (self-review). As Reeve and Brown (1984, p. 15) note, in reciprocal teaching young learners of varying competencies and a competent teacher take turns "being the teacher," with each participant leading a dialogue on what is informationally relevant to a problem-solving task, and jointly ascertaining what needs to be understood and remembered. All of these metacognitive requirements are embedded in as natural a dialogue as possible, with the adult teacher and students giving feedback to each other. Gradually, however, as students become better able to perform some aspects of the task, the teacher increases the demands such that students' behavior becomes increasingly like that of the competent teacher, who in turn decreases the level of participation and acts as a supportive audience. The purpose of the reciprocal teaching method is for the teacher to get the child to master important metacognitive skills, such as paraphrasing important informational contents, asking questions of clarification, and making statements of interpretation and prediction. These are metacognitive requirements essential to task performance. However, the child does not engage in them spontaneously and they must be elicited by the teacher.

Typically, in the reciprocal teaching method, instructors and learners model thinking-aloud procedures, present cues to stimulate self-questioning during the planning state, and ask strategy questions on how to resolve conflicting ideas.* Perhaps the most practical outcome of the reciprocal teaching method is the child's increased ability to reflect on the steps involved in the problem-solving activity, and the development of conscious self-regulation. Perhaps, most importantly, the children's increased feelings of personal competence and control enable them to go farther and improve their metacognitive skills and conscious thought processes through a self-mastery approach.

This is not to suggest that the reciprocal teaching method must be strictly on a one-to-one tutoring basis or that teaching interventions cannot be conducted in a group context. The point to be stressed in the reciprocal teaching method is that teachers should be aware that children of different ages and abilities will be at different phases in the development of metacognitive skills. The teacher's vigilance in the social interaction process is a key to enhancing the child's metacognitive

---

*See Scardamalia, Bereiter and Steinbach (1984) for details.

experience and knowledge. The degree of individual aid the teacher gives must also vary with the learner's cognitive entry level. Gradually, this will lead to the emergence of conscious self-regulation skills of the child.

Discerning teachers will recognize the similarity between the concept of reciprocal teaching of metacognitive skills and Greenfield's (1984) approach to teaching children self-mastery and self-regulation. Greenfield suggests that remedial programs aimed at fostering in children insights into their own metacognitive processes should be so organized by the teacher that elements of the degree of teacher involvement and scaffolding is adapted to the learner's current state; the amount of scaffolding decreases as the skill level of the learner increases, till ultimately the externally provided aid is completely internalized by the learner, permitting independent skilled performance or self-mastery of the problem-solving task. It should be noted, however, that, for whatever the reason, children will continue to require explicit instruction and direct teaching of metacognitive skills for a much longer time than do most adults. The point of identifying this distinction between child and adult learner is not to undermine the conceptualization or the development of conscious control and metacognitive skills in children, but to emphasize for the teacher the complexities involved in reciprocal teaching of metacognitive skills to young learners.

(3) Teaching Children More Positively Oriented Self-Evaluation and Self-Judgment Skill

Although it is unclear what underlies the development of self-appraisal and self-regulation skills (i.e. whether these are developmental changes or whether they are related to the emergence of metacognitive processes), the important point for the teacher to recognize is that more attention ought to be given to fostering in children conscious self-regulation of thought and conscious attention to self-evaluation issues.

As described earlier in the chapter teachers and educators have ignored the influence of self-perceptions, motivations, and past metacognitive experiences on the child's performance (Loper & Murphy, 1985; Cullen, 1985). From studying and interpreting the literature on social comparison, motivational and attributional processes, however, it is clear that the children's assessment of their own abilities greatly affects their self-confidence and performance on problem-solving tasks. For example, it is apparent (Ruble, Boggiano, Feldman & Loebl, 1980; Harter, 1981; Dweck & Elliott, 1983) that different-aged children possess different kinds of social comparison processes and, as a consequence, draw different conclusions from previous experiences of success and failure in performance on academic tasks.

As most teachers and educators should recognize, young children do not have a realistic perception of their competence, metacognitive abilities, and quality of performance on academic tasks. The repeated negative evaluation and labeling by self that accompanies continuing academic failure has a damaging effect on the child's metaperceptions. Such children often label themselves as being dull, stupid, incompetent and unable to succeed at anything. According to Cole and Traupman (1980), the children's negative perceptions of their prospects for success in academic tasks are of utmost importance in their self-evaluation. Children unconsciously begin to formulate strategies designed to defend against exposure to evaluations that will further document their own inadequacies. Children frequently expend so much energy in efforts to avoid negative evaluations and prognosis that they become victimized by their metaperceptions and experience a formidable barrier to learning (Dweck & Elliott, 1983). Such children view temporary failure to be an indication of long-term incompetence, and they typically derogate their capabilities. By contrast, children who participate in reciprocal teaching and are frequently praised, reinforced and encouraged for their efforts and receive constructive feedback and clarification in task performance are more likely to develop metaperceptions of mastery. Master-oriented children in turn formulate strategies designed to elicit positive feedback and support from competent adults. Rather than attributing their failures to personal shortcomings, they view obstacles in problem solving as a challenge to be overcome by developing more effective strategies of verbalization, organization, and systematic goal setting. In practical terms, therefore, teacher interventions should be more sensitive to the learner's current distorted, inaccurate or sometimes unrealistic perceptions of the self. Interventions should be aimed at fostering self-confidence and positive self-evaluation development. This does not mean that all children who are reinforced and guided in self-evaluation will necessarily develop a positive self-evaluation. The point we want to emphasize is the importance of social interaction and reciprocal feedback between the teacher and child. The goal of the procedure is to keep children fully and accurately informed of their strengths, abilities and shortcomings to facilitate the emergence of conscious self-evaluation skills. Once started, the progress will follow an orderly developmental course in later years.

In addition, it is possible to facilitate in the child self-evaluation skills that are flexible and task-dependent. For example, from a reality-based position a child may evaluate his competence and skills in composition quite highly but may conversely rate his capabilities poorly when it comes to developing peer relationships. In all events, the teacher and student's reciprocal feedback, clarification, and interpretation will facilitate the development of good metacognitive skills required for self-regulation and evaluation.

The foregoing discussion has mentioned several components of children's self-knowledge, self-monitoring, self-recording, self-reinforcement, self-instruction, and self-assessment, which have been hypothesized to be important for training in self-regulative strategies. However, all children will need the help of teachers in recognizing when and how strategies can be effectively implemented. Teachers need to be aware of the significance of a positive teacher-student relationship if students are to be motivated to engage in strategies such as self-recording and verbal self-instruction in behaviors that are problematic. In teaching children self-regulative strategies, it is suggested that training can be considerably improved if teachers are sufficiently familiar with the child's prior knowledge, and the proficiency or deficiencies of his or her metacognitive knowledge and executive control.

Borkowski, Levers and Gruenenfelder (1976) have suggested for the benefit of the teacher the following components that should be included in strategy training of the children: (a) consistent use of the same self-regulatory procedures and specific steps; (b) teaching the self-regulatory strategy by using a variety of materials; and (c) provision of detailed instructions on how each procedure should be used. Depending on the age of the learner, the younger the child, the more assurance needs to be provided that the strategy will be useful. The young learner needs to be actively involved during strategy instruction. Extensive practice should be provided in strategy implementation, and teacher prompts must be gradually faded out.

In sum, it appears that the components to be included in training children in self-regulative strategies very much depend on the age of the learner and the child's motivation to change behaviors through self-instruction.

METAMEMORY

By far the most work on metacognitive research has been concerned with metamemory. Metamemory refers to one's awareness of the memory state—that is, what one knows, as well as awareness of one's strategies for storing, retaining, or retrieving information from memory. With respect to metacognitive knowledge about memory, teachers should note a number of educational implications and classroom applications.

First, even young children are aware what is an easy memory task and what factors are conducive or detrimental to memorization. For example, children's early realization that retrieval from memory storage is affected by the amount of prior study time (Kreutzer, Leonard, & Flavell, 1975) should be of interest to teachers and practitioners.

Second, based upon the research findings of Appel, Cooper, McCarrel, Sims-Knight, Yussen, and Flavell (1972), who instructed children to "remember" as compared to "look at" instructions, teachers should recognize that although young children do distinguish between a memory task (remember) and perception task (look at), they are unable to use strategies that would allow them to remember better. The implications of these findings for teachers seem to be that young children may often give unreliable accounts of their memory ability and may overestimate their memory functioning at a number of levels. Children may report that they know something when in fact they do not. Thus, it is encumbent on the teacher to ensure and check that children do indeed remember, and will be able to retrieve information in critical situations. When children overestimate their memory ability (as often happens) and fail to retrieve, this has a negative effect on their metaperceptions. Opportunities for self-monitoring, self-testing, and self-instruction in memory tasks should be encouraged by the teacher to reinforce accurate self-assessments in children.

Third, teachers need to be alert to the fact that children often have a very poor understanding of when something has been fully committed to memory, and whether they have had sufficient time provided for the memorization. The poor performance of young children on memory tasks is probably related to a number of gaps in their metamemory awareness. Young children, for example, do not recognize the value of rehearsing or labeling (Brown, 1978a, 1978b; Kreutzer et al., 1975), nor do they know that certain strategies such as organized materials or retrieval cues are particularly important to memory functioning. These data are instructive in cautioning teachers to guard against inferring what children know about their memory states from their (children's) verbal reports.

If teachers want to foster efficient memory functioning in their children, it is important that they recognize the following characteristics of children's memory functioning:

- Regardless of the amount of time assigned to a memory task, young children as compared to older children will spend most of their study time in unproductive, nonstrategic activities unrelated to the memory task.
- Young children, as compared to older children, are unable to distinguish between the difficulty level of recall and recognition tasks and will approach both in unproductive and nonstrategic ways.
- Young children, as compared to older children, are capable of generating retrieval cues to a very limited degree only and, whenever able to, they will use retrieval cues that are strictly task-dependent. For example, on relatively simple memory tasks, young children may use simple mnemonic cues (pointing and body orientation) for remembering where concrete things go, for example, "How would you remember where you put your dollar?" (Wellman, Ritter, & Flavell, 1975), but will have obvious difficulty in generating a mnemonic cue or plan for recovering an abstract idea, for example, "How could you remember when your mother's birthday was?" (Drozdal & Flavell, 1975).

As seen in this summary review, young children do not spontaneously generate recall or retrieval strategies for unfamiliar tasks. At best there appears to be only low-to-moderate correspondence between metamemory knowledge and memory performance. In critical memorization tasks important to children's successful metacognitive performance, it is encumbent on the teacher or practitioner to help both young and old to apportion their study time more productively. This means that children must be helped (to the extent that children can comprehend the task) in generating simple retrieval cues. Children who are highly motivated to succeed in memory tasks may also be keen to learn what the task is like, perhaps discovering with the teacher's help how much and what is to be remembered, and the information that is most important to the memory task (Brown, 1978a, 1978b). By and large, teachers must accept that young children are relatively unconcerned about these matters and are somewhat confused about what memory is. Therefore, if too many external demands are placed on them to recognize, remember or recall, this pressure will only lead to a generalized state of confusion and anxiety.

Discerning teachers will note, however, that older children, not unlike adults, can be trained to approach tasks more systematically. They also develop an awareness that certain strategies are important to memory functioning. They are able to generate and use retrieval cues that are both task-dependent and task-independent. For those older children who have a good metamemory (i.e. they are more knowledgeable of strategies that facilitate the retention of information, and conditions that facilitate its retrieval), teachers may more logically presume that they would also be good memory users. This is not to imply that all children can necessarily be trained to become efficient memory users. Both memory and metamemory skills are a complex interaction of the learner's motivations, age, knowledge about specific tasks, and knowledge about situations. Overall, it is reasonable for the teacher to assume that the older child will more spontaneously use a greater number of active strategies (rehearsal and organization) than does the younger child (Cavanaugh & Borkowski, 1980; Yussen & Berman, 1981). From a cost-benefit perspective, teachers may more profitably invest their time in training older children in the use of active retrieval strategies and in devising both logical and personalized or individualized plans for retrieving information. Although all children use external cues to search the environment before they use external cues to search their own memories, Brown (1975, 1978a, 1978b) contends that many of the same strategies (retrieval cues, organizing, self-instruction) are relevant to both activities and should be encouraged.

With assistance from competent adults, the child is increasingly able to direct and control the search procedures in retrieval, including planning ahead to facilitate later retrieval according to a logical plan. Younger children often start the search with zeal, but in the midst of conducting the search they may frequently forget the goal and subsequently cease those behaviors originally directed toward achieving it. An important role that the teacher may play in the retrieval efforts is to assist the child through self-instruction to keep the goal in mind and to stay on track for a sufficient period of time and in the face of distractions. This is done by the teacher assisting children to develop specific cues that will help in recalling the location of objects and having them engage in some concrete activity or self-instructions that will help them remember during the delay. Teachers should note that external retrieval cues are easier to learn than is memory scanning—a task in which the child must deliberately adopt the goal of remembering and must initiate and maintain a purely internal, cognitive orientation to information in memory (Brown, 1975, 1978a, 1978b). The latter requires a greater degree of metacognitive control that comes only with age, experience, and motivation. Given age-related differences, young children can be trained to do something deliberate **at the time of storage** to facilitate later retrieval until their attempts at retrieval become developmentally more systematic, efficient and spontaneous. During the early stages of development, the need for increased involvement of teachers and other competent adults with children is most desirable. The teacher's function is to provide the young child with continual encouragement for monitoring memory output and to check memory output against a criterion of external acceptability.

META-ATTENTION

In Chapter 3 many facets of attention such as selective attention, attention during discrimination learning, and attention in perceptual learning were examined. That chapter focused primarily on attentional skills overlooking the possibility that the child's metacognitive awareness of how attention develops, and factors conducive to the facilitation or deterioration of attention, may also be very significant to effective attentional skills. It is likely that as a part of the general cognitive development children develop concepts of attention which may be intimately related to the development and utilization of attentional skills. The present section on meta-attention processes is concerned with examining and promoting the child's knowledge of the development of attention and factors that are conducive to selective attention.

As indicated in earlier chapters, children's understanding of how attention works is also ultimately linked with their knowledge about other metacognitive developments such as memory, perception and information manipulation. Taken together, they provide many insights into the emergence of selective attention in the young learners and developmental changes that occur in their initially limited capacity to attend selectively.

The teacher's essential function is to help children with strategy development that will assist them in various functions:

- increasing their ability to pay attention
- avoiding distractions and developing strategies for removing distractions
- attending to selective stimuli in the environment
- enhancing visual search strategies

Miller and Bigi's (1979) research findings note that children's motivations, attentional capacity, self-control, age, and intellectual level influence the amount of awareness that children have of their attentional abilities. Even young children recognize that sometimes they are able to pay attention with little effort, while at other times intense effort is required. Second, there is the knowledge that the nature of the setting is important to whether or not they pay attention. For example, young children are aware that some objects or situations (such as having the TV and radio on, seeing friends playing) are potential distractors that interfere with the task at hand. Children quickly acquire an awareness that they are apt to listen more carefully if they are looking at the teacher and sitting in one place rather than moving around (Miller & Bigi, 1979). Overall, the teacher's function is three fold:

- Impressing on the child the importance of self-monitoring attentional states — both temporary and long-term.
- Directing the child's attention to the fact that environmental factors, such as amount of noise, the visual similarity of materials, the type of potential distractions present, all affect attention.
- Stressing on the child that planning and self-initiated action are necessary to the development of selective attention. Thus, the child who is encouraged to develop systematic looking, to remove himself or herself from the distracting situation, or removing the distraction will develop a better awareness of one's attentional abilities with respect to task performance.

Ultimately, the child's choice of correct attentional strategies depends on the child's judgment of personal attentional abilities within specific situations, and the demands of the task. It is important for teachers to be aware that children who can recognize a good attentional strategy may never use that strategy for a number of reasons: The child may not realize that a strategy would be helpful. Conversely, a child may think of a good strategy but may lack the skill for carrying it out. These, therefore, are areas in which the teacher can help the child by providing direct instruction and reciprocal teaching for developing meta-attention knowledge and attentional skills. Reciprocal teaching of attentional skills must have as its underlying basis the child's entry level of self-awareness. One would expect that a child who recognizes a good strategy in a multiple-choice or forced-choice situation is ready for learning about its application in a broader, more open-ended real-life situation. A child who can verbalize a good attentional strategy is probably ready to implement a good strategy in a real-life situation, but seldom without the help of a teacher or competent adult.

Steps inherent in the reciprocal teaching approach to meta-attention are as follows:

1. Helping the child in **identifying** attentional strategies that are personally interesting, stimulating and make sense.
2. **Verbalizing** a good attentional strategy in response to a series of structured questions.
3. **Organizing rehearsals and practice and self-instructions** in using the strategy in a number of settings.
4. Teaching the child to **monitor the outcomes of the attentional strategy.**
5. Last but not least, teaching the child to appraise and **evaluate the effectiveness of the attentional strategy** in real-life tasks and activities.

It is up to the teacher to require the child to examine various aspects of the meta-attention process. It is the teacher's task to ascertain the degree of awareness that the child shows about attention through verbal expression of this knowledge, and the use of the knowledge in attention-relevant situations. Ultimately, the child will need help in selecting good attentional strategies congruent with one's abilities. Day (1975) stresses the importance of visual scanning—a process by which the young learner "actively, selectively, and sequentially acquires information from the visual environment" (p. 154). With the teacher's help, children's visual scanning strategies can be made more systematic so that through direct instruction children can be taught to pay more selective attention to stimuli that are task-relevant. Visual scanning is a naturally occurring response for a wide variety of children's attentional tasks. However, with teacher help and direction, it can achieve a useful refinement. Many aspects of the development in children's visual scanning can be attributed to the expanding role of the teacher in directing the child's attention to what aspects of the stimulus need to be scanned, and what aspects of the stimulus are more task-relevant and therefore need to be brought under closer scrutiny of the observer.

Summary

The relationship between children's metacognitive knowledge and performance in terms of attention, perception and memory is a complex one. Teachers observe that in some instances particular types of conceptual knowledge and awareness precedes task competence; however, teachers also recognize that their classroom environment has a powerful influence on how children conceptualize their experience. There is a widespread agreement among practitioners and researchers that meta-cognitive knowledge and awareness in the child is intrinsically impor-tant to task performance and self-competence. On the whole, older children have a much better knowledge than do younger children of their cognitive attentional, memory and perceptual states, and variables affecting that state. It is the function of the teacher to help children re-late what they know about the task (competence) and their practical abil-ity (performance), and to give direct instruction in the basic skills of metacognition including **predicting** the consequences of an action, **checking** the results of one's actions, **monitoring** one's ongoing activity, **reality testing,** and bringing one's efforts and cognitions under **volun-tary control.**

REFERENCES

Alessi, S. M., Anderson, T. H., & Goetz, E. T. (1979). An investigation of lookbacks during studying. *Discourse Processes, 2,* 197-212.

Anderson, T. H., & Armbruster, B. B. (1980). *Studying.* (Technical Report No. 155). Champaign: University of Illinois, Center for the Study of Reading.

Appel, L. F., Cooper, R. B., McCarrel, N., Sims-Knight, J., Yussen, S., & Flavell, J. H. (1972). The development of the distinction between perceiving and memo-rizing. *Child Development, 43,* 1365-1381.

Baker, L., & Brown, A. L. (1984). Metacognitive skills in reading. In P. D. Pearson (Ed.), *Handbook of reading research* (pp. 353-394). New York: Longman.

Baldwin, M. J. (1909). How children study. *Archives of Psychology, 12,* 65-70.

Belmont, J. M., & Butterfield, E. C. (1977). The instructional approach to develop-mental cognitive research. In R. V. Kail, Jr., & J. W. Hagen (Eds.), *Perspectives on the development of memory and cognition* (pp. 437-481). Hillsdale, NJ: Lawrence Erlbaum Associates.

Borkowski, J. G., Levers, S., & Gruenenfelder, T. M. (1976). Transfer of media-tional strategies in children: The role of activity and awareness during strategy acquisition. *Child Development, 47,* 779-786.

Brown, A. L. (1973). Temporal and contextual cues as discriminative attributes in retardates' recogntion memory. *Journal of Experimental Psychology, 98,* 1-13.

Brown, A. L. (1974). The role of strategic behavior in retardate memory. In N. R. Ellis (Ed.), *International review of research in mental retardation,* Vol. 1 (pp. 55-111). New York: Academic Press.

Brown, A. L. (1975). The development of memory: Knowing, knowing about know-ing, and knowing how to know. In H. W. Reese (Ed.), *Advances in child development and behavior,* Vol. 10 (pp. 103-152). New York: Academic Press.

Brown, A. (1977). Development, schooling and the acquisition of knowledge about knowledge. In R. Anderson, R. Spiro & W. Montague (Eds.), *Schooling and the acquisition of knowledge* (pp. 241-253). Hillsdale, NJ: Lawrence Erlbaum.

Brown, A. L. (1978a). Theories of memory and the problem of development: Growth, activity, and knowledge. In F. I. M. Craik, & L. Cermak (Eds.), *Levels of analysis approaches to cognition*. Hillsdale, NJ: Erlbaum.

Brown, A. L. (1978b). Knowing when, where and how to remember: A problem of metacognition. In R. Glasser (Ed.), *Advances in instructional psychology*, Vol. 1 (pp. 77-165). Hillsdale, NJ: Erlbaum.

Brown, A. L. (1980). Metacognitive development and reading. In R. J. Spiro, B. C. Bruce, & W. F. Brewer (Eds.), *Theoretical issues in reading comprehension: Perspectives from cognitive psychology, linguistics, artificial intelligence and education* (pp. 453-481). Hillsdale, NJ: Erlbaum.

Brown, A. L., Bransford, J. D., Ferrara, R. A., & Campione, J. C. (1983). Learning, remembering, and understanding. In J. H. Flavell & E. M. Markman (Eds.), *Handbook of child psychology, Vol. 1: Cognitive development* (pp. 77-168). New York: Wiley.

Brown, A. L., Campione, J. C., Bray, N. W., & Wilcox, B. L. (1974). Keeping track of changing variables: Effects of rehearsal training and rehearsal prevention in normal and retarded adolescents. *Journal of Experimental Psychology, 78,* 446-453.

Brown, A. L., Campione, J. C., & Day, J. D. (1981). Learning to learn: On training students to learn from texts. *Educational Researcher, 10,* 14-21.

Brown, A. L., Campione, J. C., & Murphy, M. D. (1974). Keeping track of changing variables: Long-term retention of a trained rehearsal strategy by retarded adolescents. *American Journal of Mental Deficiency, 78*(4), 446-453.

Brown, A. L., Campione, J. C., & Murphy, M. D. (1977). Maintenance and generalization of trained metamnemonic awareness by educable retarded children. *Journal of Experimental Child Psychology, 24,* 191-211.

Brown, A. L., & DeLoache, J. S. (1983). Metacognitive skills. In M. Donaldson, R. Grieve, & C. Pratt (Eds.), *Early childhood development and education* (pp. 280-289). Oxford, England: Basil Blackwell.

Brown, A. L., & French, L. A. (1979). The zone of potential development: Implications for intelligence testing in the year 2000. *Intelligence, 3,* 255-373.

Brown, A. L., & Lawton, S. C. (1977). The feeling of knowing experience in educable retarded children. *Developmental Psychology, 13,* 364-370.

Brown, A. L., & Scott, M. S. (1971). Recognition memory for pictures in preschool children. *Journal of Experimental Child Psychology, 11,* 401-402.

Brown, A. L., & Smiley, S. S. (1977). Rating the importance of structural units of prose passages: A problem of metacognitive development. *Child Development, 48,* 1-12.

Brown, A. L., & Smiley, S. S. (1978). The development of strategies for studying texts. *Child Development, 49,* 1076-1088.

Cantor, J. S., & Spiker, C. C. (1978). The problem-solving strategies of kindergarten and first-grade children during discrimination learning. *Journal of Experimental Child Psychology, 2,* 341-358.

Cavanaugh, J. C. & Borkowski, J. G. (1980). Searching for metamemory-memory connections: A developmental study. *Developmental Psychology, 16,* 441-453.

Cavanaugh, J. C. & Perlmutter, C. J. (1982). Metamemory: A critical examination. *Child Development, 53,* 11-28.

Chi, M. T. H. (1976). Short-term memory limitations in children: Capacity or processing deficits? *Memory and Cognition, 4,* 559-572.

Cole, M., & Traupman, K. (1980). Comparative cognitive research: Learning from a learning disabled child. In A. Collins (Ed.), *Minnesota Symposium on Child Development,* Vol. 13 (pp. 125-154). Hillsdale, NJ: Erlbaum.

Collins, A., Brown, J..S., & Larkin, K. M. (1980). Inference in text understanding. In R. J. Spiro, B. C. Bruce & W. F. Brewer (Eds.), *Theoretical issues in reading comprehension* (pp. 385-407). Hillsdale, NJ: Erlbaum.

Collins, A., & Smith, E. E. (1980). *Teaching the process of reading comprehension.* (Technical Report No. 182). Urbana: University of Illinois, Centre for the Study of Reading.

Craik, F. I. M., & Lockhart, R. S. (1972). Levels of processing: A framework for memory research. *Journal of Verbal Learning and Verbal Behavior, 11,* 671-684.

Cullen, J. L. (1985). Metacognitive approaches to classroom failure. In Forrest-Pressley, D. L., MacKinnon, G. E., & Waller, T. G. (Eds.), *Metacognition, cognition, and human performance* (pp. 267-300). New York: Academic Press.

Cullen, J. L., & Carver, J. (1982). *The educational relevance of metacognition: Some preliminary issues.* Paper presented at the Second National Child Development Conference, Melbourne.

Day, M. C. (1975). Developmental trends in visual scanning. In H..W. Reese (Ed.), *Advances in child development and behavior,* Vol. 10 (pp. 153-193). New York: Academic Press.

DeCecco, J. P. (1968). *The psychology of learning and instruction: Educational psychology.* Englewood Cliffs, NJ: Prentice-Hall.

Drozdal, J. G., & Flavell, J. H. (1975). A developmental study of logical search behavior. *Child Development, 46,* 389-393.

Dweck, C. S., & Elliott, E. S. (1983). Achievement motivation. In E. M. Hetherington (Ed.), *Handbook of child psychology (Vol. 4): Socialization, personality and social development* (pp. 643-692). New York: Wiley.

Flavell, J. H. (1976). Metacognitive aspects of problem solving. In L. B. Resnick (Ed.), *The nature of intelligence* (pp. 231-235). Hillsdale, NJ: Lawrence Erlbaum Associates.

Flavell, J. H. (1978). Metacognitive development. In J. M. Scandura & C. J. Brainerd (Eds.), *Structural or process models of complex human relations* (pp. 213-245). Netherlands: Sijthoff & Nordhoff.

Flavell, J. H. (1979). Metacognition and metacognitive monitoring: A new area of cognitive developmental inquiry. *American Psychologist, 34,* 906-911.

Flavell, J. H. (1981). Cognitive monitoring. In W. P. Dickson (Ed.), *Children's oral communication skills* (pp. 35-60). New York: Academic Press.

Flavell, J. H., Friedrichs, A. G., & Hoyt, J. D. (1970). Developmental changes in memorization processes. *Cognitive Psychology, 1,* 324-340.

Flavell, J. H., Speers, J. R., Green, F. L., & August, D. L. (1981). The development of comprehension monitoring and knowledge about communication. *Monographs of the Society for Research in Child Development, 46,* (Serial No. 192).

Flavell, J. H., & Wellman, H. M. (1977). Metamemory. In R. V. Kail, Jr., & O. W.
Hagen (Eds.), *Perspectives on the development of memory and cognition* (pp. 3-33). Hillsdale, NJ: Erlbaum.

Forrest, D. L., & Waller, T. G. (1979). *Cognitive and metacognitive aspects of reading.* Paper presented at the biennial meetings of the Society for Research in Child Development, San Francisco.

Forrest, D. L. & Waller, T. G. (1980). *What do children know about their reading and study
skills?* Paper presented at the annual meeting of the American Educational Research Association, Boston.

Forrest-Pressley, D. L., MacKinnon, G. E., & Waller, T. G. (1985). *Metacognition,
cognition and human performance, Vol. 2: Instructional practices.* New York: Academic
Press, Inc.

Forrest-Pressley, D., & Waller, T. G. (1984). *Cognition, metacognition and reading.* New
York: Springer-Verlag.

Fry, P. S. (1977). Success, failure, and resistance to temptation. *Developmental Psychology, 13,* 519-520.

Fry, P. S., & Grover, S. C. (1982). The relationship between father absence and children's social problem solving competencies. *Journal of Applied Developmental Psychology, 3,* 105-120.

Garner, R. (1981). Monitoring of passage inconsistency among poor comprehenders: A preliminary test of the piecemeal processing explanation. *Journal of Educational Research, 74,* 159-162.

Garner, R., & Reis, R. (1981). Monitoring and resolving comprehension obstacles:
An investigation of spontaneous text lookbacks among upper-grade and poor
comprehenders. *Reading Research Quarterly, 16,* 569-581.

Geva, E. (1981). *Facilitating reading comprehension through flow charting.* (Technical Report
No. 211). Champaign: University of Illinois, Center for the Study of Reading.

Goodwin, S. E., & Mahoney, M. J. (1975). Modification of aggression through modeling: An experimental probe. *Journal of Behavioral Therapy and Experimental Psychiatry, 6,* 200-202.

Gow, L., & Ward, J. (1980). Effects of modification of conceptual tempo on acquisition of work skills. *Perceptual Motor Skills, 50,* 107-116.

Greenfield, P. M. (1984). A theory of the teacher in the learning activities of everyday life. In B. Rogoff & J. Lave (Eds.), *Everyday cognition: Its development of social
context* (pp. 117-138). Cambridge, MA: Harvard University Press.

Hagen, J. W., Barclay, C. R., & Newman, R. S. (1982). Metacognition, self-
knowledge, and learning disabilities: Some thoughts on knowing and doing. *Topics in learning and learning disabilities, 2,* 19-26.

Hare, V., & Pulliam, C. (1980). College students' metacognitive awareness of reading behaviors. In M. L. Kamil & A. J. Moe (Eds.), *Perspectives on reading research
and instruction.* Twenty-ninth Yearbook of the National Reading Conference.
Washington, DC: National Reading Conference.

Harter, S. (1981). A model of mastery motivation in children: Individual differences and developmental changes. In A. Collins (Ed.), *Aspects of the development of competence: The Minnesota Symposium of Child Development,* Vol. 14 (pp. 215-225). Hillsdale, NJ: Erlbaum.

Hayes, J. R. (1981). *The complete problem solver.* Pittsburgh, PA: The Franklin Institute Press.

Hobbs, S. A., Moguin, L. E., Tyroler, M., & Lahey, B. B. (1980). Cognitive behavior therapy with children: Has clinical utility been demonstrated? *Psychological Bulletin, 87,* 147-165.

Huey, B. E. (1908). *The psychology and pedagogy of reading.* Cambridge, MA: M.I.T. Press. (Republished 1968).

Ironsmith, M., & Whitehurst, G. J. (1978). The development of listener abilities in communication: How children deal with ambiguous information. *Child Development, 49,* 348-352.

James, W. (1890). *The principles of psychology,* (Vol. 1). New York: Henry Holt and Company. (Republished by Dover, 1950.)

Kail, R. (1979). *The development of memory in children.* San Francisco: W. H. Freeman & Co.

Kanfer, F. H., & Zich, J. (1974). Self-control training: The effects of external control on children's resistance to temptation. *Developmental Psychology, 10,* 108-115.

Kreutzer, M. A., Leonard, C., & Flavell, J. H. (1975). An interview study of children's knowledge about memory. *Monographs of the Society for Research in Child Development, 40* (1, Serial No. 159).

Kuhlmann, F. (1907). On the analysis of the memory consciousness for pictures of familiar objects. *American Journal of Psychology, 18,* 389-420.

Loper, A. B., & Murphy, D. M. (1985). Cognitive self-regulatory training for underachieving children. In Forrest-Pressley, D. L., MacKinnon, G. E., & Waller, T. G. (Eds.), *Metacognition, cognition and human performance* (pp. 223-265). New York: Academic Press.

Lupart, M. (1984). *Reading comprehension monitoring.* Unpublished Doctoral Dissertation. University of Alberta.

Luria, A. R. (1976). *Cognitive development: Its cultural and social foundations.* Cambridge, MA: Harvard University Press.

Luria, A. R. (1982). *Language and cognition.* New York: Wiley.

Markman, E. M. (1977). Realizing that you don't understand: A preliminary investigation. *Child Development, 48,* 986-992.

Markman, E. M. (1979). Realizing what you don't understand: Elementary school children's awareness of inconsistencies. *Child Development, 50,* 643-655.

Markman, E. M. (1981). Comprehension monitoring. In W. P. Dickson (Ed.), *Children's oral communication skills* (pp. 61-84). San Francisco: Academic Press.

Meichenbaum, D. (1977). *Cognitive-behavior modification: An integrative approach.* New York: Plenum Press.

Meichenbaum, D., & Goodman, J. (1969). Reflection — impulsivity and verbal control of motor behavior. *Child Development, 40,* 785-797.

Meichenbaum, D., & Goodman, J. (1971). Training impulsive children to talk to themselves: Means of developing self-control. *Journal of Abnormal Psychology, 77,* 115-126.

Meichenbaum, D., & Goodman, J. (1975). The nature and modification of impulsivitiy. Paper presented at the First International Congress of Child Neurology. Toronto, Ontario.

Miller, P. H., & Bigi, L. (1979). The development of children's understanding of attention. *Merrill-Palmer Quarterly, 25,* 235-250.

Miller, P. H., & Weiss, M. G. (1982). Children's and adults' knowledge about what variables affect selective attention. *Child Development, 53,* 543-549.

Myers, M., & Paris, S. G. (1978). Children's metacognitive knowledge about reading. *Journal of Educational Psychology, 70,* 680-690.

Nisbett, R., & Winson, T. (1977). Telling more than we can know: Verbal reports on mental processes. *Psychological Review, 84,* 231-259.

Olshavsky, J. E. (1976-77). Reading as problem solving: An investigation of strategies. *Reading Research Quarterly, 12,* 654-674.

Olshavsky, J. (1978). Comprehension profiles of good and poor readers across materials of increasing difficulty. In P. D. Pearson & J. Hansen (Eds.), *Reading: Disciplined inquiry in process and practice.* Twenty-seventh Yearbook of the National Reading Conference. Washington, DC: National Reading Conference.

Orlando, V. (1980). A comparison of notetaking strategies while studying from text. In M. L. Kamil & A. J. Moe (Eds.), *Perspectives on reading: Research and instruction.* Twenty-ninth Yearbook of the National Reading Conference. Washington, DC: National Reading Conference.

Pace, A. J. (1979). The effect of inconsistent script information on children's comprehension of stories about familiar situations. Paper presented at the annual meeting of the American Educational Research Association, San Francisco.

Palinscar, A. S., & Brown, A. L. (1984). Reciprocal teaching of comprehension-fostering and comprehension monitoring activities. *Cognition and Instruction, 1,* 117-175.

Paris, S. G., & Myers, M. (1981). Comprehension monitoring, memory and study strategies of good and poor readers. *Journal of Reading Behavior, 13,* 5-22.

Patterson, C. J., Cosgrove, J. M. & O'Brien, R. G. (1980). Nonverbal indicants of comprehension and noncomprehension in children. *Developmental Psychology, 16,* 38-48.

Peterson, P. L., & Swing, S. R. (1983). Problems in classroom implementation of cognitive strategy instruction. In M. Pressley & J. R. Levin (Eds.), *Cognitive strategy research: educational applications* (pp. 267-284). New York: Springer-Verlag.

Reeve, R. A., & Brown, A. L. (1984). *Metacognition reconsidered: Implications for intervention research.* Technical Report No. 328, Center for The Study of Reading, University of Illinois at Urbana-Champaign.

Reis, R., & Spekman, N. J. (1983). The detection of reader-based versus text-based inconsistencies and the effects of direct training of comprehension monitoring among upper-grade poor comprehenders. *Journal of Reading Behavior, 2,* 49-60.

Ritter, D. J. (1978). The development of knowledge of an external retrieval cue strategy. *Child Development, 49,* 1227-1230.

Rosenblatt, L. M. (1978). *The reader, the text, the poem: The transactional theory of the literary work.* Carbondale, IL: Southern Illinois University Press.

Ruble, D. N., Boggiano, A. K., Feldman, N. S., & Loebl, J. H. (1980). Developmental analysis of the role of social comparison in self-evaluation. *Developmental Psychology, 16,* 105-115.

Scardamalia, M., & Bereiter, C. (1982). Assimilative processes in composition planning. *Educational Psychologist, 17,* 165-171.

Scardamalia, M., Bereiter, C., & Steinbach, R. (1984). Teachability of reflective processes in written composition. *Cognitive Science, 8,* 173-190.

Steinberg, E. R. (1980). Evaluation process in young children's problem solving. *Contemporary Educational Psychology, 5,* 276-281.

Thorndike, E. L. (1917). Reading as reasoning: A study of mistakes in paragraph reading. *Journal of Educational Psychology, 8,* 323-332.

Vygotsky, L. S. (1963). Learning and mental development at school age. In J. Simon & B. Simon (Eds.), *Educational psychology in the U.S.S.R.* Stanford, CA: Stanford University Press.

Vygotsky, L. S. (1978). *Mind and society: The development of higher psychological processes.* (M. Cole, V. John-Steiner, S. Scribner, & E. Souberman, Eds. and Trans.). Cambridge, MA: Harvard University Press.

Winograd, P., & Johnston, P. (1980). *Comprehension monitoring and the error detection paradigm.* (Technical Report No. 153). Cambridge, MA: Bolt, Bernack and Newman; Urbana: University of Illinois, Center for the Study of Reading.

Wellman, H. M., & Lempers, J. D. (1977). The naturalistic communicative abilities of two-year-olds. *Child Development, 48,* 1052-1057.

Wellman, H. M., Ritter, K., & Flavell, J. H. (1975). Deliberate memory behavior in the delayed reactions of very young children. *Developmental Psychology, 11,* 780-787.

Wertsch, J. V. (1979). From social interaction to higher psychological processes: A clarification and application of Vygotsky's theory. *Human Development, 22,* 1-22.

Wood, J., Bruner, J., & Ross, G. (1976). The mode of tutoring in problem solving. *Journal of Child Psychology and Psychiatry, 17,* 89-100.

Yussen, S. R. (1975). Some reflections on strategic remembering in young children. In G. H. Hale (Chair), *Development of selective processes in cognition.* Symposium presented at the meeting of the Society for Research in Child Development, Denver.

Yussen, S. R., & Berman, L. (1981). Memory predictions for recall and recognition in first-, third-, and fifth-grade children. *Developmental Psychology, 17,* 224-229.

CHAPTER SEVEN

CONCLUDING REMARKS

PSYCHOLOGY and especially educational psychology are relatively new scientific disciplines and as such there is no one guiding theory to account for all that is important about human behavior, or the specific relationships between classroom teaching and student learning. Instead, we have access to several views about student learning which vary substantially with respect to initial assumptions about human learning.

Within this century, for example, the two primary theoretical stances have been behaviorism and cognitive psychology. The behaviorist psychologists believe that the true scientific study of human learning must be solely based upon objective, observable reactions. Research studies of this type focus upon the presentation and manipulation of environmental stimuli and the observable effects on human performance. In contrast, cognitive psychologists are specifically interested in the component omitted from behaviorist theories: mental activity. The study of cognition involves an analysis of the way we take in, store, retrieve and use knowledge.

Although behaviorism has dominated the field of psychology for the greater part of this century, there has been a marked shift in interest toward cognitive psychology since the 1960s. Such shifting views have been instrumental in bringing change, productivity and excitement to the field but have also resulted in untested ideas, competing new perspectives, and confusion in attempting to fit existing and current research into a framework that can have any practical significance.

Despite the current upheaval in the developing field of cognitive psychology, we as educational psychologists believe that the approach is significant with respect to its potentials for understanding what is important to children's learning. We also believe that although the field of cognitive ology is far from being perfectly meshed into a unifying theory, the of a number of areas of mental processing over the last couple of decades has yielded ideas and findings that are significant for teachers and all professionals associated with the education of children.

Given that these ideas exist but remain somewhat piecemeal and unorganized, in this book we have attempted to unify what is known and what might be helpful to the educator. The five areas that we have dealt with include perception, attention, memory, problem solving, and metacognition. Our principle theme for this book — that cognitive processes play a very large role in children's learning — is evident in each individual chapter. At this point we feel it is important to draw attention to the major points emerging from each of the five areas and, then, to unify our own thinking by suggesting emerging themes most important to educational practice.

Perception

In the chapter on perceptual development we traced for the benefit of the teacher how perceptual sets develop in children and how each experience of the young child determines the manner in which new events are perceived. It was shown in this chapter how children's perception becomes more refined with increasing age level and how older children's perceptual ability can be facilitated by means of strategy training for recognizing distinctive features and dimensions of objects in the environment and relationships among them. Information-processing accounts of perceptual development stress that children's perceptual ability is refined as they learn to discriminate between distinctive dimensional and featural variations, and to respond to meaningful dimensions of their environment.

Piagetian accounts, by contrast, stress that perception is rooted in intellectual structures that organize perception and place a construction on reality. Discerning teachers will note that both positions advocate that perceptual development occurs through the child's active interaction with the environment, through action and experience, and through strategy training for abstracting prototypical information from sensory experience.

The need for increased involvement of the teacher with the child in order to bring about effective perceptual integration is undeniable. Through increasing perceptual ability, the child transforms information about the environment by coding it into conceptual categories in an attempt to make the information easier to recognize, recall and remember (memory). Through increasing perceptual ability, the child learns to recombine what he or she perceives creatively and insightfully to meet new demands of a task. The child can use expectancies about the task as a basis for selecting ways of attacking it (problem solving).

Attention

More than any other area of mental processing, attention has been the most difficult to conceptualize and define. Early 1960 views relegated attention to a stopgate position of blocking sensory input to allow processing of the relevant information. The view figured prominently in studies of children with attention problems, and indeed most teachers are well familiar with the term "attention deficit," used predominantly in defining learning disability students. Although it was at one time sufficient to provide such labels to account for the child's learning problems, teachers are now expected to provide specialized instructions to remediate such learning problems. A model which attributes poor attentional behavior to a faulty screening mechanism has limited practical utility for teachers.

Alternatively, the interactive model has considerable pedagogical implications. The approach calls for the full consideration of the child within the learning context. Both child and task characteristics and specific task variables are important to instructional planning. This perspective involves an exploration of the conditions in which children exhibit both attention and inattention. Among task characteristics, for example, the teacher must be aware of those tasks requiring a high degree of voluntary attention (sometimes called tasks with active demands) and other tasks making less rigorous demands for voluntary attention. Another task characteristic that appears to influence expressions of attention/inattention is difficulty level.

Given that there are so many individual variations in children's attention capacities, it is reasonable to suggest that the link between child characteristics, task variables and voluntary attention is an intimate one. Although these links are manifest in a more direct and automatic fashion in most children, there is evidence that children with cognitive limitations and cognitive-style rigidities may not have the usual attention skills readily available to them. Poor sustained attention in such children can be remedied through the use of specially designed instructional procedures and strategy management. Even though it is usually the psychologist or special education consultant who provides the programs for such remediation, it is often the responsibility of the teacher to implement these.

In formulating strategies for improving children's attentional capacities, the teacher must bear in mind both the developmental lag assumption and the deficit assumption. The developmental lag position assumes that some children are slower in development although not qualitatively different from other children. Deficit positions imply that children show a wide range of variability in both qualitative and quantitative dimensions of attention. Teachers should note that attention is such an all-encompassing process that it would be almost impossible for the teacher to develop cognitive strategies for improving attention unless child characteristics are well understood and substantial contextual information is available about specific tasks, and task demands are clearly spelled out.

Memory

In presenting the levels-of-processing and multistore models of memory in Chapter 4, our objective was to draw the teacher's attention to two important aspects of the memory phenomenon: The acquisition of information and its retrieval from memory. To deny the importance of either aspect of memory functioning in children's learning would be indeed premature. Explanations that have been offered by the levels-of-processing theorists and multistore theorists have served to identify a number of processes that contribute conjointly to memory development in the child and the improvement of memory performance. Cumulative rehearsal as a process for prolonging the duration of information in working memory is recognized to be one of the most important cognitive mechanisms for transferring information from the short-term to the long-term store. Discerning teachers will note, for example, that the only way children can be expected to remember locker combinations, telephone numbers, addresses, names, dates and motor movements is to commit this information to memory through cumulative rehearsal or practice.

For long-term store, however, the teacher must ensure that information is processed at and elaborated to some semantic level. This suggests to the teacher that some level of multiattribute encoding of information facilitates the acquisition and retention of information. If children can be encouraged to remember even a few attributes of an item of information (meaning, color, or location), it is likely that information about other attributes associated with it will also be remembered.

Overall, as teachers, it is important for us to note that in order to facilitate recall, we must assist children to relate their lessons to a network of associations and experiences that they have already acquired. The improvement in children's memory performace is attributed to their growing appreciation of semantic features of informational items, the amount of semantic elaboration that they are required to impose upon situations, and their ability to generate suitable and compatible cues for retrieving the contents of information. In regard to these last points, the teacher's intervention is vitally imperative, especially with young children. The teacher's essential function is to arrange retrieval environments designed to direct the child's attention to at least a few meaningful semantic features of information to be remembered. These same semantic features will serve to generate perceptual, mnemonic and physical retrieval cues which will, in turn, facilitate the child's recall. It is important for teachers to note that children at all levels can profit from activities design to generate retrieval cues, although as children age they are more apt to elaborate information spontaneously or profit from contexts that prompt such processing. An important aspect of the teacher's function therefore is to arrange retrieval environments that are congruent with the maturational level, cognitive development, and background experiences of the child. Teachers must be sensitive to the fact that young children are limited in terms of their operative knowledge and will therefore be less able to conserve information about operative properties of objects and events unless they have some corresponding operational schemes that can assimilate the information. Teachers, therefore, need to ensure sufficient cognitive readiness in the child before introducing new materials to be remembered. It is only through gradual experience and cumulative rehearsal that the child develops a repertoire of proficient memory abilities. As Piaget and Inhelder note, we as teachers cannot discount the notion of stage-related changes in children's memory capacities and the age-related operative effects seen in children's limited capabilities for developing strategies for encoding or retrieving information.

The teacher can further facilitate memory performance and development in the learner by an increased sensitivity to the characteristics of learning tasks. Factors such as difficulty level, organization of materials, activities to stimulate previously acquired knowledge, and the degree to which the activity promotes strategy utilization all need to be considered.

An area that will need to be explored further is one that concerns the teacher's role in teaching children content versus generalized strategies for memory acquisition and retention.

Problem Solving

In Chapter 5 we stressed how processes by which children perceive, acquire, store and assimilate information are fundamentally important to virtually all kinds of problem-solving tasks confronting children in daily living. The recognition that problem-solving behavior in children can be made strategic has led to a curiosity in researchers, teachers and educators alike about what types of rules are used in problem solving and what kinds of perceptual, mnemonic and cognitive variables integrate information gained from rule use. We observed that there are two major frameworks in which children's problem solving can be examined: synthesis and analysis. The synthesis or systems modeling method is directed at the specification of precise rule systems or algorithms that define and represent the problem-solving process.

In the chapter on problem solving (Chap. 5), we have described a number of rule systems and strategies for improving children's problem-solving skills, although we acknowledge that the position we have tentatively espoused is a controversial one. We recognize that a steady diet of well-structured strategies for problem solving might ultimately produce children and adolescents who have learned a number of cognitive tricks but who do not actively become involved with the true elements of the problem-solving world. Therefore, under the section of the analysis approach to problem solving, we stress that one of the important functions of the teacher is to impress upon the child the basic value of a problem-solving orientation, i.e. the expectancy that very young children can and should solve problems by acquiring an inhibiting set "to stop and think" before responding impulsively to a problem. We suggest that the teacher teach problem solving by a guided-discovery approach. The teacher has the responsibility for stressing **problem identification** by encouraging children to consider the relevant and irrelevant elements of the problem with respect to setting short- and long-term goals. Before a child can decide on a course of actions for solving a problem, it is important that the child consider the potential **obstacles components** and the **alternative solutions components** in problem solution. This suggests that the child must be cognitively advanced enough to consider a unified integration of skills, rules and strategies that must be applied to the problem.

Implicit in our comparison of the Piagetian view of problem solving and the information-processing view is the concept that teachers must consider the interaction of developmental, perceptual and cognitive abilities of children prior to challenging them for problem-solving tasks. In terms of perceptual capacities, teachers need to assess whether children are capable of discriminating the stimulus field accurately and appropriately (i.e. Are they able to decenter and consider several dimensions of the stimulus simultaneously? Do they have a variety of control processes including skills in rehearsal, chunking, interactive imagery and capacity for subjective organization of materials?). We suggest that these deficiencies in perception and memory capacity reduce the child's problem-solving proficiency and limit cognitive abilities to coordinate the use of strategies and rules for solving problems.

Also to be considered by the teacher are specific child characteristics such as reflexivity-impulsivity (Kagan, 1966), state and trait anxiety (Sinclair, 1969), aggression (Goodwin & Mahoney, (1975) and social extroversion-introversion (Jakibchuk & Smergilio, 1976) which limit the degree to which children may profit from rules and strategy training for problem solving (Mueller, 1976; Nottelmann & Hill, 1977).

Research reviewed under the analysis approach to problem solving also suggests that it may be necessary for teachers to incorporate into their accounts of development a **maturational factor** much like that advocated by the Genevans. Gholson (1980) and Gholson and Cohen (1980) speculate that lack of operative knowledge (the ability to decenter, reverse thought, and understanding of class inclusion) may limit the degree to which children can benefit from problem-solving strategy implementation. Preschool children, for example, have operative knowledge limitations that impede the efficient use of logical rules. Although training specific to preschool children's level of operative knowledge may facilitate certain communication skills, such training does not contribute to their skills in problem solving. Operative limitations apparently negate the effectiveness of training programs that require higher levels of operative knowledge (e.g. abstracting problem-solving principles, focusing, etc.), and operative factors may place an upper limit on the amount of gains that a child may derive from strategy training programs. Piaget further argues that experience alone is not a sufficient condition for problem solving, because maturation of the nervous system is not complete until about the fifteenth or sixteenth year and the formation of mental structures vitally necessary to problem solving is incomplete for many years of the child's development. Effective problem solving, according to Piaget, also involves sequencing which is a product of cognitive development. For these reasons effective problem solving must be viewed by the teacher as a complex interaction of maturation, experience, and strategy skills.

We advocate a position which is more closely in tune with the position of the information-processing theorists who typically advocate a bottom-to-top approach to problem solving based on the premise that over a long term problem-solving deficiencies are thought to stem from skill and strategy deficiency, although maturation, experience and operative knowledge are all key ingredients of effective problem solving. What is centrally important is that the teacher consider specific child characteristics and characteristics of problem-solving traits. By identifying critical child traits and by narrowing down the parameters of the task, the teacher can assist the child in using step-by-step procedures for problem solution.

Metacognition

The newest and currently the most prolific area of investigation in cognitive psychology is metacognition, an area that will perhaps ultimately be the most significant for teachers and learners. Growing out of the early studies of metamemory, the term "metacognition" subsumes other areas such as metaperception, meta-attention and metalinguistics. Important stable constructs inherent in the concept of metacognition suggest that individuals' self-knowledge of mental activity can promote in them a sense of executive self-control and self-mastery. As seen in Figure 7-1 the acquisition of these executive controls leads to higher levels of metacognitive knowledge. Lawson (1984) (see Fig. 7-1) hypothesizes that metacognitive knowledge is an outcome of executive processes emerging from a reflection of cognitive processes. The application of this concept to children's learning suggests that acquisition of metacognitive knowledge by the child must be viewed by both teacher and learner as being a controlled, effortful process requiring constant and conscious monitoring and vigilance. Consideration of the nature of executive processing and the extent to which metacognitive knowledge and executive processes can be developed in children are questions that require much further study. In the meanwhile, one point that is obvious is that metacognitive knowledge requires a learner's active involvement in the learning activity. Metacognitive knowledge is conscious and will require the young learner's conscious reflection on personal cognitive attributes, cognitive style, strategies and knowledge schemes (see Fig. 7-2). Therefore, the teacher's active mediation is essential to the child's acquisition of executive processes and metacognitive knowledge. Students will need to become aware of their own thought processes at higher and higher levels of metacognitive experience. Teacher intervention aimed at encouraging children to talk about and share ideas, knowledge schemes, strategies and cognitive style is necessary to the progressive development of children's knowledge of their cognitive state and variables affecting that state.

FIGURE 7-1

Metacognitive Knowledge as the Outcome of Executive Processes

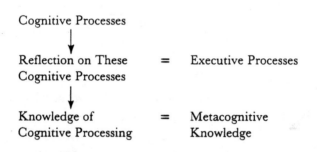

Source: Lawson, Michael. J. (1984). Being executive about metacognition. In John R. Kirby (Ed.), *Cognitive strategies and educational performance* (pp. 89-109). New York: Academic Press (Harcourt Brace Jovanovich, Publishers).

FIGURE 7-2

Metacognitive Knowledge as an Outcome of Reflection on the Self

Discerning teachers will note that older children, on the whole, have much better metacognitive knowledge than younger children who will need more of the teacher's help in establishing achievable goals, in planning learning tasks, in identifying relevant features of the learning task, and in monitoring and checking their cognitive activities. Teachers' intervention will take the form of explicit instructions and explanations for carrying out tasks, providing demonstrations, modeling, and opportunities for rehearsal and practice. At first, teacher mediation must be considerable. However, it is important that at all times the teacher provides assistance only as required, the ultimate objective being to have the learner assume independent control or regulation over the cognitive tasks and functions. It has been shown that, provided with difficult and unfamiliar tasks, we should expect all children to perform poorly. However, given tasks that are simple and easily understood, even young children will show some metacognitive knowledge. This rather unremarkable finding must be tempered with the knowledge that what children know is often affected by a variety of task and situational variables. The teacher's role in all this is to facilitate metacognitive knowledge by adapting task and situational demands to the operative knowledge base of the child and the child's relative competence in implementing strategies.

Unifying Themes

Within this book we have identified a number of ways in which cognitive psychologists have helped us to understand those processes in learning, and how to determine and analyze the needs of the individual learner. We believe that this work is particularly useful for teachers and all professionals in the education field, because it should similarly help us to understand the nature of effective learning environments. To this end, we feel that there are a number of major themes that pervade all of the learning processes examined in the various chapters. These are deserving of the teacher's attention.

Learning Requires Active Involvement

The student is not a passive vessel into which curriculum content is poured. The learning process depends upon dynamic interaction between the learner and the learning context. The teacher's role is to gauge the entry level of the student and to present learning conditions that motivate the learner to become cognitively involved in the learning task. This means that the teacher should use a number of cognitive techniques such as posing questions involving inferential reasoning, activities of modeling, role playing and perspective taking, all requiring active involvement of the learner.

Cognitive Processes are Interrelated

It is important for teachers to note that cognitive processes discussed in separate chapters of this book do not in fact develop as uniquely discrete processes but are interrelated with one another. For example, when we ask a child to read a paragraph, perceptual processes are necessary to identify the letters according to configuration. Attention must be deployed to process the information, and memory must be tapped to associate, comprehend and retain the information. Metacognitive processes would help the child monitor and evaluate his responses. Depending upon the particular reading task, other cognitive processes such as problem solving, decision making, or inferencing may be involved. Moreover, these interrelated processes are not directly observable and this fact makes it more important for teachers to bear in mind the interrelationships of these cognitive processes when designing intervention programs for children.

Teachers As Custodians of Individual Differences in Children's Cognitive Processing

Although planning or control processes seem to be well-accepted in information-processing models of children's performance, this is usually without reference to individual differences. It is the teacher's function to ensure that individual differences are considered and safeguarded when cognitive strategies of control are introduced and when intervention programs are organized for the individual learner. Following a number of cognitive intervention models (Hunt, 1980; Sternberg, 1977), we suggest that the teacher work toward a reconciliation of relationships among cognitive processes, educational performance, and individual differences (see Fig. 7-3). Until recently, the hypothetical relationship between individual differences, cognitive processes, and educational performance shown in Figures 7-2 and 7-3 has not been a dominant concern in education or in the psychology of individual differences. Briefly, educational performance is seen to be the result of common, underlying cognitive processes suggesting a two-way interaction. Increasingly, however, we recognize that there is a three-way relationship that influences educational performance and that individual differences also contribute to educational performance. Individual differences in terms of cognitive style, strategies, knowledge schemes, and metacognitive awareness are not only recognized but must be preserved by the teacher. Clearly, not all individual differences will be equally influential in educational performance, although all may continue to be useful areas of consideration for the teacher (see Figs. 7-2 & 7-3), since from this study should flow improvement in the school performance and metacognitive knowledge of the individual child.

FIGURE 7-3

Relationships among individual differences, educational performance, and underlying cognitive processes

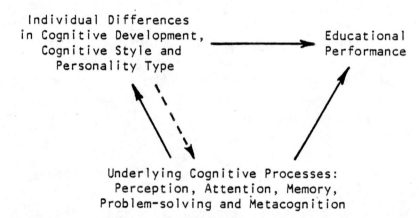

Individual Differences
in Cognitive Development,
Cognitive Style and
Personality Type

Educational
Performance

Underlying Cognitive Processes:
Perception, Attention, Memory,
Problem-solving and Metacognition

Teachers as Remediators of Children's Processing Deficiencies

Overall, it is important for teachers to note a number of well-substantiated subprocessing deficiencies in children's cognitive functioning that can be remediated through **pretraining** in subprocessing skills, simplification of strategies developed for somewhat older children, and through cognitive behavior modification and restructuring. The principal reason for providing **pretraining** at all age levels of children is that young children exhibit processing deficiencies that older children do not and older children show processing deficiencies that adults do not. Pressley's (1983, p. 240) report has ordered processing deficiencies in children as follows:

1. Children are less able to deal with poorly structured, illogical, and ambiguous materials than are adults.
2. Children are less capable of going beyond the information given and deriving inferences from input than are adults.

3. Children are not as adept at using strategies when working with meaningful materials.

The message for the teacher seems clear. Teachers concerned about improving children's processing in attention, memory, problem solving and the like should do all they can to present materials in well-structured ways (logical order versus arbitrary order) (Mandler, 1978). Because children's cognitive processing can be affected pejoratively by nonoptimal organization, it is encumbent on teachers as producers and presenters of materials to generate well-structured presentations.

There are several recent developments (Shatz, 1977; Pratt & Bates, 1982) that are heartening for teachers with respect to remediating deficiencies and developing interventions for children. Pratt and Bates (1982) have speculated that children's deficiencies in processing can be improved and success is more likely **when processing load is minimized.** Other child psychologists have posited that processing capabilities of children can be improved if **information and materials are made maximally explicit** through (1) additional verbalizations (Nelson, 1980) and (2) concretization in the form of videotapes and pictorial presentations (Chandler, Greenspan & Barenboim, 1973). The essential theme that we wish to reiterate here is that it is possible for teachers to help the immature mind by presenting learning information in a format that is highly individualized, more concrete, more explicit, and more likely to trigger the individual child's existing schemata (Pressley, 1983; Pressley, Heisel, McCormick & Nakamura, 1982).

Education Should Be an Interactive Process

Virtually all of the recommendations given in this chapter are variants of the general prescriptions presented in Chapters 1-6. In short, what we have advocated in individual chapters of the book is a broad base of support for an interactionist position in which the teacher considers: (1) developmental capabilities of the child as a learner, (2) child characteristics in terms of state and trait components, (3) task characteristics in terms of information-processing load, and (4) teaching format in terms of explicit strategy, structure and concretization (Smith & Cotten, 1980; Brown & French, 1979). It is sufficient to conclude that the "interactionist" and "explicitness" framework proposed here requires that any cognitive functioning of perceiving, comprehending or remembering by the child involves the simultaneous consideration of the various underlying cognitive processes. It is apparent that each cognitive process contributes to the child's educational performance, and the teacher needs to understand them all.

What is not all that apparent is the fact that the influence of the cognitive processes may vary considerably in the individual learner. By systematically observing and adapting instruction to meet the individual learner's developmental needs, the teacher can help the child to achieve optimal learning. In order to function in this role the teacher must be well-trained in techniques for influencing children's attentional and selection processes, techniques for influencing the developmental construction processing, and, finally, and most important, techniques for influencing children's problem-solving and integration processes (Cook & Mayer, 1983).

Teachers As Designers of Strategy Training

In organizing the various chapters of this book for the classroom teacher, we have presumed in the teacher some background or prerequisite knowledge for designing and implementing strategy training. Wherever relevant, we have elaborated on developmental skills and abilities of younger and older children that need to be considered by the teacher in cognitive strategy planning. We have also commented on cognitive strategies for improving perception, attention, memory, problem solving or metacognition that would be appropriate or inappropriate for children at different ages and developmental stages. We have suggested that sometimes strategy usage is difficult for children with limited operative knowledge, no matter how explicit and well-structured the instructions provided by the teacher may be. We have been reminded that some educators are particularly critical of these types of strategy approaches to children's learning, observing that they are typically receptive and often devoid of meaningful context. In fact, the Piagetions have largely rejected the idea that training could positively affect children's cognitions — a position that we consider untenable given the evidence of positive perceptual, attentional, memory and problem-solving strategy-training effects reviewed in the chapters of this book. We take the position that teachers should continue to experiment with strategy development, taking into account the developmental abilities of the learner, the specific requirements of the task, the cognitive style of the child, and the child's level of metacognitive knowledge.

Readers must not infer that our enthusiasm for individualized cognitive strategies indicates by any means a reduced concern for the increasing responsibilities of the classroom teacher. We believe that the quest for more individualized strategy programs for the young learner will undoubtedly continue. Their value is not so much in what they are now but in what they might become in the future. We recognize that such an individualized approach to cognitive training can be very taxing on the teacher's time and energy and may not be very viable given the economics of the classroom. However, it should be reassuring for classroom teachers that (as discussed in Chapter 5) recent advances in microcomputer technology and production systems may open up ways to apply the fruits of cognitive strategy research findings to the individual child (Dickson, 1983). The microcomputer serves as the adult-speaker and will both think aloud and will verbalize for the individual child a specifically designed strategy along cognitive behavior-modification lines of Meichenbaum (discussed earlier), and the referential communications lines of the work by Asher and Wigfield (1981). The microcomputer technology has not yet had much impact upon educational or classroom intervention, although it would seem to provide the most logical foundation for individualized instruction and strategy implementation.

Teachers As Primary Observers of the Learning Process

Since teachers, unlike reseachers, work with children on a day-to-day basis, they have the unique advantage of observing the gradual unfolding of children's learning capabilities and skills. We suspect that many of the tactics or approaches that teachers use in the classroom are intuitive. They are based not so much on theoretial constructs but rather on the collective experience of approaches that have been found to be effective with individual children. It is our belief that recent developments in cognitive psychology (cognitive strategy training, metacognitive awareness, metalinguistics, study of cognitive styles) have much to offer to the teacher.

Although much work remains to be done in understanding the cognitive processes of the child, there are a number of potentially productive routes discussed in the chapters that the teacher can take. Along with Norman (1980, p. 97) we propose the development of a team of "cognitive engineers" in the classroom capable of bringing about in teaching and instruction an effective merger of cognitive psychological principles and their pedagogic application.

We would like to conclude this chapter by inviting teachers to take up the challenge of incorporating ideas and constructs emerging from cognitive psychology into their own educational practice.

REFERENCES

Asher, S. R., & Wigfield, A. (1981). Influence of comparison training on children's referential communication. *Journal of Educational Psychology, 73*, 232-241.

Brown, A. L., & French, L. A. (1979). The zone of potential development: Implications for intelligence testing in the year 2000. *Intelligence, 3*, 255-273.

Chandler, M. J., Greenspan, S., & Barenboim, C. (1973). Judgments of intentionality in response to videotaped and verbally presented moral dilemmas: The medium is the message. *Child Development, 44*, 315-320.

Cook, L. K., & Mayer, R. E. (1983). Reading strategies training for meaningful learning from prose. In M. Pressley & J. R. Levin (Eds.), *Cognitive strategy research: Educational applications* (pp. 87-132). New York: Springer-Verlag.

Dickson, W. P. (1983). Training cognitive strategies for oral communication. In M. Pressley & J. R. Levin (Eds.), *Cognitive strategy research: Educational applications* (pp. 29-43). New York: Springer-Verlag.

Gholson, B. (1980). *The cognitive-development basis of human learning: Studies in hypothesis testing.* New York: Academic Press.

Gholson, B., & Cohen, R. (1980). Operativity and strategic hypothesis testing. *The Genetic Epistemologist, 9*, 1-5.

Goodwin, S. E., & Mahoney, M. J. (1975). Modification of aggression through modeling: An experimental probe. *Journal of Behavioral Therapy and Experimental Psychiatry, 6*, 200-202.

Hunt, E. (1980). Intelligence as an information-processing construct. *British Journal of Psychology, 71*, 449-474.

Jakibchuk, Z., & Smergilio, V. L. (1976). The influence of symbolic modeling on the social behavior of preschool children with low levels of social responsiveness. *Child Development, 47*, 838-841.

Kagan, J. (1966). Reflection-impulsivity: The generality and dynamics of conceptual tempo. *Journal of Abnormal Psychology, 71*, 17-24.

Lawson, M. J. (1984). Being executive about metacognition. In J. R. Kirby (Ed.), *Cognitive strategies and educational performance* (p. 89-109). New York: Academic Press.

Mandler, J. M. (1978). A code in the node: The use of a story schema in retrieval. *Discourse Processes, 1*, 14-35.

Mueller, J. H. (1976). Anxiety and cue utilization in human learning and memory. In M. Zuckerman & C. D. Spielberger (Eds.), *Emotions and anxiety: New concepts, methods, and application* (pp. 197-229). Hillsdale, NJ: Erlbaum.

Nelson, S. A. (1980). Factors influencing young children's use of motives and outcomes as moral criteria. *Child Development, 51*, 823-829.

Norman, D. A. (1980). Cognitive engineering and education. In D. T. Tuma & F. Reif (Eds.), *Problem solving and education* (pp. 88-105). Hillsdale, NJ: Erlbaum.

Nottelmann, E. D., & Hill, K. T. (1977). Text anxiety and off-task behavior in evaluative situations. *Child Development, 48,* 225-231.

Pratt, M. W., & Bates, K. R. (1982). Young editors: Preschoolers' evaluation and production of ambiguous messages. *Developmental Psychology, 18,* 30-42.

Pressley, M. (1983). Making meaningful materials easier to learn: Lessons from cognitive strategy research. In M. Pressley & J. R. Levin (Eds.), *Cognitive strategy research: Educational applications* (pp. 239-266). New York: Springer-Verlag.

Pressley, M., Heisel, B. E, McCormick, C. G., & Nakamura, G. V. (1982). In C. J. Brainerd & M. Pressley (Eds.), *Verbal processes in children* (pp. 82-101). New York: Springer-Verlag.

Shatz, M. (1977). The relationship between cognitive processes and the development of communication skills. In C. B. Keasey (Ed.), *Nebraska symposium on motivation.* (Vol. 25). Lincoln: University of Nebraska Press.

Sinclair, K. E. (1969). The influence of anxiety on several measures of classroom performance. *Australian Journal of Education, 13,* 196-307.

Smith, L. R., & Cotten, M. L. (1980). Effect of lesson vagueness and discontinuity on student achievement and attitudes. *Journal of Educational Psychology, 72,* 670-675.

Sternberg, R. J. (1977). *Intelligence, information processing, and analogical reasoning: The componential analysis of human abilities.* Hillsdale, NJ: Erlbaum.

NAME INDEX

SUBJECT INDEX

249